Comprehensive edition published: December, 2017

Comprehensive edition ISBN: 978-0-9966454-4-7

Edited by Carol Gajus

ה נ ב '

(הִנֵּנִ')

From Bethel to Peniel
A Study of Jacob

Genesis 25:19--35:29

By

Frank G. Carver

To the members of "Come and Go" Sunday School class at the San Diego, California, First Church of the Nazarene, who under the leadership of Arthur Seamans allowed Herbert Prince and me as co-teachers, to spend over two years exploring the text of Genesis.

Contents

Preface

Prologue: Why Jacob?
(32:22-32)

Part One: To Bethel
(25:19—28:22)

I.
Isaac and Rebekah
(25:19—26:30)

II.
The Brothers and the Blessing
(27:1—28:22)

Part Two: To Peniel
(29:1—33:17)

I.

Jacob and Laban
(29:1—31:55)

Chapter Seven: Rachel and Leah

Chapter Eight: The Children

Chapter Nine: Jacob Prospers

Chapter Ten: Jacob Leaves for Home: Part One

Chapter Eleven: Jacob Leaves for Home: Part Two

II.
Jacob and Esau
(32:1—33:17)

Chapter: Twelve: Esau is Coming

Chapter Thirteen: Jacob at Peniel

Chapter Fourteen: The Face of God

Epilogue: Jacob in Canaan
(33:18—35:29)

The story of Jacob, too, is a highly artistic composition combining very diverse, separate traditions, and this composition is clearly marked by two narratives which by virtue of their programmatic content stand out from all the others and thus provide, in a thematic respect, a decisive and distinctive stamp to the whole: these two are the Bethel story and the Peniel story. In both of them the paradoxical character of the divine action is as sharp as can be imagined.[1]

For it is God who said, "Let light shine out of darkness," who has shone in our hearts to give the light of the knowledge of the glory of God in the face of Jesus Christ (2 Cor. 4:6).

---

[1] Gerhard Von Rad, *Biblical Interpretations in Preaching,* trans. John E. Steely (Nashville: Abingdon, 1977), 40.

4.11 Jacob—Bethel to Peniel

Preface

"[Biblical] history unfolds a theology in action."[2]

The character of Jacob in Genesis fascinates me whenever I delve into his story. Someday, I mused, I will give quality time to a study of this complex, illuminating, and crucial patriarchal character. The theological nature of the patriarchal stories, the rhetoric with which they are told, and their place and function in the account of God's people possess a unique attraction, especially the story of Jacob. So much is imbedded in these narratives; they are so artfully constructed. What all they are saying and how they tell it is an enticing challenge to the reader.

Although I write within the contemporary context as a spiritual and theological heir of the Anglican divine, John Wesley, I am not necessarily attempting to write a Wesleyan theology of Jacob. I am concerned rather with the biblical picture of Jacob and how in his family structure and setting God works in him and with him to form him into

---

[22] Meir Sternberg, *The Poetics of Biblical Narrative: Ideological Lit6eraturre and the Drama of Reading* (Bloomington: Indiana University Press, 1985), 45.

the spiritual as well as the biological father of an elect people. It is a story told through the eyes of the faith of ancient Israel. I seek to discover how God's transformation of Jacob speaks to us within our particular heritages, wherever we are in the providence of God. I write as a Christian without apology. The text of Genesis confronts us with a view of the relationship between God and humankind that can speak to, confirm, and inform our New Testament faith.

Jacob is one of three patriarchs who belong together in biblical history—Abraham, Isaac, and Jacob. When their descendants were slaves in Egypt, the God of the Israelites identified himself to Moses at the burning bush as "the God of your father, the God of Abraham, the God of Isaac, and the God of Jacob" (Exod. 3:6). Jesus cited this text against the Sadducees to affirm that the Lord "is God not of the dead, but of the living" (Luke 20:37). The three patriarchs are named together twenty-one times in the Old Testament and seven times in the New Testament.[3] They are the unique three who are the beginning of a specific called-out, elect people, Israel, through whom the biblical God

---

[3] Matt. 8:11, 12:32; Mark 12:36; Luke 13:28, 20:37; Acts 3:13. 7:32.

chose to reveal himself to the world. Abraham is called "the Father" of a people, but it is Jacob who bears the name "Israel" and whose sons were the ancestors of the twelve tribes.

The story of Jacob proper is best seen as beginning in the womb of his mother Rebekah (25:19) and ending with Jacob's return to Bethel and the death of his father Isaac (35:29). At that point the plot shifts to the descendants of Esau. The several sections of the Jacob story (25:19—35:29) can be analyzed structurally in a chiastic (ab**xba**) arrangement. Gordon Wenham points out that when they are viewed as such, the central account (**x**) is the "Birth of Jacob's sons" (29:31—30:24) and serves as the turning point of the Jacob story.[4] The Israelites are literally "the sons of Israel." We, the Church of New Testament revelation, can see much of ourselves in Jacob's life and experience of God—who and what we are as frail humans, and who we are by the grace, calling, and presence of God.

The occasion to write this study comes through the indulgence of the "Come and Go" Sunday School Class at First Church of the

---

[4] Gordon J. Wenham, *Genesis 16-50*, Volume 2, Word Biblical Commentary (Dallas, Texas: Word Books, Publisher, 1994), 169-170.

Nazarene in San Diego, California. Included foremost are my co-teacher Herbert L. Prince and our esteemed leader Arthur Seamans. From May 2011 to July 2013 we immersed ourselves in a study of the book of Genesis. When we came to the Jacob stories, they allowed me the privilege of concentrating on the figure of Jacob for as long as it takes.

I give the primary title "From Bethel to Peniel" to our journey into Jacob's heart and character. Part I: "To Bethel" covers the treatment of Jacob from conception in Rebekah's womb to his discovery of himself in "the house of God" (28:17). Part II: "To Peniel" indicates Jacob's story as climaxed in his mysterious wrestling match that takes place in the context of his meeting with his estranged brother Esau. Jacob named that place "Peniel" (32:30) meaning "the face of God." The Jacob story concludes with The "Epilogue" that brings Jacob back to Bethel and wraps up the essence of the story as "the descendants of Isaac" (25:19--35:29).

I have chosen the Hebrew expression הִנֵּנִי (*hinēnî*) "Here I am!" as a secondary and more personal title. This Hebrew expression has long fascinated me—a prayer for life! On Jacob's lips, it expresses his response when the angel of God called him by name in a dream, "Jacob," and he replied, "Here I am" (31:11). With this same response, his brother Esau responds obediently to his Father Isaac (27:1) and Jacob answers Isaac deceitfully (27:11) earlier in the Jacob narrative.

Although not a key phrase in the Jacob story, "Here I am," does appear meaningfully earlier in the patriarchal stories. Its significance comes mainly from Genesis 22:1, 7 and 11 where Abraham responds with "Here I am!" to God's call to take his only son Isaac to "the land of Moriah, and there offer him as a burnt offering." Then, when Isaac becomes concerned about the absence of "the lamb for a burnt offering," he calls out "Father," and Abraham answers, "Here I am, my son." And third, when "the angel of the LORD called to him from heaven, . . . 'Abraham, Abraham,'" and tells Abraham not to lay his hand on his son Isaac, Abraham responds, "Here I am!" In the prophecy of Isaiah even God uses it to announce his presence to a rebellious people:

> I was ready to be sought out by those who did not ask,
>   to be found by those who did not seek me.
> I said, "Here I am, here I am,"
>   to a nation that did not fall on my name (65:1).

The response of "Here I am" from the Abraham and Isaac account is an appropriate response as we give our minds and hearts to the Jacob story. I invite the reader along with me to discover ourselves in the study of Jacob and God's providential dealings with him. The expression captures for us the presence and call of God according to his purpose in human life. We see this vividly as well in Moses' response to the divine voice in the burning bush (Exod. 3:4), the boy Samuel's use of the phrase (1 Sam. 3:4-10), and Isaiah's answer to the call of God in his vision of the holiness of the LORD in the Temple (6:8).

The writer to the Hebrews reports the crowning use of this significant expression (10:5-7). He writes that "when Christ came into the world" Christ prayed that "a body you have prepared for me." In Hebrews, as Jesus was facing his coming death, his exclamation, "See God, I have come to do your will O God," reflects Psalm 40:7-8. The Psalmist says, "'Here I am,' , , , I delight to do your will, O my God." The Christ on the path to the Cross is One who fully says, *"hinēnî"*-- "Here I am"!

"Jacob as Israel" is a theme that penetrates these stories. Jacob is a person in his own right whose character is carefully and subtly delineated with a clearly defined personality that develops and matures over the course of the story. But Jacob is more than an individual. In Jacob, Israel, both man and nation, saw God face to face, lived and was blessed--a great mystery. The generations of the faithful in Israel who heard this story could affirm that what had happened to Jacob was true, because it also had happened to them. As the traditions develop that tell his story, Jacob becomes the nation Israel as such, and the later experiences of the Israelite people shaped how the story of Jacob is told. As Israel saw themselves in these stories of promise, conflict, and blessing, so we can as the disciples of him who in his person fulfilled the destiny of the nation Israel. Karl Barth declares that "this Israel's name is now Jesus of Nazareth,"[5] the one faithful Israelite!

I invite you on a quest with me for the "biblical" Jacob and the witness of these narratives as scripture to the God of Abraham, Isaac, and Jacob, now known to us as the "Father of our Lord Jesus Christ" (2

___

[5] Karl Barth, *Dogmatics in Outline,* trans. G. T. Thompson (New York: Harper & Brothers, 1959), 79.

Cor. 1:3). Our goal is the Jacob of divine promise and blessing in as much depth as possible. On this quest we face stories of a very human man, stories that in the providence of the God of the Bible have become scripture for the Jewish and Christian faith-communities. We will look at them "as they are" in the biblical text with Meir Sternberg, that is, in the "historiographic terms"[6] of the Bible itself. The literary structure and style of the biblical narrative will furnish the subtle clues that contribute to the interpretation of the events recounted in the text. We seek to appreciate the power of the rhetoric as it releases to our hearts the theological witness of the text.

I explore this sacred literature in its final wholeness as the remembered traditions of a people whom God has formed through whom to bless the nations. These traditions retell the story of Jacob as the witness of a called-out people to the meaning of the God who invaded their history and whose chosen people they believe they are. These are "faith stories" of how faith is operative in the rawness of human experience, yet stories designed to stir the imagination and

---

[6] Sternberg, *The Poetics of Biblical Narrative*, 34.

transform the faith of the reader. Robert Alter concludes his book on *The Art of Biblical Narrative* with a word of encouragement for such reading:

> Subsequent religious tradition has by and large encouraged us to take the Bible seriously rather than to enjoy it, but the paradoxical truth of the matter may well be that by learning to enjoy the biblical stores more fully as stories, we shall also come to see more clearly what they mean to tell us about God, man, and the perilously momentous realm of history.[7]

The LORD of hosts is with us;
the God of Jacob is our refuge.[8]

---

[7] Robert Alter, *The Art of Biblical Narrative* (New York: Basic Books, Inc., Publishers, 1981), 189.

[8] Psalm 46:7, 11.

Acknowledgments

In this study I have relied heavily on the highly stimulating work of J. P. Fokkelman, *Narrative Art in Genesis: Specimens of Stylistic and Structural Analysis* (1991), the very informative commentary by Gordon J. Wenham, *Genesis 16-50,* Word Biblical Commentary, Volume 2 (1994), and Kevin Walton, *Thou Traveller Unknown: The Presence and Absence of God in the Jacob Narrative* (2003). Fokkelman looks at the text from a modern literary perspective apart from historical questions. Wenham is a thorough commentary employing the state of research at the time of writing. Kevin Walton's study is primarily theological with the aim of bringing together theological, literary, and historical tools.

The influence of these three is present even when precise documentation is lacking. I do, however, endeavor to be faithful in documenting their contributions in direct quotations and occasional unique insights into the Genesis text. The valuable works of Robert Alter, Walter Brueggemann, Franz Delitzsch, Michal Fishbane, Terrence E. Fretheim, Gerhard von Rad, John H. Walton, and not least Claus Westermann, are employed in the same manner. The influence of one or all of the above mentioned sources may be detected by the informed reader on almost every page whether or not documentation is present.

Herbert L. Prince, my theologian/philosopher co-teacher, ploughed the way ahead of me through the narrative in "Part II: To Peniel" and I relied often on his excellent work and his continuing critique of the manuscript as it took full manuscript form. I am grateful also to friends Dean Nelson and Ernie J. Loos who have read and responded to the completed work.

Prologue: Why Jacob?
(Genesis 32:22-32).

The name "Jacob" occupies a very prominent role in our Bibles even beyond the Genesis record. It occurs over 250 times in the Old and New Testaments combined. The various ways in which it appears indicate the name's significance in biblical tradition. In Moses' day the God of the Israelites described himself to Moses at the burning bush as "the God of your father, the God of Abraham, the God of Isaac, and the God of Jacob" (Exod. 3:6, 15, 16). Jesus quoted this patriarchal description in answer to the Sadducee's question about the resurrection (Matt. 22:32; Mark 12:26; Luke 20:37) and it is found twice in Acts, once on the lips of Peter (3:13) and again in the speech of Stephen (7:32).

The name "Jacob" in the expression, "The God of Jacob," stands most often for the nation of Israel from Exodus on in the Old Testament, particularly in the Psalms and the Prophets. With this meaning, "Jacob" can stand alone (Ps. 53:6) or appear in phrases such as "the house of Jacob" (Isa. 2:5), "the fortunes of Jacob" (Ps. 85:1), "the Mighty One of Jacob" (Ps. 132:2), and "the glory of Jacob" (Isa. 17:4), among others less frequent.[9] With good reason we take comfort and courage from the

Psalmist whose faith exclaims,

Happy are those whose help is the God of Jacob,
whose hope is in the LORD their God (146:5).

James S. Stewart in a sermon on this Psalm text published after

his death on "The God of Jacob," asks "Why the God of *Jacob* in

particular? . . . Why not the God of Abraham? Why not the God of

Moses?" The "old psalmists and prophets," he writes,

> prayed with greater confidence when they remembered it was the
> God of Jacob they were praying to. They sang with more
> glowing rapture when they reflected that it was the God of Jacob
> who was listening to their praises. They faced life with firmer
> courage when they knew that it was the God of Jacob who was
> with them.[10]

"Why the God of Jacob?" We shall see as we probe his story.

Meir Sternberg startles us by the assertion that "the Bible

habitually generates ambivalence."[11] This is true especially of the Jacob

---

[9] Such include "dwelling places" (Ps. 82:7); "survivors" (Isa. 10:21); "the Holy One" (Isa. 29:23); "offspring" (Isa. 45:19); "tribes" (Isa.49:6); "habitations" (Lam. 2:2); "transgression" (Mic. 1:5); "majesty" (Nah. 2:2).

[10] James S. Stewart, *Walking With God,* ed. Gordon Grant (Edinburgh: Saint Andrew Press, 1956), 63. This   book was compiled at the instigation of his son, the Reverend Robin Stewart, with a memoir by his father's friend and parish minister, the Very Reverend Bill McDonald.

[11] Sternberg, *The Poetics of Biblical Narrative,* 38.

stories. Typical of these accounts, for example, is the discord between divine election and moral stature, yet, they display an underlying harmony. Kevin Walton reminds us in the opening sentence of his fascinating study that "the story of Jacob is theologically complex." He sees this complexity in terms of a paradox. On the one hand, indications of divine revelation and purpose are clear to Jacob. On the other hand, the character and actions of Jacob as well as the events surrounding him "show little evidence of divine presence." Jacob's story thus "centres around the presence and absence of the divine."[12]

Illustrative of the axiom quoted by Meir Sternberg that "the Bible has many secrets but no Secret"[13] is one of the most fascinating, enigmatic, and mysterious accounts in Scripture that appears at a crucial point in the life of the patriarch Jacob:

> [22]The same night he got up and took his two wives, his two maids, and his eleven children, and crossed the ford of the Jabbok.[23]He took them and sent them across the stream, and likewise everything that he had.[24]Jacob was left alone; and a man wrestled with him until daybreak.[25]When the man saw that he did not prevail against Jacob, he struck him on the hip socket;

---

[12] Kevin Walton, *Thou Traveller Unknown: The Presence and Absence of God in the Jacob Narrative* (Waynesboro, Georgia: Paternoster, 2003), 1.

[13] Sternberg, *The Poetics of Biblical Narrative*, 49.

and Jacob's hip was put out of joint as he wrestled with him.[26]Then he said, "Let me go, for the day is breaking." But Jacob said, "I will not let you go, unless you bless me."[27]So he said to him, "What is your name?" And he said, "Jacob."[28]Then the man said, "You shall no longer be called Jacob, but Israel, for you have striven with God and with humans, and have prevailed."[29]Then Jacob asked him, "Please tell me your name." But he said, "Why is it that you ask my name?" And there he blessed him.[30]So Jacob called the place Peniel, saying, "For I have seen God face to face, and yet my life is preserved."[31]The sun rose upon him as he passed Penuel, limping because of his hip.[32]Therefore to this day the Israelites do not eat the thigh muscle that is on the hip socket, because he struck Jacob on the hip socket at the thigh muscle (32:22-32).

One of Charles Wesley's most outstanding poems is "Wrestling Jacob" inspired by Jacob's experience at Peniel. [14] Isaac Watts (1674-1748), himself no mean composer of hymns from the same period, was quick to say that this single poem, "Wrestling Jacob," was worth all the verses he himself had written. John Wesley, a little over two weeks after his brother's death, "tried to give out this hymn at Bolton, but broke down when he came to the lines,

My company before is gone,

---

[14] Charles Wesley, "Wrestling Jacob," Franz Hildebrandt, Oliver A. Beckerlegge, and James Dale, ed., *A Collection of Hymns for the use of the People called Methodists,* Volume 7, *The Works of John Wesley* (Nashville: Abingdon Press, 1983), 250-252. It was first published in 1742.

And I am left alone with thee." [15]

Although we are not seeking a Wesleyan interpretation of the Jacob stories, we do set before us Charles Wesley's hymn as a link to our heritage as Wesleyans:

> Come, O thou Traveller unknown,
>   Whom still I hold but cannot see!
> My company before is gone,
>   And I am left alone with thee;
> With thee all night I mean to stay,
> And wrestle till the break of day.
>
> I need not tell thee who I am,
>   My misery or sin declare;
> Thyself hast called me by my name;
>   Look on thy hands, and read it there.
>
> But who, I ask thee, who art thou?
> Tell me thy name, and tell me now.
>
> In vain thou strugglest to get free;
>   I never will unloose my hold;
> Art thou the Man that died for me?
>   The secret of thy love unfold:
> Wrestling, I will not let thee go
> Till I thy name, thy nature know.
>
> Wilt thou not yet to me reveal
>   Thy new, unutterable name?

---

[15] Hildebrandt, Beckerlegge, and Dale, ed., *A Collection of Hymns for the use of the People called Methodists*, 250.

Tell me, I still beseech thee, tell'
     To know it now resolved I am:
Wrestling, I will not let thee go
Till I thy name, thy nature know.

What   though   my   shrinking   flesh
complain
     And murmur to contend so long?
I rise superior to my pain,
     When I am weak, then I am
strong;
And when my all of strength shall fail
I shall with the God-Man prevail.

Yield to me now--for I am weak,
     But confident in self-despair!
Speak to my heart, in blessings speak,
     Be conquered by my instant
prayer:
Speak, or thou never hence shalt move,
And tell me if thy name is LOVE.

'Tis Love! 'Tis Love! Thou diedst for me;
     I hear the whisper in my heart.
The morning breaks, the shadows flee,
     Pure Universal Love thou art:
To me, to all, thy bowels move--
Thy nature, and thy name, is LOVE.

My prayer has power with God; the grace
     Unspeakable I now receive;
Through faith I see thee face to face;
     I see thee face to face, and live!
In vain I have not wept and strove--
Thy nature, and thy name, is LOVE.

I know thee, Saviour, who thou art—
    Jesus, the feeble sinner's friend;
Nor wilt thou with the night depart,
    But stay and love me to the end:
Thy mercies never shall remove:
Thy nature, and thy name, is LOVE.

The Sun of Righteousness on me
    Hath rose with healing in his
  wings;
Withered my nature's strength; from thee
    My soul its life and succor brings;
My help is all laid up above;
Thy nature, and thy name, is LOVE.

Contented now upon my thigh
    I halt, till life's short journey end;
All helplessness, all weakness, I
    On thee alone for strength depend;
Nor have I power from thee to move:
Thy nature, and thy name is LOVE

Lame as I am, I take the prey,
    Hell, earth, and sin with ease
  o'ercome;
I leap for joy, pursue my way,
And as a bounding hart fly home,
Through all eternity to prove,
The nature, and thy name, is LOVE.[16]

Frances M. Young (b. 1939), a British theologian and

[16] Hildebrandt, Beckerlegge, and Dale, ed., *A Collection of Hymns for the use of the People called Methodists*, 250-252, Hymn #136. Verses 5 and 7 are taken from Frank Baker, ed., *Representative Verse of Charles Wesley* (Nashville: Abingdon Press, 1962), 38.

Methodist minister, in her *Brokenness and Blessing* devotes an entire chapter to "Wrestling Jacob." [17] An undercurrent in the book is her life with her first-born son, Arthur, who was born with profound learning disabilities, and failing to progress as a child, was extremely physically handicapped. As she and her husband supported him in their home, she described him in his late thirties as "totally dependent for all his everyday functions, such as feeding, washing, dressing, [and] mobility."[18] Frances Young shares how caring for Arthur affected her faith:

> For years I found holding onto faith profoundly difficult. God seemed absent. But then one day, as I got up from my chair to do some household chore, I suddenly heard a voice, as it were: "It makes no difference to me whether you believe in me or not!" It was meaningful at all kinds of levels: for one thing I was absolved of responsibility for deciding about God, for God no longer depended on me for existence—God just "is," independent of what I thought or felt.[19]

It is understandable why Frances Young found Jacob at Peniel helpful for her own "wrestling." As part of her study she sketches how

---

[17] Francis M. Young, *Brokenness and Blessing: Towards a Biblical Spirituality* (Grand Rapids: Baker Academic, 2007), 39-59. .Frances Young is the retired Edward Cadbury Professor of Theology at the University of Birmingham, England, where she taught from 1971 to 2005.

[18] Young ,*Brokenness and Blessing,* 31.

[19] Young ,*Brokenness and Blessing,* 32.

the Genesis 32 account was understood in the Church Fathers including

Augustine (354-430) and concluding with Gregory Nazianzen (329-

389). These Fathers approached the account with interpretive freedom as

did Charles Wesley who related the biblical text to his own soul and the

story of its salvation:

> He is left alone to wrestle (v. 1), demanding to know who is the
> stranger with whom he struggles (vv. 2-4). Like Jacob, he knows
> himself a sinner (v. 2) and wrestles for release, wanting to know
> the name and nature of God in Christ. To see God face to face is
> to receive God's grace, to know that God is love (vv. 5-8). The
> soul limps on life's journey as a result (v 9), and yet is
> empowered, because it is dependent on God alone (vv. 9-10).[20]

Our study of Jacob sets its long range sight on this climax in the

Jacob story. Along with the Creation narratives and Genesis 22, Jacob's

wrestling match is a high peak account in the Genesis narratives. It is the

tip of the mountain in Genesis *as* "revelation." The entire Jacob story is

in itself most fascinating and instructive. We see who the people of God

are, and thus who you and I are in process as a people who have come

into being as the culmination of scriptural revelation.

---

[20] Young, *Brokenness and Blessing*, 42.

We begin what is entitled the *"Tol^{e}dot* of Isaac" in Genesis 25:19—35:29: "These are the descendants (*tol^{e}dot*) of Isaac, Abraham's son" (25:19).[21] The eleven occurrences of the Hebrew word *tol^{e}dot* is a significant feature of the structure of Genesis. This we are familiar with as the King James' "generations." For the Hebrew *tol^{e}dot,* the *New Revised Standard Version* employs "generations" in 2:4, "descendants" in 5:1; 6:9; 10:1; 11:10, 27; 25:12, 19; 36:1, 9; and "story" in 37:1, which then reads, "this is the story of the family of Jacob." This latter heading, and Jacob now as the head of the family, is how the quite different story of Joseph (37:2—50:26) begins, which occupies the rest of Genesis.

We understand the noun *tol^{e}dot* in Genesis as introducing what follows it in the text, whether narrative, genealogy, or a combination of both. The *"Tol^{e}dot* of Isaac" (25:19—35:29), the account of Jacob's life, thus ends appropriately with the report of Isaac's death in 35:28-29; Isaac lived to be one hundred eighty "and his sons Esau and Jacob

---

[21] We are following the structural analysis of Genesis proposed by John H. Walton, *Genesis,* The New Application Commentary (Grand Rapids: Zondervan, 2001), 58-59.

buried him." So with 25:19, "These are the descendants (*tol^edot*) of Isaac," the family history or lineage of Isaac, we enter the story of Jacob and his family. Characteristically in the patriarchal narratives, the heading mentions the father and the stories focus on the sons.

Some biblical scholars, however, disagree both about the meaning of the Hebrew *tol^edot* in any given occurrence and whether it follows or precedes the section to which it refers. For example, many interpreters take its use in Genesis 2:4 to refer to what precedes rather than to what follows. Although not a *tol^edot,* however, Genesis 1:1 can be viewed as a literary introduction to what follows, that is, it functions as a *tol^edot*.

To begin the account of "the descendants (*tol^edot*) of Isaac" (25:19—35:29), we leave the story of Abraham entitled in Genesis as "the descendants of Terah" (11:27-25:11). Before the stories of Jacob begin at 25:19, his grandmother Sarah has died (23:1-20) as well as his grandfather Abraham (25:1-11). The brief account of "the descendants of Ishmael" follows that takes note of Ishmael's children by Hagar, Ishmael's death, and where his family has settled (25:12-18).

But after Jacob's grandmother dies and before the death of his grandfather Abraham, Jacob's father to be, Isaac, needs a wife. The covenant with Abraham demands a new generation; the covenant is to be fulfilled through a distinct family. The ethnic people of the land, the Canaanites, are not related to the family of Abraham in any way. So lest Isaac assimilate with the people whom his descendants are eventually to drive out of the land, Isaac must find a wife from among his family members back in the city of Nahor.

To do this Abraham deploys his oldest servant "who had charge of all that he had" (24:2) to find a suitable wife for Isaac among Abraham's kindred. Significantly, a non-Canaanite wife must be willing to go with the servant back to Canaan to marry Isaac and live with him there. The account is a delightfully constructed love story (24:1-67): "Isaac brought her into his mother Sarah's tent. He took Rebekah, and she became his wife; and he loved her. So Isaac was comforted after his mother's death" (24:67).

So what about Jacob's father, Isaac? Who and what kind of man is Isaac? Is he merely the shadow figure in the patriarchal narrative as

Thomas Mann describes him?[22] Isaac seems to appear only as a copy or reflection of Abraham in chapter 26. Isaac is blessed for Abraham's sake—a seemingly passive, deferential, character. The LORD appears to Isaac and the promise given to Abraham is now passed on to Isaac (vv. 1-5; see vv. 23-25). Isaac resides in Canaan, becomes involved with Abimelech, and interestingly, in fear, lies about his wife to Abimelech just like his father before him (26:6-11). And then in chapter 27, Isaac appears as an old man, blind and gullible on his deathbed. Is he simply a transition figure whose main distinction is being the son of Abraham and the father of Jacob?

A reader would normally expect that with the death of Abraham the Genesis narrator would fully focus on Isaac. After all, traditionally, Isaac is given equal billing with Abraham and Jacob as Israel's founding patriarchs: "I am the God of your father, the God of Abraham, the God of Isaac, and the God of Jacob" (Exod. 3:6-16). Instead, the narrative quickly shifts its attention from Isaac to his children; Isaac serves primarily as the link between Abraham and Jacob. There is no *tol^edot* of

---

[22] Thomas W. Mann, *The Book of the Torah: The Narrative Integrity of the Pentateuch* (Atlanta: John Knox Press, 1988), 51.

Abraham or story of Isaac; only a *tol^edot* of Isaac, the story of Isaac's children, Jacob and Esau (25:19—35:29), an account that ends with the death of Isaac (35:28-29).

As one looks ahead, this story is in a real sense a story of conflict, flight and return, and as such is a Jacob-Esau story. The major movements in the story can be seen as twofold, first as Jacob and Esau—deception, and then Esau and Jacob—reconciliation. Further, all the way through the narrative, the prominence of blessing, not to exclude the promise, characterizes the foreground of this Jacob-Esau story.

A threefold look at the accounts gives us perspective.[23] The Jacob story begins with "Jacob in Canaan" (25:19—28:22). The stories are told of the birth of the twin boys, the birthright and the blessing, followed by Jacob's hasty and fearful departure. The section closes with Jacob's dream at Bethel: "Surely the LORD is in this place—and I did not know it!" (28:16). "Jacob in Haran" (29:1—31:35) finds Jacob now with his larger family headed by his uncle Laban. Jacob marries, has

---

[23] The threefold division is that of John Walton, *Genesis*, 58-59.

children, and prospers materially even beyond his benefactor, uncle Laban. Again Jacob flees and he and Laban agree to part: "The LORD watch between you and me, when we are absent one from the other" (31:49). "Jacob returns to Canaan" (32:1—35:29) finds him dealing again with the reality of his wronged brother Esau. A mysterious wrestling match takes place at Peniel after which Jacob meets with Esau: "Truly to see your face is like seeing the face of God" (33:10). Jacob then returns to Bethel.

While Abrahams' character was questionable, Jacob's is unscrupulous as will be seen—and God and his ways are inscrutable! Yet, a people, a nation, God's people, are being formed. God is at work purposively. In view is a servant people for the blessing of the nations, a people whose loins contain the line of the Servant: "The Son of Man came not to be served, but to serve, and to give his life a ransom for many" (Mark 10:45).

The end figure of the redemptive history beginning with Abraham, Isaac, and Jacob—Jesus, taught us to pray, "Your kingdom come." Scriptures teaches us plainly that the kingdom of God is *always* at work in and through people--*such we are*! When we pray the prayer that Jesus taught us to pray, our request for the kingdom includes our own day-to-day lives—in and through us Lord, now, who we are and where we are: "Your kingdom come" (Luke 11:2).

Part I: To Bethel
(Genesis 25:19—28:22)

I.
Isaac and Rebekah
(25:19—26:30)

ONE
What's In a Name?
(Genesis 25:19-26)

Genesis 25:22:

The children struggled together within her; and she said, "If it is to be this way, why do I live?" So she went to inquire of the LORD.

Come, O thou Traveller unknown,

Whom still I hold but cannot see!

My company before is gone,

And I am left alone with thee;

With thee all night I mean to stay,

And wrestle till the break of day. [24]

Twin boys are born. A story of depth and density, a story that one can read at more than one level begins. A fascinating perspective from which to view the story of Jacob is that of character development, and at a profound level, an account of a spiritual pilgrimage. Jacob did

---

[24] Hildebrandt, Beckerlegge, and Dale, ed., *A Collection of Hymns for the use of the People called Methodists*, 250.

not leave home on such a quest; he was simply fleeing his brother's fury. Our lives are often similar; we do not intend their circumstances, their true significance; it just overtakes us unawares—providentially—with a hidden purpose.

I am, and perhaps you are as well, fascinated by biography and autobiography. specially, I enjoy novels that deal with personal growth and enrichment. We are fascinated with the expansion of intellect and spirit and the course of life transformation—this is the power of the Jacob story.

On Hitler's Mountain by Irmgard A. Hunt is one such account. Irmgard was born in 1934, the year following Adolf Hitler's rise to power in Germany. She lived with her parents in Berchtesgaden, Bavaria, a village resting in the shadow of Hitler's Eagle's Nest and near the lair of the Nazi elite. Hitler had made Obersalzberg, a hamlet up the mountain from Berchtesgaden, his home and headquarters. Irmgard Hunt writes that Hitler's "presence on that mountain stamped my early years with a uniqueness that could not be claimed by other middle-class children elsewhere in Germany. The mountain loomed large over every aspect of my childhood."[25]

Irmgard Hunt's parents were pro-Nazi largely because the Nazis had reversed the economic chaos of the Weimar Republic—now they had jobs! But her mother's parents and an aunt saw through the prosperity façade to the brutal totalitarian nature of the Nazi regime. Irmgard's aunt lived nearby in Berchtesgaden and her grandparents resided elsewhere in Germany. During these childhood years—she was ten when the American army arrived in May, 1945—Irmgard, as she admits with her precocious talent for eavesdropping and spying, thrived on local gossip, word-of-mouth news, adult conversations, and repeatedly told tales.

Irmgard Hunt shares her life under the Nazis in this memoir of her early years. She describes how she dealt with it all as a child, how various villagers acted, what she thought as the war and its deprivations made their relentless impact on her life, and how her understandings and attitude slowly changed. At three years of age, she sat on Hitler's knee,

---

[25] Irmgard A. Hunt, *On Hitler's Mountain: Overcoming the Legacy of a Nazi Childhood* (New York: HarperCollins Publishers, 2005), 2.

which in later years she remembered in horror. Her account ends with depictions of life under American occupation. She eventually emigrated to the United States in 1968 for she had married an American doctor. Irmgard Hunt's story is not a Jacob story, yet it is a story of an intellectual and spiritual journey as only a child could experience it, a life as she later began to view as life under the rule of monsters.

We first meet our anti-hero Jacob in the womb of his mother Rebekah, identified there as one "who struggles with his brother." As his story moves to its climax, Jacob becomes Israel, he "who struggles with God!" What kind of transformation of perspective is taking place in Jacob's mind? Is he undergoing a change of heart? How did such an apparently spiritual journey come about? Jacob's story leads us to ask, "Who *were* we?" And now, "Who *are* we?" Will we and Jacob answer with Dietrich Bonhoeffer's "Whoever I am, thou knowest me; O God, I am thine."[26]

---

[26] Dietrich Bonhoeffer, *Letters and Papers from Prison,* Dietrich Bonhoeffer Works, Volume 8, ed. John W. de Gruchy, trans, Isabel Best, Lisa Dahill, Reinhard Kraus, and Nancy Luiens (Minneapolis: Fortress Press, 2010), 460.

We can say with Jacob that our lives have a divine perspective. In the plot of Jacob's life, God is not an obvious character, yet he can be observed as a mysterious mover behind the scenes. God's providential scheme creates its own paradoxes. Here the younger twin is favored over the elder, it seems, by the sheer grace of God. Yet, Esau is seen as unworthy—he "despised his birthright" (25:34). With us, as with Jacob, observes Kevin Walton, God "works through agents, with a strong sense of paradox and mystery."[27]

As our story marches toward Bethel it begins with a birth report in Genesis 25:19-34, specifically in verses 21-26. This is the first of the many biblical scenes that make up the narrative of Jacob's life. Many view the birth account as both a conclusion to the Abraham-Isaac narrative and a prologue or introduction to the Jacob story binding the two accounts together. The report foreshadows how the entire scope of the Jacob story will develop as an account of strife in the family. The predominant tension in the Jacob cycle is set in motion in Thomas

---

[27] K. Walton, *Thou Traveller Unknown,* 25-27.

Mann's vivid description as "Esau and Jacob 'crash together' in Rebekah's womb":[28]

> The children struggled together within her; and she said, 'If it is to be this way, why do I live?' So she went to inquire of the LORD" (25:22).

From here on throughout the Jacob accounts until chapter 33, Jacob continues as one "who struggles with his brother."

After the death of his wife Sarah and the marriage of his son Isaac to Rebekah, Abraham takes another wife, Keturah, and has more children by her. As Abraham solved the threat to Isaac's status in regard to Ishmael, so to Keturah's sons "Abraham gave gifts, while he was still living, and sent them away from his son Isaac, eastward to the east country." In contrast, the narrator states that "Abraham gave all he had to Isaac" (25:1-6). Then at the age of 175 years, Abraham died and was buried in the cave of Machpelah. Isaac then settled at Beer-lahai-roi (25:7-11).

Beer-lahai-roi is difficult to locate, but the name means "the well of the Living One who sees me." When an angel appeared to Hagar at

---

[28] Mann, *The Book of the Torah*, 52.

the well, she named it Beer-lahai-roi (16:14). The short *Tol^edot* of

Ishmael (25:12-18)—the naming of his descendants and account of his

death at 137 years—follows the death of Abraham and brings us to

25:19.

The story of Jacob begins in earnest with

Isaac's Family
(25:19-20)

[19]These are the descendants of Isaac, Abraham's son: Abraham
was the father of Isaac, [20]and Isaac was forty years old when he
married Rebekah, daughter of Bethuel the Aramean of Paddan-
aram, sister of Laban the Aramean.

These verses lead us into Genesis 25:19--35:29 as "the

descendants" or *Tol^edot* "of Isaac." This is the family history of Isaac

that consists of the Jacob-Esau narrative. Although the focus is on the

wiles and drive of Jacob, the ancient narrator does not allow him to be

simply an isolated individual. Relatives are significant. Jacob—and

Esau—belong to the family of Abraham; their grandfather is the

exemplary blessed one.[29]

---

[29] Genesis 12:1-3, 7; 13:14-17; 15:5-7, 18; 17:1-8, 15-20; 22:16-18; 24:1.

Rebekah, the mother of Esau and Jacob, is even more important than Isaac for the progress of the story. She is the daughter of a man worth naming and locating: "Bethuel the Aramean of Paddan-aram," the land from which Abraham came. As the homeland of Rebekah and Laban, Paddan-aram was somewhere in northern Mesopotamia, possibly in the vicinity of Haran (11:31).[30] Rebekah is the "sister of Laban the Aramean," a clever character in his own right. Laban's life becomes life intimately intertwined with that of Jacob who becomes his son-in-law—doubly so! Laban will dictate Jacob's life for almost twenty years in Paddan-aram (29:1—31:55).

Two significant separations have taken place in the progress of Israel's patriarchal history: the separation of Abraham from the other nations and the separation of the son of promise, Isaac, from Abraham's other offspring. Abraham's other children were Ishmael the son of Hagar, the Egyptian maid, and his sons by Keturah whom he married after Sarah dies (25:1-6). The process of separation by divine election

---

[30] Paddan-aram, unique to Genesis, occurs at 28:2, 5-7; 31:18; 33:18; 35:9, 26; 46:15; 48:7.

and yet fully human, now continues; we see its beginnings between the twin sons of Isaac, Esau the elder son and Jacob the younger.

The narrative spends minimum time on Isaac, primarily as the son of Abraham and as one described as "the son of forty years" when he married Rebekah. The narrator mentions his age of "forty years" apparently because Isaac had to wait until he was sixty for an offspring—twenty long years of anxious waiting. Now to the heart of the account:

Pregnancy
(25:21-23)

[21]Isaac prayed to the LORD for his wife, because she was barren; and the LORD granted his prayer, and his wife Rebekah conceived. [22]The children struggled together within her; and she said, "If it is to be this way, why do I live?" So she went to inquire of the LORD. [23]And the LORD said to her, "Two nations are in your womb, and two peoples born of you shall be divided; the one shall be stronger than the other, the elder shall serve the younger."

The narrator begins with Isaac in the foreground but quickly shifts to Rebekah as the focus of attention as Isaac moves to the background. With her, we meet the familiar obstacle of barrenness prominent in the Abraham narratives,[31] a motif that defines Rebekah's firstborn sons as the gift of God. They are therefore special—sons born special like Sarah's Isaac foreshadow the dramatic significance of the initial barrenness of Jacob's future wife, Rachel.

Rebekah has been barren for twenty years, a miserable condition in ancient society, thus Isaac's anxiety. Her long barrenness makes Isaac's life an enigma; as a child of the promise to Abraham, Isaac has no children. Isaac functions as the intercessor in keeping with patriarchal custom. For the first time in the story, Isaac takes the initiative as he "prayed to the LORD for his wife" for many years. The verbs used in "Isaac prayed to" and "the LORD granted his prayer" are active and passive forms of the same verb—"entreated" and "was entreated"; they stress the effect of his prayer as the text reports in quick sequence that "his wife Rebekah conceived."

Apart from Rebekah's despairing "Why," her cry of lament is difficult to translate, it is literally, "If so, why such [this]?" Most satisfactory is probably *The Torah*'s suggestion that Rebekah is asking.

---

[31] Gen. 11:30; 15:1-6; 16:1-6; 17:15-22; 18:1-15; 21:1-7.

"What good is life if I have to suffer like this?"[32] Claus Westermann notes that Rebekah's cry "is the primeval cry of 'Why?' about the meaning of life, an expression of anguish across the whole of human history." [33] The cause of her cry appears more than natural female anxiety. Is it a premonition or portent of dreadful things to come? The silence of the text may suggest that Isaac is apparently unaware of Rebekah's suffering, mental surely, and perhaps even of her physical discomfort.

The crucial point in the birth story is not the birth of the twins but the future fate of the struggle between the two boys. The striving within Rebekah sets the tone for the motif of struggle that will characterize the lives of the characters in the Jacob stories, beginning even between their parents. Rebekah's thoughts become even more threatening after the boys have grown: "Your brother Esau is consoling himself by planning to kill you" (27:42).

---

[32] *The Torah: A Modern Commentary* (New York: Union of American Hebrew Congregations, 1974), 247. See Genesis 25:32.

[33] Claus Westermann, *Genesis 12-36: A Commentary,* trans. John J. Scullion S.J. (Minneapolis: Augsburg Publishing House, 1985), 413,

Rebekah's desperate prayer sets the stage for an unambiguous oracle from the LORD, the focus of the birth account (v. 23). The LORD speaks directly "to her." The poetic craft of the divine oracle is instructive. Each of the two halves of two brisk poetic sentences characterizes its composition. J. P. Fokkelman observes that "all the four sentences take one step forward in giving information; each one step farther than its predecessor":[34]

"Two nations are in your womb, and
　　　two peoples born of you shall be divided;
　　　　　the one shall be stronger than the other,
　　　　　　　the elder shall serve the younger."

The first and third sentences tell what is going on with an assurance to Rebekah that she is the ancestress of two nations ("two nations . . . one shall be stronger"). The second and fourth sentences, however, each contain a barb ("divided . . . elder shall serve"). First, the two sons or the two peoples cannot live together; they will separate in more ways than one. Second, while the one son is to be stronger than the other, it is the younger son who will prevail over the elder. The cultural

---

[34] J. P. Fokkelman, *Narrative Art in Genesis: Specimens of Stylistic and Structural Analysis* (Eugene, Oregon: Wipf & Stock Publishers, 2nd ed., 1991), 89.

norm of the relationships between brothers is turned upside down; in Babylonian family law, the eldest son inherited a double heritage. The struggle in the womb now means that Rebekah will face a future full of anxiety as she observes her twin boys from youth into adulthood.

The oracle has created maximal tension by its preview of the outcome; it raises the wonderment as to how Jacob will succeed and how the divine promises will be fulfilled through human actions. Will the oracle provide Rebekah with the foreknowledge that her younger son will prevail? Will she do all in her human power to fulfill the oracle? Like Genesis 12:1-3, Gordon Wenham points out, Genesis 25:23 is programmatic for the narrative which follows: "it announces the God-determined career of Jacob to be one of conflict culminating in ultimate triumph."[35]

The extraordinary poetry of the oracle joins two separate historic periods together—Jacob and Esau, Israel and Edom. Esau and Jacob were the forefathers of two nations, Edom and Israel who were bitter rivals throughout the Old Testament period. The essence of the

---

[35] Wenham, *Genesis 16-50,* 173.

prophetic oracle is that in a simple family event from the patriarchal period, the narrator sees the experience of a later people. This fusion of individuals and peoples, the two essential levels of the Jacob story, explains why the patriarchal stories continued to live on in later Israelite periods.

Following the divine oracle we come directly to

The Birth
(25:24-26).

[24]When her time to give birth was at hand, there were twins in her womb. [25]The first came out red, all his body like a hairy mantle; so they named him Esau. [26]Afterward his brother came out, with his hand gripping Esau's heel; so he was named Jacob. Isaac was sixty years old when she bore them.

The narrative moves from the divine perspective to the human event--even Isaac is mentioned. Probably only Rebekah was aware of the oracle. The literal translation of the *New American Standard Version* of verse 24, "When her days to be delivered were fulfilled, behold (*hinnēh*), there were twins in her womb," reveals the presence of the Hebrew *hinnēh* that can indicate emphasis or a call to attention. "Behold" affirms the oracle; the ordeal in her womb is over. J. P. Fokkelman suggests that here *hinnēh* "makes us share the surprise which the parents experience when their offspring is born—the oracle has really come true."[36]

As the first to be born in a family, the birth of twins everywhere raises the special situation of who is the "first born." Such determination was all the more crucial in patriarchal times. Claus Westermann asks, "Could not the one born at least on the same day lay claim to the same right?"[37] How can one twin be older than the other? In that culture it appears that the question narrows down to who came first out of the womb. A somewhat similar account appears later in Genesis.

In the account of Tamar, the wife of a deceased grandson of Jacob (Genesis 38:27-30), when twins were being born to her, one of them put out his hand, Zerah, and the midwife bound a crimson thread on his hand and announced that "this one came out first." But "he drew back his hand, and out came his brother," Perez. Then "his brother came out with the crimson thread on his hand." Which brother possessed the right of the firstborn? The text does not say, but it is Perez who carries on the line that leads to David. When Perez came out the midwife said,

---

[36] Fokkelman, *Narrative Art in Genesis,* 89-90.
[37] Westermann, *Genesis 12-36,* 414.

"What a breach you have made for yourself." The narrator comments that "therefore he was named Perez," that is, "breach." What does she mean? That he tore things up physically, or figuratively?

The narrator describes Esau's appearance and pictures Jacob as already in action. Esau was born "red, all his body like a hairy mantle" as a kind of Endiku figure who appears in the Gilgamesh Epic: "shaggy with hair was his whole body"[38] quoting E. A. Speiser. Esau is named "Esau," a "red-man" as he is later understood in relation to the land of Edom (v. 30). Edom meant "red" or "ruddy" like the sandstone of the area. The Endiku-like description corresponds to the qualities of Esau in verses 27 and 29-34; these depict him as an "uncouth man of the field"[39] In Robert Alter's words. The description "red" points ahead to the "red stuff" (v. 30) Esau craved in the next scene, and the description "hairy mantle" sets the stage for the deception of Isaac in chapter 27.

Jacob, born "with his hand gripping Esau's heel," is portrayed as one who wants to overtake and outstrip his brother—already a man of

---

[38] E. A. Speiser, *Genesis,* The Anchor Bible (Garden City, New York: Doubleday & Company, Inc., 1964), 196, quoted from the Gilgamesh Epic, Tablet I, column ii, line 36.

[39] Alter, *The Art of Biblical Narrative*, 43.

action! He is already fighting for the best starting position! He is given the name "Jacob," which is a folk-etymological explanation taken from his action at birth. It comes from the Hebrew for "heel" and later came to mean deceiver. Jacob's further life and actions will reveal the true significance of his grasping of his brother's heel.

This first scene ends as it began—with the announcement of Isaac's age, "Isaac was sixty years old when she bore them." Twenty years have gone by since he married Rebekah: "Isaac was forty years old when he married Rebekah" (v. 20). Twenty years was an unusual long period for a woman to wait in her day, painful indeed. The story, however, is not that "Isaac has begot," but that Rebekah has given birth. These two boys are not so much begot of Isaac as they are an affair between Rebekah and the LORD, an affair between a barren woman who receives children only by divine help. We meet with Jacob and Esau the irony of their story as children in conflict almost from the moment of conception.

Rebekah wants an answer to the crashing pain in her womb so she inquires of the LORD. She receives an oracle, a not too comforting word of revelation. Or is it a word of "predestination"? The Apostle Paul apparently thought so as he quoted the divine word of Malachi 1:2 to the effect that "I have loved Jacob, but Esau I have hated" (Rom. 9:13). Rebekah is a mother caught up in "the mystery of election" as God begins to work out his self-revelation and his redemptive purpose for the nations of the world even in her womb!

What kind of life is ahead for Rebekah? Does her life hint of the way of the Cross as she functions as a mother in all her humanness? But God is truly at work in her and her sons—even Esau! No wonder Paul ended the enigmatic chapters of Romans 9-11 with an outburst of praise:

> O the depth of the riches and wisdom and knowledge of God! How unsearchable are his judgments and how inscrutable are his ways!
>> "For who has known the mind of the Lord?[40]
>> Or who has been his counselor?" (11:33-34)

---

[40] See Job 35:7; 41:11.

TWO
Whose Birthright?
(Genesis 25:27-34; 26:34-35)

Genesis 25: 27, 34: "Jacob was a quiet man. . . . Esau despised his birthright."

> I need not tell thee who I am,
> My misery or sin declare;
> Thyself hast called me by my name;
> Look on thy hands, and read it there.
> But who, I ask thee, who art thou?
> Tell me thy name, and tell me now. [41]

Birthright is a crucial issue in the story of Esau and Jacob. The right of the first-born was a concept widespread in both Israel and the Ancient Near East. Somewhat similarly, what our cultural history knows as primogeniture is the right by law or custom of the first born male to inherit the entire estate. Such a one was responsible for the inheritance and its passing on to eligible relatives. It was applied to the inheritance of real property (land) and inherited titles and offices. Variations have taken place in the West over the years differing in each country. After World War II the preference of male over female siblings was largely

---

[41] Hildebrandt, Beckerlegge, and Dale, ed., *A Collection of Hymns for the use of the People called Methodists*, 250.

eliminated. In the US, the inheritance laws vary slightly from state to state. Wills are the normally determinative factor.

At the time of the patriarchs, the birthright went to the first born son, whether the son of a wife or concubine. The first-born son in Israel was esteemed as special. He was the "first fruits of [his father's] vigor" (49:3) and dedicated to God (Exod. 22:29). During his lifetime, he was a privileged son (43:33), and when the inheritance was divided up he received a double portion (Deut. 21:17). For example, if there were three children, there would be four portions, two of them going to the first born and one to each of the other two sons.

The father could disregard this pattern in certain cases. This took place with the birth of Isaac by Abraham's wife Sarah; Ishmael the older son by Hagar was set aside. Later Deuteronomic law, however, prohibits the father from giving the birthright to the younger son just because his mother is especially loved (Deut, 21:15-17). Texts from the archeological sites of Mari and Nuzi show that the birthright could be traded among members of the family for certain considerations, and that the possession of the household images attested to the ownership (31:30-35).

What kind of life lies ahead for this mother of twins, Esau and Jacob, in Rebekah's situation? How will Rebekah react to the events of her pregnancy, the oracle, and giving birth to the twins? Does the oracle affect her behavior? Although Rebekah, as in the previous scene, is not the focus (vv. 19-26), yet, undeveloped in the account, silently her presence in all her motherly humanness is inescapable. As we observe the two boys growing up, they develop and act according to their natures as the next scene reveals. We anticipate how the prophetic word to their mother will relate to the lives of Esau and Jacob. What will be Rebekah's and Isaac's part in the future lives of their twin boys?

The Twins
(25:27-28)

[27]When the boys grew up, Esau was a skillful hunter, a man of the field, while Jacob was a quiet man, living in tents. [28]Isaac loved Esau, because he was fond of game; but Rebekah loved Jacob.

These two compact verses set up the entire Jacob-Esau narrative. The chief figures are fully introduced with their contrasting characterizations—the personifications of two ways of life—the hunter and the shepherd. The two occupations were typical of life in that land at the time. The relationship between the two was often tense. Here the point of tension is reinforced by parental preferences, a tension not only between Jacob and Esau, but also implicitly between Isaac and Rebekah.

The simple statement that "the boys grew up" opens the scene and marks a new stage in the narrative. How old were they? They are obviously old enough to act in accord with their characters; they are at least in late adolescence. ng Esau had developed into "a skillful hunter, a man of the field," and Jacob is described as "a quiet man living in tents." Do these descriptions give a clue as to why Isaac preferred Esau, while Rebekah's favorite was Jacob? Was Isaac's preference for Esau because for Isaac, literally, "game was in his mouth"? But the Hebrew text is not fully clear whether the taste for game was in Isaac's mouth or Esau's.

Contrasting dialogues are often used in biblical narrative to expose differences. This technique tends to limit scenes to two characters at a time. The more important a narrative event is to the narrator, the more apt he is to render it in dialogue form. The introduction of two brothers in narratives embracing different occupations is common throughout the whole of world literature. Esau is pictured as a man of the outdoors, of the open air, and unfettered horizons. He loved the chase and the kill. But as a hunter, Esau was naturally not always successful—oftentimes no prey was found, otherwise, why was he so desperately hungry? A hunter does not always have enough to eat!

While Esau was a real country man, a man of the open skies, Jacob lived in tents. This does not mean that Jacob stayed home all the time doing domestic tasks with his tent pitched next to his mama's. He was in charge of the herds and flocks with their herders who were not always kept at home base, but were taken seasonally to outlying pastures. One is reminded of Jacob's son Joseph, who, at "seventeen years old, was shepherding the flock with his brothers" (37:2). This makes for a more economically secure life for Jacob than Esau could have with his hunting. In contrast to a possibly boisterous Esau, Jacob is described as "a quiet man."

How to translate the Hebrew *tam* here rendered "quiet" is a fascinating inquiry. Other suggestions include "mild," "simple," "plain," and even "retiring." The interpretive puzzle arises because all other biblical occurrences of *tam* refer to the moral quality of the person's character. Job, for example, appears as a man "blameless (*tam*) and upright" (1:1; 1:8; 2:3). Somehow that quality does not seem suit Jacob at this point in his life. The Hebrew adjective, however, can also carry the sense of "complete."

John Walton suggests that if *tam* takes this direction here, Jacob may be described as "sophisticated and refined, . . . an organized, administrative type of person who is conscientious, detail-oriented, well-rounded, and efficient." [42] J. P. Fokkelman has it right when he believes that the only possible interpretation of *tam* is "bent on one purpose,"[43] a single-minded man who knew what was of value, sensitive to the worth of his familial traditions in the culture of the day. Gerhard Von Rad may be helpful when he speaks of Jacob "belonging to the solidarity of

---

[42] J. Walton, *Genesis,* 550.
[43] Fokkelman, *Narrative Art in Genesis*, 91.

community life with its moral regulations, a solidarity that the hunter does not know because he is much more dependent on himself."[44]

Isaac and Rebekah humanly have their favorites. On the one hand, Isaac, seemingly out of self-interest, prefers Esau because of his fondness for the game the older twin brings to his table. Gordon Wenham describes Isaac as "not only a passive, peaceable man of prayer, but a gourmand who loves his food."[45] On the other hand, the narrative states without explanation that Rebekah loves Jacob. This suggests that Rebekah's affection for Jacob is not found in any material convenience that her son can provide her, but is a preference more justly grounded.

Did Rebekah sense a spiritual quality in Jacob missing in Esau? Perhaps so, although it may have been only as Franz Delitzsch, an Old Testament scholar from the late 1800s, suggests, that Rebekah was "better pleased with his quiet, gentle and thoughtful disposition, than

[44] Gerhard von Rad, *Genesis: A Commentary,* The Old Testament Library, trans. John H. Marks (Philadelphia: The Westminster press, 1961),, 261.
[45] Wenham, *Genesis* 16-50, 177.

with the boisterous, wild, clumsy Esau."[46] Is Jacob more easily

manipulated by her than Esau? Anticipating what is to come, Rebekah

will use Isaac's appetite and Jacob's disposition to gain the blessing for

the son she loves, yet setting the stage to lose him.

The parental favoritisms of Isaac and Rebekah continue in line

with the preferred lifestyles and dispositions of the twins. Man-to-man

talk was no doubt easier for Isaac with Esau and Jacob could better share

Rebekah's interests. Yet, the text neither excuses Rebekah's preferential

treatment of Jacob nor condemns Isaac's contrasting love for Esau.

Parenting is not the issue. Nor does the text suggest that in either case

the other son is unloved. Rather, the Hebrew verb translated "loved" is

more the love of primary choice than that of affection as in

Deuteronomy 6:4-5: "Hear, O Israel, the LORD is our God, the LORD

alone. You shall love the LORD your God with all your heart, and with

all your soul, and with all your might."

Affection is not the point in this great summary commandment,

but that of primary loyalty or first choice above all others--first place in

---

[46] Franz Delitzsch, *A New Commentary on Genesis,* Volume II, trans. Sophia
Taylor (Minneapolis: Klock & Klock Christian Publishers [T. & T. Clark], 1988), 135.

all of life! Rebekah no doubt loves both her children as any mother would, but Jacob is special. This brief statement of parental preferences with its characterization of husband and wife anticipates the unfolding of the story for both the brothers and their parents as we shall see.

The Sale
(25:29-34)

[29]Once when Jacob was cooking a stew, Esau came in from the field, and he was famished. [30]Esau said to Jacob, "Let me eat some of that red stuff, for I am famished!" (Therefore he was called Edom.) [31]Jacob said, "First sell me your birthright." [32]Esau said, "I am about to die; of what use is a birthright to me?" [33]Jacob said, "Swear to me first." So he swore to him, and sold his birthright to Jacob. [34]Then Jacob gave Esau bread and lentil stew, and he ate and drank, and rose and went his way. Thus Esau despised his birthright.

"Birthright" ($b^e kor\bar{a}h$) is the key-word in this scene, occurring four times (vv. 31, 32, 33, 34). Over this right of the first born, the twins, Jacob and Esau, negotiate. When the report of the scene is viewed as a chiastic construction (abcdx*dcba*), the center line (**x**), "Esau said, 'I am about to die; of what use is a birthright to me?'" (v 32) stands out. The presence of the untranslated "behold" (*hinnēh*) before "I am" points this up. A Jacob line both precedes (d), "Jacob said, 'First sell me your birthright,'" and follows the central line (*d*), "Jacob said, 'Swear to me first.' So he swore to him, and sold his birthright to Jacob" (vv. 31, 33). Thus Esau, in rhetorical structure as well as story, is hemmed in by his brother's cunning design.[47]

That Esau wants food is the bottom line. Jacob has food: "Once when Jacob was cooking a stew, Esau came in from the field, and he was famished. . . . 'Let me eat some of that red stuff'" (vv. 29-30). Esau's very language reveals his coarse personality; he cannot even use the right word for the stew, but carelessly calls it "that red stuff." A Hebrew particle (*nā'*) would allow a "please" from Esau. Perhaps Esau thinks that the "red stuff" is a meaty "blood soup." When he receives only a dish of lentils instead, he finds himself already.

Esau has just come in from strenuous hunting; he is exhausted and desperately hungry: "Let me eat some of that red stuff, for I am famished!" The verb for "eat," occurring nowhere else in the Hebrew Bible, means "devour greedily." The narrator pictures Esau as a creature caught at that moment by the demands of a terrfic appetite, even to the

---

[47] Fokkelman, *Narrative Art in Genesis,* 95.

point of exaggeration: "I am about to die." Is Esau being depicted as one hardly worthy of the birthright?

Jacob, on the other hand, is calmly in charge of the food preparation. His cool head, calculating with the legal implications in mind, takes advantage of Esau's impulsive outburst rising out of a growling stomach: "First sell me your birthright. . . . Swear to me first." "First . . . . first" is literally "today . . . today." "At once" could also be a translation. "To 'me'" is placed emphatically at the end of the Hebrew sentence. Gordon Wenham interprets Jacob to be stating his demand in a way that "suggests long premeditation and ruthless exploitation of his brother's moment of weakness."[48] Jacob wants Esau to confirm the sale with an oath guaranteeing that the agreement cannot later be rescinded. Moral ambiguities pursue Jacob as the story continues.

Esau surrenders his birthright to Jacob with a binding oath: "So he swore to him." Esau bargains away his pride and dignity as he forgets his legal rights in the family and fails to honor his birthright. Jacob has scored his first hit; he knows the value of the future—he looks ahead!

---

[48] Wenham, *Genesis 16-50,* 178.

Esau only hurriedly gulps down Jacob's stew, "that red stuff. . . . (Therefore he was called Edom)" or "the Red-Man" (vv. 30 and 25). Two nations as well as two individuals are again in view.

Fortunately for Jacob, Esau was too absorbed in his own immediate hunger pain to notice that Jacob was acting obviously out of self-interest, "I am about to die." Thomas Mann crudely characterizes the actions of each twin who appear as "the victims of their own cussedness rather than the helpless pawns of fate. . . . Jacob has a sharp mind and no conscience, but Esau is all belly and no brains."[49]

Esau quickly "ate and drank, and rose and went his way"—thoughtless, or already too bitter to talk to his brother? This rapid-fire chain of verbs expresses the precipitous manner in which Esau gulps down his food and spurns his birthright. "Thus Esau despised his birthright," the conclusion of the scene is an explicit moral commentary that rarely occurs in biblical narrative. Esau's failure is the focus; he

---

[49] Mann, *The Book of the Torah*, 51-52.

flippantly preferred "the palpable and present to the unseen and future"[50] In Robert Alter's apt phrasing.

Fifteen hundred years later in the course of biblical history, the writer to the Hebrews was perhaps a little harsh in his evaluation, but not far off target: "See to it that no one becomes like Esau, an immoral and godless person, who sold his birthright for a single meal" (12:16). Esau was lacking in sensitivity to traditional family custom; he was not "a quiet man," a *tam* man! May we say that even at this stage in his story Jacob encourages us to be *tam* folk people with an eye to what is of future value?.

In the story of Jacob and Esau, we keep facing the question of how God works out his purposes in the lives of individuals and peoples. One encounters an inescapable sense of paradox and mystery in the relative roles of the human and the divine. A clearly indicated divine perspective to this point .in the story is as yet ambiguous. It leaves many questions open.[51] Human need on Esau's part and cleverness on Jacob's govern the action, but the brothers are not aware of all they are doing.

---

[50] Alter, *The Art of Biblical Narrative,* 44.
[51] K. Walton, *Thou Traveller Unknown,* 26, 28.

God is present behind the scenes. Human behavior is as much a factor in the story as the guidance of providence. As his personality develops, the character of Jacob is becoming the most fully and subtly sketched of all the patriarchs

Do we see any likeness in the story as to how God has worked in our lives in the past? Can we find any encouragement here for the present, and for the future? Are we able to empathize with Joseph when he said to his brothers in Egypt of the ways of God, "Even though you intended to do harm to me, God intended it for good. . . ." (Gen. 50:20)? We do we take heart with Paul's confidence that

> He who began a good work in you will perfect it until the day of Christ Jesus.[52]

---

[52] Phil. 1:6, NASB.

THREE
The Promise Goes On
(Genesis 26:1-33)

Genesis 26:2-5, 24   The LORD appeared to Isaac and said, . . . "I will
fulfill the oath that I

swore to your father Abraham. [4]I will make your
offspring as numerous as the stars of heaven, and
will give to your offspring all these lands; and all
the nations of the earth shall gain blessing for
themselves through your offspring," . . .

And that very night the LORD appeared to him and
said, "I am the God

of your father Abraham; do not be afraid, for I am
with you and will bless you and make your
offspring numerous for my servant Abraham's
sake."

In vain thou strugglest to get free;
    I never will unloose my hold;
Art thou the Man that died for me?
    The secret of thy love unfold:
Wrestling, I will not let thee go
    Till I thy name, thy nature know.[53]

The final week of August, 2012, was dotted with headlines about
Isaac:

Deadly Isaac brings misery; drenches Haiti, Cuba.
Isaac forces Republicans to adjust convention plan.
Isaac gaining strength.

---

[53] Hildebrandt, Beckerlegge, and Dale, ed., *A Collection of Hymns for the use of the People called Methodists*, 251.

Gulf braces as Isaac hits.[54]

Isaac was one mean hombre! Hardly the Isaac we know from the biblical record as Gordon Wenham describes—"a timid ,peace-loving man"![55]

The peace-loving Isaac is integral to the Jacob saga. Jacob's father's appearance is prominent as he intrudes into the Jacob stories. Isaac, when residing in Gerar, as did his father Abraham before him, when the men there found his wife desirably attractive, passes her as his sister--"like father, like son"! Sarah and Rebekah must have been beautiful, handsome women by the cultural standards the time. But why is chapter 26 even here? What does it have to do with Jacob? One can read directly from chapter 25 into chapter 27 and not miss 26. Is it truly out of place—anomalous in the present context?

All three patriarchs, Abraham, Isaac, and Jacob, not just Isaac, are involved or implied in chapter 26, enlarging our sense of who the patriarchs were. Although the writer employs the narrative device of intrusion here with a digression in plot, the theme remains the same. The chapter's essential theme is "promise," inextricably intertwined with

---

[54] *Union-Tribune San Diego* (August 26-29, 2012).
[55] Wenham, *Genesis 16-50,* 188.

"blessing." The initial promise to Abraham shines through all the patriarchal stories:

> I will make of you a great nation, and I will bless you, and make your name great, so that you will be a blessing. I will bless those who bless you, and the one who curses you I will curse; and in you all the families of the earth shall be blessed (12:2-3).

The promise is spoken exclusively to Abraham up to this point in the Genesis narrative; Jacob is yet "afar off." Between the partriarchal promise and Jacob stands his father Isaac and his older brother Esau. Yet, Jacob alone becomes "Israel"! The significance of chapter 26 is seen in its frequent reference back to Abraham and the covenant promises. The advance in this chapter is that Isaac will become the direct recipient of God's blessing and now owns the promises as did his father Abraham before him. Isaac is now in charge of the blessing! Jacob has come a wee bit closer to the promise--his father has it!

As we move from the material birthright to the more spiritual promise and blessing, This account serves as a buffer between the two. Chapter 26 thus functions appropriately in the story of Jacob as it deals with

Abraham's Promise
(26:1-5)

[1]Now there was a famine in the land, besides the former famine that had occurred in the days of Abraham. And Isaac went to Gerar, to King Abimelech of the Philistines. [2]The LORD appeared to Isaac and said, "Do not go down to Egypt; settle in the land that I shall show you. [3]Reside in this land as an alien, and I will be with you, and will bless you; for to you and to your descendants I will give all these lands, and I will fulfill the oath that I swore to your father Abraham. [4]I will make your offspring as numerous as the stars of heaven, and will give to your offspring all these lands; and all the nations of the earth shall gain blessing for themselves through your offspring, [5]because Abraham obeyed my voice and kept my charge, my commandments, my statutes, and my laws."

Isaac is faced with "a famine in the land" as was his father Abraham. Unlike his father, Isaac did "not go down to Egypt" (12:10-12). Abraham, whom God called with a promise of blessing and protection to leave his country and go to a land that he would show him, in a "failure of faith," did go to Egypt. But Isaac, responding to a word from the LORD, "went to Gerar, to King Abimelech of the Philistines." Gerar was located south of Jerusalem, just west of Beer-sheba.

After the destruction of Sodom and Gomorrah and his nephew Lot's escape (19:1-38), Abraham did go and reside as an alien in Gerar (20:1-18). While there Abimelech "took Sarah" as his wife (20:2). Will Isaac act in Gerar as his father did? Isaac's behavior in Gerar will reveal more of the kind of father Jacob had in Abraham's son. The narrator consciously compares the career of Isaac with that of his father Abraham inviting the reader to reflect on the differences and the similarities between the careers of Abraham and Isaac—Jacob's immediate ancestors.

In Gerar, the LORD himself promises Isaac that "I will be with you." Isaac was the first of the patriarchs to receive such a clear word from the LORD himself. Such an assuring word did come later to his son Jacob on several occasions (28:15; 31:3; 46:4). The presence of God is seen as the guarantee of protection and success (28:15; 39:2). The divine "I will be with you" is here conditioned by a command, "Reside in this land as an alien." The promise to Isaac logically follows: "to you and to your descendants I will give all these lands." Specifically, "land" was first linked directly to the patriarchal promise in 15:18-19 and then in 17:8. The original promise to Abraham was similarly prefaced by: "Go from your country and from your kindred and your father's house to the land that I will show you" (12:1). To Isaac , however, the promise of land appears to extend beyond the land of Canaan: "to you . . . I will give all these lands."

The promise, "I will fulfill the oath that I swore to your father Abraham," motivates this gracious gift now given to Isaac. Previously, the divine word to Abraham was that of a "covenant" both with him (15:18; 17:2-19) and with his yet-to-be-born son, Isaac (17:19, 21). The "oath" that God will fulfill for Isaac is the one that follows the great testing of Abraham on Mount Moriah where he heard God's command to offer Isaac as a burnt offering (22:1-14). There in Genesis 22:16-18 the angel of the LORD for the second time called to Abraham from heaven:

> "By myself I have sworn, says the LORD: Because you have done this, and have not withheld your son, your only son, I will indeed bless you, and I will make your offspring as numerous as the stars of heaven and as the sand that is on the seashore. And your offspring shall possess the gate of their enemies, and by your offspring shall all the nations of the earth gain blessing for themselves, because you have obeyed my voice."

The promise to Abraham was a covenant confirmed by an oath. The writer to Hebrews many centuries later describes it: "When God made a promise to Abraham, because he had no one greater by whom to swear, he swore by himself" (6:13), for "an oath given as confirmation puts an end to all dispute" (6:16).[56] This covenant promise, confirmed by an oath, is what Isaac now receives that he may pass it along to his own descendants:

> "I will make your offspring as numerous as the stars of heaven, and will give to your offspring all these lands; and all the nations of the earth shall gain blessing for themselves through your offspring."

Abraham's obedience, reflecting his behavior on Mount Moriah, appears as the key to the promise: "because Abraham obeyed my voice and kept my charge, my commandments, my statutes, and my laws" (26:5). The terminology is similar to the language of the law given at Sinai. In the pre-Sinai period beginning with creation, divine commands emerged no doubt along the way for the law given at Sinai does not emerge as a completely new reality but " stands in basic continuity with

---

[56] See Gen. 21:27, 31; 26:28, 31.

earlier articulations of God's will for the creation." [57] The concern here, however, is that the promise of God to Abraham, and now to Isaac, and eventually to Jacob and his posterity, inherently involves obedience. This truth of the biblical witness to obedient faith and life is demonstrated, often tragically, by the entire subsequent history of the people of Israel, all the way to Jesus the Christ of the new covenant in his blood.

But again, what about Isaac? And what about

Isaac's Sister?
(26:6-11)

⁶So Isaac settled in Gerar. ⁷When the men of the place asked him about his wife, he said, "She is my sister"; for he was afraid to say, "My wife," thinking, "or else the men of the place might kill me for the sake of Rebekah, because she is attractive in appearance." ⁸When Isaac had been there a long time, King Abimelech of the Philistines looked out of a window and saw him fondling his wife Rebekah. ⁹So Abimelech called for Isaac, and said, "So she is your wife! Why then did you say, 'She is my sister'?" Isaac said to him, "Because I thought I might die because of her." ¹⁰Abimelech said, "What is this you have done to us? One of the people might easily have lain with your wife, and you would have brought guilt upon us." ¹¹So Abimelech

---

⁵⁷ Terence E. Fretheim, "The Book of Genesis: Introduction, Commentary, and Reflections," *The New Interpreter's Bible,* Volume I (Nashville: Abingdon Press, 1994), 529.

warned all the people, saying, "Whoever touches this man or his wife shall be put to death."

Isaac obeyed--a significant theme in relation to the patriarchal promise. He heeded the divine word and "settled in Gerar." Yet, all is not well; Isaac's presence there as a resident alien has its dark side. The positive side is that this episode continues the link with father Abraham; Negatively it reminds the reader of Abraham's poor behavior that his son appears to duplicate. This account by its brevity and similarity presupposes the two earlier episodes concerning Abraham and Sarah, one in Egypt (12:10-20) and the other in Gerar (20:1-18).

The patriarchal fear is similar in all three accounts, caused in the first and third stories by the wife's beauty (20:11; 26:7; see 24:16). Sarah was "very beautiful" as the text has it (12:14) and Franz Delitzsch interprets that Rebekah may even have been "seductively beautiful."[58] Abraham and Isaac fear for their very lives—"they will kill me" (12:12; 26:9): the pronoun is personal. Abraham twice and Isaac once identify their wives as their sisters (12:13; 20:2; 26:7). Pharaoh rebukes

---

[58] Delitzsch, *Genesis,* II, 135.

Abraham, and Abimelech rebukes both Abraham and Isaac for their white lies.

Significant differences take place in relation to the circumstances of the two wives, Sarah and Rebekah. Of Sarah in 12:15, "the woman [Sarah] was taken into Pharaoh's house." Pharaoh in his rebuke to Abraham uses explicit sexual language:

> "Why did you not tell me that she was your wife? Why did you say, 'she is my sister,' so that I took her for my wife? Now then, here is your wife, take her, and be gone." (12:18-20).

The same Hebrew verb, "to take" in "Abimelech . . . took Sarah"[59] is used also with Abraham in Gerar (20:2). But in this second account with Abraham, God, in a reported dream, after threatening Abimelech with death and Abimelech protests, says to him, "Yes, I know that you did this in the integrity of your heart; furthermore it was I who kept you from sinning against me. Therefore I did not let you touch her" (20:6).

Of Rebekah ere in Gerar (26:7-9), although Isaac identifies her as his sister to Abimelech, she remains with Isaac. The intimacy of husband and wife is not broken as it was in the previous stories. For

---

[59] See 24:67 and 25:1, 20 for the use of the same Hebrew verb in the context of marriage..

after "a long time, King Abimelech of the Philistines looked out of a window and saw him fondling his wife Rebekah." The mention of "a long time" suggests that Isaac's fears may be somewhat unfounded. Apparently Esau and Jacob had not yet been born. Earlier the patriarchal duplicity concerning their wives was exposed by plagues in Egypt (12:17) and by revelation in Gerar (20:3).

This time the discovery of Isaacs' duplicity came by chance when Abimelech happened to notice Isaac's interaction with Rebekah. Surprise is indicated by a twofold *hinnēh* ("behold") translated literally in verse 8, "and saw, and behold (*hinnēh*)," and in verse 9, "Surely, behold (*hinnēh*), she is your wife!" As a result of his discovery of Isaac and Rebekah's intimate behavior, Abimelech called for Isaac and bluntly rebukes him,

> "What is this you have done to us? One of the people might easily have lain with your wife, and you would have brought guilt upon us," So Abimelech warned all the people, saying, "Whoever touches this man or his wife shall be put to death."

Rebekah, it seems, had been in less danger than Sarah; she was never taken into the king's harem as Sarah apparently was.

Abimelech's edict assures the couple of a secure situation in which God's blessings can now flow freely to Isaac. The danger to the chastity of the patriarchal wife, and thus to the promise, has decreased with each of the three incidents to almost no danger. Now more significantly, as with Abraham in both Egypt and in Gerar, the encounter results in another report of patriarchal prosperity. The very next verse tells us that God blessed Isaac so that even in the midst of famine, he "prospered more and more until he became very wealthy" (26:13).

The keyword in our narrative is promise. The initial promise to Abraham is at the heart of this Isaac story. As "The Promise Goes On" it is wrapped in blessing. Blessing, however, runs a close second to promise, or is even the more prominent theme as the emphasis turns to

Isaac's Prosperity
(26:12-25)

[12]Isaac sowed seed in that land, and in the same year reaped a hundredfold. The LORD blessed him, [13]and the man became rich; he prospered more and more until he became very wealthy. [14]He had possessions of flocks and herds, and a great household, so that the Philistines envied him. [15](Now the Philistines had stopped up and filled with earth all the wells that his father's servants had dug in the days of his father Abraham.) [16]And Abimelech said to Isaac, "Go away from us; you have become too powerful for us."

81

[17]So Isaac departed from there and camped in the valley of Gerar and settled there.[18]Isaac dug again the wells of water that had been dug in the days of his father Abraham; for the Philistines had stopped them up after the death of Abraham; and he gave them the names that his father had given them.[19]But when Isaac's servants dug in the valley and found there a well of spring water, [20] the herders of Gerar quarreled with Isaac's herders, saying, "The water is ours." So he called the well Esek, because they contended with him. [21]Then they dug another well, and they quarreled over that one also; so he called it Sitnah. [22]He moved from there and dug another well, and they did not quarrel over it; so he called it Rehoboth, saying, "Now the LORD has made room for us, and we shall be fruitful in the land." [23]From there he went up to Beer-sheba.

[24]And that very night the LORD appeared to him and said, "I am the God of your father Abraham; do not be afraid, for I am with you and will bless you and make your offspring numerous for my servant Abraham's sake." [25]So he built an altar there, called on the name of the LORD, and pitched his tent there. And there Isaac's servants dug a well.

Settled comfortably in Gerar, Isaac turns to agriculture and reaps abundant harvests: "the LORD blessed him." Isaac appears to prosper as the psalmist later expressed it:

> Trust in the LORD and do good;
> > so you will live in the land, and enjoy security.
> Take delight in the LORD,
> and he will give you the desires of your heart (37:3-4).

The LORD is looking after Isaac; his wealth is not due to Abimelech's

or Pharoah's compensation as it was with Abraham, but a gift of God.

Isaac "became rich," indeed, prospering "more and more until he became very wealthy." Isaac possessed "flocks and herds, and a great household" arousing great envy on the part of the Philistines. They were so threatened by Isaac's wealth that early on they had plugged with dirt all the wells that Abraham's servants had dug. "Open range" often comes with territorial problems. Earlier on a similar occasion Abraham had protested to Abimelech about such behavior (21:25), but Isaac, a more passive personality, apparently says nothing.

One cannot help but think back as far as the account of Abraham and his son Isaac on Mount Moriah. The father was under the heavy command of God to sacrifice the son as a burnt offering. When Abraham raised his knife to slay his son on the altar, Isaac is silent. He is seemingly fully submissive to his father's will. Does this scene simply display Isaac's future character? Or can we see in this event a traumatic experience that contributed to the formation of the kind of person we see him later to be?

Wells belonged to the person who dug them and rendering them useless was a serious invasion of property rights: In that kind of country where water was precious it was a matter of life and death for man and beast. As a boy "home on the range" in the cattle country of the Nebraska sandhills, I would go with my father almost daily to check the windmills and the condition of the water tanks in the pastures where there was no natural running water. In the winter we would break the ice in the water tanks to make sure the livestock could drink.

Abimelech, siding with his subjects, sent Isaac away to the outskirts of Gerar: "Go away from us; you have become too powerful for us." God's blessing became the means of Isaac becoming an important person in the land of the Philistines—too important it seems: "Enduring Isaac," as Franz Delitzsch characterizes him, submits willingly and leaves the area.[60]

But the Philistine's paranoiac hostility regarding the land was so great that trouble follows. Isaac and his servants dig two more wells over which the two sets of herders continue to quarrel. There they found "a well of spring water," in Hebrew, "living water." They named the first well appropriately "Esek" (contention or quarrel) and the second

---

[60] Delitzsch, *Genesis,* II, 141.

"Sitnah" (enmity or hostility). So Isaac, again in character, "moved from there and dug another well," over which there was finally no quarrel—a tribute to Isaac's power--and named it "Rehoboth" meaning ample or broad place: "Now the LORD has made room for us, and we shall be fruitful in the land." The terminology of "be fruitful," so prominent in Genesis 1-11, appears here for the first time in the patriarchal stories.

Isaac now moves on from Gerar southeast to Beer-sheba where the LORD again appears to him. Beer-sheba was an important location in relation to Abraham as now to Isaac, and eventually will be to Jacob (28:10; 46:1, 5) [61]. Located southeast of Jerusalem, it served as a cultic center. This is the last time the LORD appears to Isaac in the biblical record. Interestingly, he has received no name change as did his father Abram before him, or as his son Jacob will after him. His birth, however, is set within a context of divine intervention (18:1-15).

The LORD repeats the oracle of promise to Isaac (26:3-5). It is introduced significantly by "I am the God of your father Abraham." Although the place is indicated, God does not represent himself as

---

[61] See 21:14, 31-33; 22:`19 for Abraham and 26:23, 33 for Isaac..

connected with one place; rather he is the God of a distinct group of people. The designation "God of your father, expressed previously in simpler terms (vv.3-5), is "do not be afraid, for I am with you and will bless you and make your offspring numerous for my servant Abraham's sake" (26:24). Again the promise is to be *with him* as well as the blessing and numerous offspring. Land is not mentioned. Prominent is the transfer of the tradition associated with Abraham to the second generation, to Isaac; "the promise goes on" in Jacob's direction.

The importance of this event for Isaac, and for the narrator, is stressed by the report that for the first time Isaac "built an altar" and "called on the name of the LORD" as did his father Abraham before him.[62] This spiritual act of faith is matched by a more earthy confirming act, "there Isaac's servants dug a well." "Wells" to this point have been a source of tension and trouble with the Philistines. Will they force Isaac again to move on? Perhaps Isaac is hopeful and determined, relying on and risking more on the promise! Isaac appears to possess an "elasticity

---

[62] See 12:7, 8; 13:18; 22:9.

of endurance."[63] Isaac may well have his strengths in relation to the promise.

    This sets the stage for

---

[63] Delitzsch, *Genesis,* II, 146.

Isaac's Blessing
(26:26-33)

[26]Then Abimelech went to him from Gerar, with Ahuzzath his adviser and Phicol the commander of his army. [27]Isaac said to them, "Why have you come to me, seeing that you hate me and have sent me away from you?" [28]They said, "We see plainly that the LORD has been with you; so we say, let there be an oath between you and us, and let us make a covenant with you [29]so that you will do us no harm, just as we have not touched you and have done to you nothing but good and have sent you away in peace. You are now the blessed of the LORD." [30]So he made them a feast, and they ate and drank. [31]In the morning they rose early and exchanged oaths; and Isaac set them on their way, and they departed from him in peace. [32]That same day Isaac's servants came and told him about the well that they had dug, and said to him, "We have found water!" [33]He called it Shibah; therefore the name of the city is Beer-sheba to this day.

The theme of the blessing that accompanies the Abrahamic promise is again center stage. Isaac is one who bears and causes blessing, not only one who receives blessing. Even "Abimelech," along with "Ahuzzath his adviser and Phicol the commander of his army," recognize that Isaac is blessed. Attitudes are reversed; they can now see that Isaac's good fortune is a potential boon for them rather than a threat. So they take the initiative, leave Gerar, and come to Isaac seeking a covenant of peace with him. Isaac bristles; he is not so sure: "Why have you come to me, seeing that you hate me and have sent me away from you?"

Abimelech and his cohort, however, seeing the blessing that Isaac enjoys from the LORD, are not put off; they want to share in it: "LORD has been with you. . . . You are now the blessed of the LORD." They appeal to the fact that they have been good to Isaac and have touched neither him nor his wife and have sent them away in peace. They ask, "let there be an oath between you and us, and let us make a covenant with you." The king and two officials seek assurance that Isaac will do them no harm. Apparently the combination of Isaac's wealth and power and thus the obvious divine blessing intimidates even Abimelech, his advisor, and the commander of his army. Again. Isaac's wealth did not stem from any material payment from Abimelech as it was with Abraham. Rebekah had never left Isaac's side in Gerar; his wealth had no relation to his wife or to the strife over the well, but solely gifted by the blessing of God.

The blessing of God, experienced by Isaac and recognized by others as such, confirms for Isaac that God's promise to his father

Abraham is now his. Isaac finds assurance in the good providences of God. Good providences do play a positive role in our lives—but what about when they are not so great? We are *graced* to believe the Apostle Paul's declaration that God is at work for our good *in* all things (Rom. 8:28). God is never absent even when there is no palpable evidence of his presence: "Am I a God near by, says the LORD, and not a God far off? Who can hide in the secret places so that I cannot see them? says the LORD. Do I not fill heaven and earth?" (Jer. 23:23-24).

Abimelech and Isaac talk through their recent history, reach an understanding, and make a covenant or pact between them. They share a feast, "they ate and drank" into the night, rise early the next morning, and exchange oaths. Their mutual oaths signify a treaty between equals. Isaac then "set them on their way, and they departed from him in peace." The "peace" (v. 29) does not reverse the expulsion of Isaac from Abimelech's territory, probably the conviction of them both. The "peace," rather, consists of their mutual pledge to do each other no harm. Fellowship appears not to be the issue, but rather a relationship in which each leaves the other alone--in peace. This story describes relationships with people outside the emerging patriarchal or tribal group.

The final note is both vital and symbolic: "That same day Isaac's servants came and told him about the well that they had dug, and said to him, 'We have found water!'" Life can be supported without fear or interruption, for conflict has now ended. Is the discovery of good water a pledge of future security in the land? Isaac names the well "Shibah" or oath and the narrator comments that "therefore the name of the city is Beer-sheba to this day," Beer-sheba meaning "well of an oath" (21:31). The names of the wells Isaac's servants dig trace the path to reconciliation--from Contention and Enmity to Room and Oath.

We began with Isaac characterized as "a timid, peace-loving man."[64] But is that an adequate summary of Isaac's character and role as a patriarch? True, narrative-wise, he lived somewhat in the shadow of his father, Abraham, and of his son, Jacob. We remember that earlier in the story Abraham concluded his grievance with Abimelech in similar fashion. The two made a covenant at a well Abraham had dug:

---

[64] Wenham, *Genesis 16-50*, 188.

"Therefore that place was called Beer-sheba; because .there both of them swore an oath" (21:31).

Isaac walked in his father's footsteps. As before noted, Isaac's life echoes that of his father. Nevertheless, this son of promise is not unworthy of his father. The faith of Abraham became a vibrant force in his life. Gordon Wenham observes that "this somewhat ineffectual man receives yet great promises and experiences their fulfillment in fuller measure than even his father Abraham did."[65] Isaac knows how to endure; he possesses a special greatness that he has transmitted to his descendants "as an ineradicably tenacious vital faculty"[66] as Franz Delitzsch continues to stress.

What then was Isaac's contribution? Nothing spectacular--he made no particular addition in idea or insight to the tradition he receives from Abraham his father. In the life of Isaac, the tradition reaches a plateau. But Isaac did preserve a tradition; he receives it, he holds on to it; and is loyal to it; he is not simply a negative character. As the son of Abraham and the father of Jacob, Isaac did not break the chain of the

---

[65] Wenham, *Genesis 16-50*, 194.
[66] Delitzsch, *Genesis,* II, 146,

tradition handed to him. In all his actions he preserves a tradition for his descendants.[67]

Along with his father Abraham and his son Jacob, Isaac is a man of faith, but not always faithful. Yet, even as a person of mixed character, the LORD is with him, protects him, and blesses him. As God used Abraham, he now works through Isaac, and will link even Jacob irrevocably to his age-long purposes in and through which we who were " strangers to the covenants of promise, having no hope and without God in the world [and] once far off" will be "brought near by the blood of Christ" (Eph. 2:13). The promise of God to Abraham, passed on to Isaac, is coming our way—"the promise goes on"—in Jacob!

---

[67] This paragraph is dependent on *The Torah,* 262.

II.
The Brothers and the Blessing
(17:1—29:22)

FOUR

The Blessing: Jacob
(Genesis 26:34--27:29)

Genesis 27:14, 22:   So he went and got them and brought them to his mother; and his mother prepared savory food, such as his father loved. . . .So Jacob went up to his father Isaac, who felt him and said, "The voice is Jacob's voice, but the hands are the hands of Esau."

Hebrews 11:20:   "By faith Isaac invoked blessings for the future on Jacob and Esau."

> Wilt thou not yet to me reveal
>   Thy new, unutterable name?
> Tell me, I still beseech thee, tell'
>   To the know it now resolved I am:
> Wrestling, I will not let thee go
> Till I thy name, thy nature know.[68]

"Bless you" is our frequent response when someone sneezes in our presence. "What a blessing!" is an observation frequently heard among Christians. Or in the Advent season we say, "May you have a blessed Christmas." Young men customarily ask the parents of their hoped-for bride for their blessing in order to marry. The language of

---

[68] Hildebrandt, Beckerlegge, and Dale, ed., *A Collection of Hymns for the use of the People called Methodists*, 251.

blessing is not limited to us religious folk in contemporary culture. Significantly the farewells in Spanish "Vaya con Dios" (Go with God), even "Adiós" (to God), and the French *Adieu* (to God), are all forms of blessing.

We church folk use the language of blessing most often. Dining out together we subtly maneuver over who will say "the blessing"! When a friend comes to us hurting, we listen sympathetically and as sincerely as we can, we say "Bless you"! Or if they are facing a critical challenge or a new opportunity, we respond with an encouraging "bless you my friend." Our prayers of intercession for those we love and for whom we care are often sprinkled with the imperative, "Bless . . . ." No one, especially we church-goers want to live an unblessed life.

Words of blessing are not empty words, but rather a "speech act." We intend our blessing to grant a special favor, a mercy, or a benefit. Blessings are a gift. Behind them are our good will, our love, our faith, our support, and our prayers. Words partake of power, especially words of blessing spoken in God's name. "Blessing" ultimately is a divine activity, "living and active" (Heb. 4:12)!

After God "created humankind in his image, in the image of God," he "blessed them" and said "Be fruitful and multiply" (Gen. 1:27-28). An attempt to count in a biblical concordance the verb "bless" and the noun "blessing" and their cognates leads to despair, they are so numerous. In Genesis alone, words of blessing appear eighty-eight times. In the lives of the patriarchs, it is first God who blesses. The God of Abraham, Isaac, and Jacob is a God who cares, makes and keeps promises, and blesses. Divine blessing is crucial in the human-divine relationship. It is a gift from God that cannot be earned.

We return to the twin brothers, Esau and Jacob, after having seemingly departed from the story of Jacob in our study of chapter 26 with its focus on Isaac. Chapter 26 was a pause that puts the activities and attitudes of Jacob and Esau into perspective within the patriarchal story. Our present story concerns both twins—equally as we shall see—as we move from the cultural birthright to the religious blessing.

The full story of the blessing of Jacob is told in seven scenes of two persons in dialogue conforming to "the law of epic"[69] according to Michael Fishbane. The story involves not only Jacob and Esau, but Rebekah and Isaac as well. The first portion of the narrative of blessing opens with its attention on Isaac and Esau (27:1-4), shifts to Rebekah and Jacob (vv. 5-17), and ends with Jacob and Isaac (vv. 18-29). The second portion of the story continues with Esau and Isaac (vv. 30-40), Rebekah and Jacob (vv.41-45), Rebekah and Isaac (v. 46), and Isaac and Jacob (27:45—28:9). . No dialogue takes place between the brothers or between Rebekah and Esau. Husband and wife do not come together until the next to the last scene.

But before the account of Isaac's blessing, the final two verses of chapter 26 deal with the marriages of Esau, Jacob's brother, a figure large in the present story. As belonging to the story of Isaac's blessing, we look briefly at.

Esau's Hittite Marriages
(26:34-35)

---

[69] Michael Fishbane, *Text and Texture: Close Readings of Selected Biblical Texts.* New York: Schocken Books, 1979), 50.

> [34]When Esau was forty years old, he married Judith daughter of Beeri the Hittite, and Basemath the daughter of Elon the Hittite; [35]and they made life bitter for Isaac and Rebekah.

Rebekah's life with her twin boys was no sunny Sunday afternoon picnic. The road she travels with them is hardly smooth as they mature into manhood. How does Esau take his loss of the birthright? For sure, he is not happy. After an intervening account (26:1-33) concerning Isaac, these two verses appear as one sentence hinting for an answer. The sentence suggests that Esau possesses a rebellious attitude toward his parents and nurses a spiteful spirit.

So at age forty, the age his father married Rebekah, Esau marries two Hittite ladies who "made life bitter for Isaac and Rebekah." The Hittites were residents of Canaan, a non-Semitic people, totally unrelated to the patriarchs. Esau apparently has little respect for or sensitivity to the normal concerns of family in that culture and marries outside the boundaries of the clan. His behavior shows a lack of consideration for his parents, their values and their feelings.

Earlier, Esau's physical hunger dictated his actions in the sale of his birthright to Jacob. This time, perhaps, one motivation is lust—the

Hittite ladies may well have been exotic foreign women in Esau's eyes, shall we say, physically constructed so as to attract a virile male such as Esau! The point, however, is that after the marriage, these two ladies "made life bitter for Isaac and Rebekah." In all fairness, the Hittite ladies may have been reacting to their perception of Isaac's and Rebekah's disapproval of them; the parents are apparently deeply scandalized by Esau's action. The Hittite beauties could very well have imbibed Esau's spiteful spirit.

On this negative note about Esau, we return to the movement of the story from the material birthright to the more spiritual promise and blessing. As we have seen, and now even more prominently, we view the promise as uniquely wrapped in blessing. The blessing becomes the issue. We begin with the dialogue between

Isaac and Esau
(27:1-4)

[1]When Isaac was old and his eyes were dim so that he could not see, he called his elder son Esau and said to him, "My son"; and

he answered, "Here I am." [2]He said, "See, I am old; I do not know the day of my death. [3]Now then, take your weapons, your quiver and your bow, and go out to the field, and hunt game for me. [4]Then prepare for me savory food, such as I like, and bring it to me to eat, so that I may bless you before I die."

The series of seven scenes composed of two-person dialogues now begins. The scenes follow the convention of biblical narrative that only two persons can be in a dialogue. We give our attention to the first three- -Isaac-Esau, Rebekah-Jacob, and Jacob-Isaac (27:1-29). The first pair is the father and his favorite son followed by the mother and her favorite son--two pairs set on opposing tracks. The third pair, the father and his second son, is at the heart of the story.

The figures of Isaac and Esau are alone. Rebekah is out of eye-sight (v. 5), listening in, as a deathbed scene opens this carefully crafted drama story of the family blessing. The story is indispensably linked to the promise to Abraham, and as we have seen, and also to Isaac (12:1-3; 26:2-5, 24). Isaac's request to his elder son Esau suggests that he was unaware of the prophetic word to Rebekah (25:23). Or was Isaac spiritually blinded by an obstinate attachment to his eldest son? Isaac is old, blind, and uncertain as to how much longer he will live. He lives, however, many more years, dying at the age of one hundred and eighty (35:29). Isaac, deprived of sight, is a man of taste (25:28) and of touch (26:8). Isaac will rely on taste, touch, and smell in sequence to identify his firstborn son; he strangely ignores the evidence of sound in this central episode of the story (27:18-25).

We come at once to Isaac's big concern as Esau answers his father's request with "Here I am" (*hinnēnî*) and Isaac responds with "See (*hinnēh-na'*), I am old." Isaac's anxiety about his age, "I am old; I do not know the day of my death," prompts his call for Esau. But why call just Esau? The usual custom is for the family head to gather all the offspring at the approach of his death. Does Isaac want to make certain that he blesses Esau and leaves nothing to Jacob"? Is his theological sensitivity overpowered by his sensuality as often happens? Isaac asks Esau to take his weapons and "go out to the field, and hunt game for me." Does Isaac's appetite for the "savory food" or tasty dish that only Esau can make blind his spiritual vision? Isaac has always loved Esau more than Jacob "because he was fond of game" (25:28).

Continuing with Isaac's intention for Esau, "that I may bless you," it may be translated as "so that my life-breath [*napshî*] may bless you" for the Hebrew *napshî* indicates the whole person: Isaac desires to bless his son with all that he is in a most solemn blessing. In the Old Testament, blessing takes its meaning primarily from its life setting as leave-taking or farewell (Gen. 24:60). Blessing passes on vitality by the one who is departing life to the one who continues to live. Because of this vitality, the blessing cannot return or be subsequently altered. The mention of Esau in Hebrews12:16-17 reflects this.

We can only speculate as to the reason Isaac was willing to overlook Esau's transgression of family custom when he married the two Hittite ladies who caused Isaac and Rebekah so much grief (26:35). The biblical text does not say if Isaac knows of the oracle God gave to Rebekah when the twins were yet in her womb. If Isaac did know of it, he overlooks it as well as the troublesome Hittite women. Has Isaac set his will against the will both of God and Rebekah? Were his motives more ulterior than tummy-oriented? How fully is Isaacaware of the issues at stake? Who will triumph, Isaac and Esau, or Jacob and Rebekah as promised?

The dialogue as the next two characters in our story meet suggests an answer to that question as we come to

Rebekah and Jacob
(27:5-17)

[5]Now Rebekah was listening when Isaac spoke to his son Esau. So when Esau went to the field to hunt for game and bring it, [6]Rebekah said to her son Jacob, "I heard your father say to your brother Esau, [7]'Bring me game, and prepare for me savory food to eat, that I may bless you before the LORD before I die.' [8]Now therefore, my son, obey my word as I command you. [9]Go to the flock, and get me two choice kids, so that I may prepare from them savory food for your father, such as he likes; [10]and you shall take it to your father to eat, so that he may bless you before he dies." [11]But Jacob said to his mother Rebekah, "Look, my brother Esau is a hairy man, and I am a man of smooth skin. [12]Perhaps my father will feel me, and I shall seem to be mocking him, and bring a curse on myself and not a blessing." [13]His mother said to him, "Let your curse be on me, my son; only obey my word, and go, get them for me." [14]So he went and got them and brought them to his mother; and his mother prepared savory food, such as his father loved. [15]Then Rebekah took the best garments of her elder son Esau, which were with her in the house, and put them on her younger son Jacob; [16]and she put the skins of the kids on his hands and on the smooth part of his neck. [17]Then she handed the savory food, and the bread that she had prepared, to her son Jacob.

The focus of story is now on the blessing. The words "bless," "blessing," and "blessed" are the key to the passage, occurring twenty-two times in 27:1—28:9. "Brother" is another significant word that underscores the centrality of the fraternal element. Also worthy of attention

is how the author uses his vocabulary to create a sensuous story--seeing, hearing, tasting, touching, and smelling--making it a story one can feel as well as imagine.

The sense of hearing is the first to appear: "Rebekah was listening when Isaac spoke to his son Esau." Like Sarah, she was eavesdropping through the tent walls (18:10). She repeats to Jacob what she heard highlighting its significance, literally, "Behold (*hinnēh*), I heard your father say to your brother Esau. . . ." The Hebrew is literally "hear my voice" (vv. 8, 13). Later when Rebekah spoke "to her son Jacob" she said "my son, obey my word." The tension between the phrasing of "his son Esau" and "her son Jacob" reflects the parent's emotional preferences, and more importantly the family rift that is already in place.

Together, Rebekah and Jacob proceed to divide the family quartet even further into two parties. J. P. Fokkelman observes that Jacob, no doubt, "wants to obtain the firstborn's (*bkr*) right, to be blessed (*brk*), even at the cost of the ties of blood that connect him with Isaac and Esau."[70] He remarks humorously, that "all the members of the family take part in the action but at the same time they must be kept apart in pairs to prevent bloodshed"![71]

Rebekah, always energetic and decisive as shown by her response to Isaac's servant's request to leave home and country to be his wife (24:1-67), moves into action. She is angry perhaps because Isaac disregards custom in not summoning both sons for the blessing. When Rebekah repeats Isaac's request to Esau to Jacob (v. 3), she omits all reference to hunting ("weapons . . . field . . . hunt game") lest Jacob hesitate. Rebekah, however, adds Isaac's intention to bless Esau "before the LORD" revealing her conviction based on the birth oracle (25:23) that

---

[70] Fokkelman, *Narrative Art in Genesis*, 98-99. Note the identical consonants. The two Hebrew words with vowels added are *b^ekorah* (birthright) and *b^erakah* (blessing).

[71] Fokkelman, *Narrative Art in Genesis*, 98.

what she is about to do is the LORD's will, at least in result even if not in means.

But why Rebekah's deceit if she believes the oracle? John Calvin, the 16th century Swiss reformer, asks, "why then does she not patiently wait till God shall confirm it in fact?" By her lie, does she compromise "the grace promised to her son"?[72] Perhaps with adding "before the LORD" to Isaac's request of Esau, Rebekah emphasizes the significance of what Isaac desires to do, that is, the blessing has divine sanction; a sense of the sacred permeates the narrative.

Exercising all the authority she can muster, Rebekah adds the note of "command" to her request that Jacob "listen" to her. Jacob is to select two choice kids from the flock that she may prepare a meat delicacy for his father "such as he likes." Why did she not have Jacob cook it? He was a good cook. Being a woman of action she probably wants to give Jacob little opportunity to hesitate, and no doubt she desires to do all she can—it was *her* scheme. This tasty stew Jacob then will take to his father that Isaac may bless Jacob before he dies.

---

[72] John Calvin, *The First Book of Moses Called Genesis,* Second volume, trans. John King (Grand Rapids: Wm. B. Eerdmans Publishing Company, 1948 [1847]), 84.

And Jacob does hesitate at the scheme: should he follow his father's will or his mother's command? But his problem is not moral principle, but the feasibility of the plan. Jacob does not want the scheme to back fire and he is found out--his only fear: "Perhaps my father will feel me, and I shall seem to be mocking him, and bring a curse on myself and not a blessing." Rebekah does not argue about the proposal, but apparently feels so strongly that she moves directly to ward off Jacob's objection by the assurance that "Let your curse be on me, my son," only listen to my voice. For her, action is urgent. But if the blessing is non-transferable once bestowed, would not the curse be non-transferable also? Does she know this? Does Jacob? If so, his submission to his mother indicates his full complicity in the scheme.

Rebekah does everything essential. Jacob only goes to get the kids, and bring them to his mother and that in haste as the abrupt sequence of verbs displays. She prepares the "savory food" to taste like game "such as his father loved," puts Esau's festive garments on Jacob, covers his hands and the smooth part of his neck with the skins of the kids, and gives the tasty meat dish along with bread to her son Jacob.

Claus Westermann judges that the narrator attributes "this deliberately calculated initiative entirely to Rebekah,"[73] that is, the initial and primary motive in the account belongs to her.

All is set for the plot to proceed—and succeed. Rebekah designates Isaac as "his," that is, Jacob's "father" rather than naming or identifying him as her husband. The narrator thus draws attention to the rift in the family that has motivated Rebekah to act as she does, and to Isaac's physical appetite that contributes to his favoritism and to the family division.

The centerpiece of the blessing narrative (27:1-45) is at hand in which we await the narrator's command for . . . "Action!"

Jacob and Isaac
(27:18-29)

[18]So he went in to his father, and said, "My father"; and he said, "Here I am; who are you, my son?" [19]Jacob said to his father, "I am Esau your firstborn. I have done as you told me; now sit up and eat of my game, so that you may bless me." [20]But Isaac said to his son, "How is it that you have found it so quickly, my son?" He answered, "Because the LORD your God granted me success." [21]Then Isaac said to Jacob, "Come near, that I may feel you, my son, to know whether you are really my son Esau or not." [22]So Jacob went up to his father Isaac, who felt

---

[73] Westermann, *Genesis 12-36,* 438.

him and said, "The voice is Jacob's voice, but the hands are the hands of Esau." [23]He did not recognize him, because his hands were hairy like his brother Esau's hands; so he blessed him. [24]He said, "Are you really my son Esau?" He answered, "I am." [25]Then he said, "Bring it to me, that I may eat of my son's game and bless you." So he brought it to him, and he ate; and he brought him wine, and he drank. [26]Then his father Isaac said to him, "Come near and kiss me, my son." [27]So he came near and kissed him; and he smelled the smell of his garments, and blessed him, and said, "Ah, the smell of my son is like the smell of a field that the LORD has blessed. [28]May God give you of the dew of heaven, and of the fatness of the earth, and plenty of grain and wine. [29]Let peoples serve you, and nations bow down to you. Be lord over your brothers, and may your mother's sons bow down to you. Cursed be everyone who curses you, and blessed be everyone who blesses you!"

Action comes in a tension filled scene. Jacob and Isaac are the actors whose dramatic encounter focuses on the question of "who is who." Without hesitation Jacob approaches Isaac, "My father." Isaac, however appears suspicious as to which son it is, "Here I am (*hinnenî*); who are you, my son?" Jacob, taken back, perhaps overreacting, asserts with an audacious lie, declaring, "I am Esau your firstborn" (*beꞥkoraka*). The deceptive scheme may not be going as smoothly as first thought by Rebekah and her favorite son.

Jacob identifies himself up front as his father's "first born" (*beꞥkoraka*); it is the firstborn's blessing (*beꞥrakah*) that he is after.

Ironically, later in the Jacob story (29:26), Jacob gets a first born that he does not want--Leah! Jacob quickly assures his father that "I have done as you told me" and brashly requests that Isaac "now sit up and eat of my game, so that you may bless me," literally, "that your soul may bless me." For the first time we learn that Isaac is not only blind but bedridden as well.

Isaac hesitates, wondering how Jacob has found the game so quickly. Jacob's answer, "Because the LORD your God granted me success"—a lame reply to a not so dim Isaac--was the worst of his lies, Indeed he blasphemes as he brings God into the picture. But to be fair, Jacob speaks of only "your God" to Isaac, for Isaac is the patriarch, the one with the direct link and relationship to God. Jacob does not yet know God. Apart from an awareness of family tradition, no relationship exists between Jacob and the God of the patriarchs.

Isaac continues the pursuit of his suspicions. He cannot see, but he can taste, hear, smell, and feel. He asks to "feel" Jacob as he says, "to know whether you are really my son Esau or not." As Jacob approaches his father who, as he feels him, remarks that the "voice is Jacob's voice, but the hands are the hands of Esau." Isaac is confused; his senses of hearing and touch conflict. Jacob craftily takes care to speak as little as possible during the rest of the encounter! But what sounds like Jacob's voice does not fully convince Isaac of Jacob's deceit because Jacob's "hands were hairy like his brother Esau's hands; so he blessed him." Jacob passes the feel test and is about to receive the blessing (vv. 28-29).

But does Isaac not know that it is really Jacob for his suspicions continue? Isaac asks again, "Are you really my son Esau?" Jacob answers simply with an emphatic, "I am." Isaac's doubts are seemingly set aside and he asks Jacob for his "game" that he may bless him. One wonders, if at some subterranean level of his heart does Isaac sense that Jacob could perhaps be a better bearer of the patriarchal promise than Esau?

However it is, the game is brought with wine, and Isaac eats the food and drinks the wine, contributing no doubt to a dulling of his critical senses. The blessing ritual calls for a kiss; Jacob comes near to his father and they exchange kisses. Word and action come together in what Claus Westermann labels the oldest sacrament; the physical contact of the kiss participates in the meal strengthening the one who blesses for the passing on of his own vital power.[74]

As they kissed, Isaac "smelled the smell of his garments, and blessed him, and said, "Ah, the smell of my son is like the smell of a field that the LORD has blessed." One last test appears to overcome Isaac's doubts. With the kiss comes the earthy smell of Esau's garments, and the smell leads to the blessing on Jacob. The fourfold mention of "smell" in the verse is striking. There is something final about the "smell" test that transcends reasoning—we say, "I don't know exactly why, but that deal, that administrative decision or political action does not smell right!" Yet even the smell test can be deceptive as our story reveals!

The blessing Isaac gives Jacob centers on fertility and dominion; it reflects the wording of the birth oracle:

> "May God give you of the dew of heaven, and of the fatness of the earth, and plenty of grain and wine. [29]Let peoples serve you, and nations bow down to you. Be lord over your brothers, and may your mother's sons bow down to you. Cursed

---

[74] Westermann, *Genesis 12-36*, 435, 440. The kiss is a fourth element in a fivefold blessing ritual that takes placed in the previous paragraphs of the narrative..

> be everyone who curses you, and blessed be everyone who
> blesses you!"

How the blessing works out in relation to "peoples . . . and nations" is

not as clear as that of "dew . . . fatness . . . and grain and wine." The

lines that reflect the oracle, "your brothers . . . your mother's sons," will

be worked out in part as the patriarchal story continues. Multiple

meanings are in view as a blessing intended for Esau is addressed to

Jacob. The curse and the blessing that close the paragraph look back in

reverse order to the promise to Abraham in 12:3. There it was "I will

bless those who bless you, and the one who curses you I will curse."

Verses 28-29 bring us to the climax of the blessing account (27:1-45)

with the irrevocable character of the blessing.

The cultural and spiritual reality of blessing is all important in

the world of the patriarchs. It is the center of our story and the Genesis

story from beginning to end. But the recipient of the blessing to this

point has a far less intimate relationship with God than did Abraham, or

even Jacob's father Isaac. Franz Delitzsch concludes that Jacob, the

"quiet man" (25:27), however, "by reason however of the fundamental tendency of his mind toward the promised blessing . . . is the more pleasing to God of the two brothers."[75]

God is at work in the transference of the blessing although his presence in the narrative is only a shadow. Rebekah brings the LORD into the picture as she adds "before the LORD" to Isaac's request to Esau for "savory food" from his hunting. Jacob uses his knowledge of family religious traditions when he attributes his quick success at finding and preparing game to Isaac's God, that is, he can seemingly only use the name of God as an excuse, to lie to his father. Isaac is much more positive about God's reality and presence as he pronounces the blessing in God's name: "May God give you of the dew of heaven . . ." The LORD God is not absent!

How aware is Jacob of the true character of the blessing and of the implications of the patriarchal promise? Certainly at this point in the story, he has little knowledge that there is another world penetrating the one in which he is lives. More was happening than he knew. Yet, as now the blessed one, he joins in his spiritual ignorance

[75] Delitzsch, *Genesis,* II, 137.

that trinity of characters that defines the God of the Old Testament, "the God of Abraham, the God of Isaac, and the God of Jacob" (Exod. 3:6). The blessing possessed Jacob more than Jacob possessed the blessing! We paraphrase his later discovery, "Surely the LORD is in this event, and Jacob knows it not" (28:16). There is more at work against Isaac than the scheming of Rebekah, God is at work for Jacob!—and for us!

FIVE
The Blessing: Esau
(Genesis 27:30-28:9)

Genesis 27:33, 34, 38: Isaac trembled violently. . . . Esau . . . cried out with an exceedingly great and bitter cry. . . . Esau lifted up his voice and wept.

> What though my shrinking flesh complain
> And murmur to contend so long?
> I rise superior to my pain,
> When I am weak, then I am strong; And when my all of strength shall fail I shall with the God-Man prevail. [76]

Our interest in "blessing" as it appears in its earliest stages in the biblical narrative continues. The pre-biblical more magical form of blessing is transcended in the Jacob-Esau stories. In them blessing is a primary concern as the power of fertility and prosperity. As Claus Westermann concludes, "the entire complex of the promises to the patriarchs consists largely of blessing."[77] Blessing appears in the whole of the Old Testament as that which upholds, sustains, and undergirds all

---

[76] Hildebrandt, Beckerlegge, and Dale, ed., *A Collection of Hymns for the use of the People called Methodists*, 251.

[77] Claus Westermann, *Blessing in the Bible and the Life of the Church,* trans. Keith Grimm (Philadelphia: Fortress Press, 1978), 33.

of life; salvation is not only deliverance, it is also blessing. All this is in view when we pronounce the ancient biblical blessing of Numbers 6:24-26:

> The LORD bless you and keep you;
> the LORD make his face to shine upon you,
>> and be gracious to you;
> the LORD life up his countenance upon you,
>> and give you peace.

A wisdom teacher wrote long ago, "Death and life are in the power of the tongue" (Prov. 18:21). Our Lord's brother observed that "the tongue is a fire. . . . With it we bless the Lord and Father, and with it we curse those who are made in the likeness of God" (Jas. 3:6, 9). Our parents warned us that words are like feathers; once we let them fly they cannot be retrieved. Politicians discover that "off the record" can inadvertently become "on the record"!   On the other hand, Pastor Rick Warren of Saddleback Church in Southern California in a sermon entitled "Blessing others with your words" declared that

> You bless others when you show courtesy (Titus 3:3);
> You bless others when you offer mercy (Col. 3:13);
> You bless others when you show sympathy (Col.3:12);
> You bless others when you speak honestly (Eph. 4:15);

You bless others when you affirm them (1 Thess. 5:11).[78]

If words have power in our digital and media saturated culture, just think of the power of a spoken word that possesses a life of its own in more primitive and ancient cultures.

With these thoughts in mind we return to the "blessing" at the heart of this Jacob-Esau narrative. The New Testament writer to the Hebrews accurately interprets our Genesis text to mean that "by faith Isaac invoked blessings for the future on Jacob and Esau." (11:20). On Esau too? "Was Esau blessed by God as well?" If so, in what sense?

We will see as we look into another account of two persons in dialogue. This time the narrator presents us with

Esau and Isaac
(27:30-40)

[30]As soon as Isaac had finished blessing Jacob, when Jacob had scarcely gone out from the presence of his father Isaac, his brother Esau came in from his hunting. [31]He also prepared savory food, and brought it to his father. And he said to his father, "Let my father sit up and eat of his son's game, so that you may bless me." [32]His father Isaac said to him, "Who are you?" He answered, "I am your firstborn son, Esau." [33]Then Isaac trembled violently, and said, "Who was it then that hunted game and brought it to me, and I ate it all before you came, and I

---

[78] March 8, 2003.

have blessed him? —yes, and blessed he shall be!"[34]When Esau heard his father's words, he cried out with an exceedingly great and bitter cry, and said to his father, "Bless me, me also, father!"[35]But he said, "Your brother came deceitfully, and he has taken away your blessing."[36]Esau said, "Is he not rightly named Jacob? For he has supplanted me these two times. He took away my birthright; and look, now he has taken away my blessing." Then he said, "Have you not reserved a blessing for me?"[37]Isaac answered Esau, "I have already made him your lord, and I have given him all his brothers as servants, and with grain and wine I have sustained him. What then can I do for you, my son?"[38]Esau said to his father, "Have you only one blessing, father? Bless me, me also, father!" And Esau lifted up his voice and wept.[39]Then his father Isaac answered him: "See, away from the fatness of the earth shall your home be, and away from the dew of heaven on high.[40]By your sword you shall live, and you shall serve your brother; but when you break loose, you shall break his yoke from your neck."

Repetition plays a significant rhetorical role in the patriarchal narratives. The biblical authors by repetition could highlight continuity, stress important aspects, provide commentary, and foreshadow events and that as Robert Alter describes, with "a wonderful combination of subtle understatement and dramatic force."[79] When occurring in differing contexts with slight change of wording, repetition affords unique insight into the telling of the story. This role of repetition is particularly evident in the present account of Isaac's blessing.

---

[79] Alter, *The Art of Biblical Narrative*, 91.

Tension and breath-taking speed characterizes the account: "Jacob had scarcely gone out from the presence of his father Isaac" when "his brother Esau came in from his hunting." The tables are turned in contrast to the birth-narrative. Jacob appears first as the Hebrew order accentuates. Esau arrives on the scene just minutes too late to expose his brother's deceitful charade as he proceeds to prepare his own tasty meat stew and bring it his father. In contrast to Jacob's earlier commanding tone to his father (v. 19), Esau politely requests his father to sit up and eat his game so that Isaac may bless him. But Isaac asks, "Who are you?" leaving off the "my son" with which he had addressed Jacob (v. 18). Does he not recognize Esau?

Esau responds to his father's "Who are you?" unknowingly using Jacob's language, "I am your firstborn son, Esau," but in reverse word order to Jacob's "I am Esau your first born" (v. 19). : Jacob's point is that he is *Esau,* while Esau's concern is that his father know him as the *firstborn!* Isaac panics at the terrifying shock of the discovery of Jacob's deceit:

Isaac trembled violently and said, "Who was it then that hunted game and brought it to me, and I ate it all before you came, and I have blessed him? —yes, and blessed he shall be!"

Although he surely knows who deceived him, Isaac pretends not to know. He finds it easier to let Esau name the deceiver; he already had his doubts when he heard Jacob's voice pretending to be Esau. But sadly for Esau, Isaac's blessing of Jacob cannot be revoked. Isaac had already "ate it all," an act he cannot take back. For the second time in our story, we see a man duped by his desire for tasty food. Both Esau and Isaac put appetite before principle (25:29-34).

At Isaac's word, it is Esau's turn to panic: "he cried out with an exceedingly great and bitter cry, and said to his father, 'Bless me, me also, father!'" The grief of both Isaac and Esau is enormous. Gordon Wenham translates, Esau "let out a loud and very anguished scream."[80] Isaac entertained suspicions before, but suppressed them. Now they burst out into full recognition; he has been deliberately blindsided by Jacob: "Your brother came deceitfully, and he has taken away your blessing"! Employing the same verb that conveys deliberate planning

---

[80] Wenham, *Genesis 16-50,* 199.

when Laban substitutes Leah for Rachel later in the Jacob narrative, Jacob cries out, "Why then have you deceived me?" (29:25).

Although not the climax of the story as such, which occurred in 27:28-29), the narrative skill in Genesis 27:1—28:9 comes to a stylistic climax at verse 36.

> Esau said, "Is he not rightly named Jacob? For he has supplanted me these two times. He took away my birthright; and look, now he has taken away my blessing."

The patriarchal blessing (*b^erakah*) is brought in line with the birthright (*b^ekorah*) Jacob has already attained. The two terms, related linguistically (*brk* and *bkr*), are key or leading words (*leitwörter*) around which the Jacob stories are structured.

That the definitive interpretation of the name of Jacob, supplanter, comes from Esau's mouth indicates that this story is concerned equally with Esau –and with the whole family. It is not just about Jacob and how he obtained the blessing he coveted. Twice, wails Esau, Jacob has cheated me: "Is he not rightly named Jacob?" Isaac should have summoned both of his sons (27:1), but intended to bless only Esau. Esau went along with his father's intent to bless him and not

Jacob, and is left with empty-handed. Had he indeed found Isaac's sole invitation to him quite attractive?

As accented by "look (*hinnēh*), now he has taken away my blessing," the account centers vividly in Jacob's cruel deception and Esau's plaintive cry, "Have you not reserved a blessing for me?" With a change from "your mother's sons bow down" (27:29), the wording of Jacob's blessing becomes to "all his brothers as servants," Isaac can only say, "I have already made him your lord, and I have given him all his brothers as servants, and with grain and wine I have sustained him." Weakly, almost pleadingly, Isaac asks Esau, "What then can I do for you, my son?"

Esau can only repeat his desperate plea as he lifts up his voice in loud weeping: "Have you only one blessing, father? Bless me, me also, father!" Esau pursues the matter because in principle the privilege of Isaac's blessing extends also to him. But will Isaac bless Jacob only? Is Esau left with only an "anti-blessing"? The writer to the Hebrews affirms that "by faith Isaac invoked blessings for the future on Jacob and Esau" (Heb. 11:20). What *are* we to think?

124

Is Isaac's blessing of Esau only "a secondary blessing"? Isaac's blessing is not especially consoling:

> "See (*hinnēh*), away from the fatness of the earth shall your home be, and away from the dew of heaven on high, [40]By your sword you shall live, and you shall serve your brother; but when you break loose, you shall break his yoke from your neck."

Esau is sent to the more arid area to the south and east of Canaan "away from" rich land and adequate rainfall. The future relationship of Esau (Edom) and Jacob (Israel) may be reflected here; one will live a wandering nomadic existence away from settled agricultural existence, while the other will enjoy the fruits of the earth.

A life marked by violence will be Esau's lot: "By your sword you shall live." Further, Isaac predicts, "you shall serve your brother; but when you break loose, you shall break his yoke from your neck." There is a glimmer of hope for Esau. Esau "shall live"! Are we being too positive? We think not. Terrence Fretheim concludes that

> for all the negative correspondence to Jacob's blessing, Esau will have a [fruitful?] land in which to dwell, life, progeny, and periods of freedom from his brother. Esau receives blessing—attenuated, compared to Jacob's—but not a curse or even nonblessing.[81]

---

[81] Fretheim, "The Book of Genesis," 536-537.

The Genesis record later indicates that Esau did prosper in Edom. Jacob

is told that Esau had "four hundred men" (32:6) coming to meet him.

When Jacob finally meets Esau face to face offering placating gifts,

Esau refuses saying, "I have enough, my brother, keep what you have

for yourself" (33:9).

Who is the next narrative couple? It looks like, it is

Rebekah and Jacob
(27:41-45)

[41]Now Esau hated Jacob because of the blessing with which his father had blessed him, and Esau said to himself, "The days of mourning for my father are approaching; then I will kill my brother Jacob." [42]But the words of her elder son Esau were told to Rebekah; so she sent and called her younger son Jacob and said to him, "Your brother Esau is consoling himself by planning to kill you. [43]Now therefore, my son, obey my voice; flee at once to my brother Laban in Haran, [44]and stay with him a while, until your brother's fury turns away—[45]until your brother's anger against you turns away, and he forgets what you have done to him; then I will send, and bring you back from there. Why should I lose both of you in one day?"

Rebekah appears up front in the story in this her final appearance in

Genesis. She is a mother who manipulates to perfection—a dominating

figure in contrast to her husband's retiring nature. Rebekah and Jacob

have won, but they are the moral losers. The family is torn apart.

Because Isaac has blessed Jacob, Esau now intensely and openly hates Jacob; he is furious and plans to kill Jacob after Isaac's death. Jacob has gained little by his deception. Esau waits for Isaac to die, why? Respect for his father? Fear that he might be further disinherited and cursed? The promise is again at risk.

Rebekah takes action. She is convinced that Jacob must be sent away immediately. Hearing of Esau's intention—Esau surely had boasted of his intent to kill his brother thereby "consoling himself." Rebekah, realizing that her plan has achieved little, urgently (*hinnēh*) informs Jacob of Esau's intentions with the exact words she used to instruct Jacob earlier (27:8). She advises Jacob, Listen to me, flee, stay with my brother Laban in Haran for your protection "until your brother's fury turns away—until your brother's anger against you turns away, and he forgets what you have done to him." When time has cooled Esau's fury, as Rebekah tells Jacob, "I will send, and bring you back from there." The repetition, "until . . . until," emphasizes Rebekah fearful concern: "Why should I lose both of you in one day?" If Esau kills

Jacob, vengeance will certainly follow; he will be dead or exiled like Cain.

Rebekah believes she must act, for she doubts that neither Isaac's blessing nor the divine oracle will protect her favorite son. Rebekah would rather lose Jacob for a time than forever. In fact, she will never see her favorite son again. Jacob will never again hear his mother's voice. He will be gone for twenty years during which time Rebekah apparently dies. Her death is not recorded, only the place of her burial with Abraham, Sarah, Isaac (49:31).

But Jacob hesitates. He is in no hurry to leave home. Does he think his mother is exaggerating the immediate danger? Rebekah appears to be unaware of Esau's murderous timeline—after Isaac dies. Is Jacob afraid to go so far away, all to the way to Paddan-aram? So the scene shifts for a moment to another pair:

Rebekah and Isaac
(27:46)

[46]Then Rebekah said to Isaac, "I am weary of my life because of the Hittite women. If Jacob marries one of the Hittite women such as these, one of the women of the land, what good will my life be to me?"

Rebekah rightfully seeks Isaac's help in getting Jacob to run away in her concern for his life--and a wife. The persuasive point she employs is the proximity of "the Hittite women" as she, in a demeaning tone, calls Esau's wives. Rebekah is apparently silent about Esau's threat as a matter of tact, for he is Isaac's adored favorite. The Hittite wives have wearied her nigh unto death; and Isaac feels the same (26:35).

Rebekah argues that Jacob should not marry "one of the Hittite women such as these, one of the women of the land." If he does, "what good will my life be to me? Her question echoes the earlier one of her troubled pregnancy (25:22). A discerning wife, Rebekah says no more. If she told Isaac what to do, her husband could balk. She just dumps the problem in his lap! Thus we conclude the story of the blessing with

Isaac and Jacob
(28:1-9)

[1]Then Isaac called Jacob and blessed him, and charged him, "You shall not marry one of the Canaanite women.[2]Go at once to Paddan-aram to the house of Bethuel, your mother's father; and take as wife from there one of the daughters of Laban, your mother's brother.[3]May God Almighty bless you and make you fruitful and numerous, that you may become a company of peoples.[4]May he give to you the blessing of Abraham, to you and to your offspring with you, so that you may take possession of the land where you now live as an alien—land

129

that God gave to Abraham."[5]Thus Isaac sent Jacob away; and he went to Paddan-aram, to Laban son of Bethuel the Aramean, the brother of Rebekah, Jacob's and Esau's mother.

[6]Now Esau saw that Isaac had blessed Jacob and sent him away to Paddan-aram to take a wife from there, and that as he blessed him he charged him, "You shall not marry one of the Canaanite women,"[7]and that Jacob had obeyed his father and his mother and gone to Paddan-aram.[8]So when Esau saw that the Canaanite women did not please his father Isaac,[9]Esau went to Ishmael and took Mahalath daughter of Abraham's son Ishmael, and sister of Nebaioth, to be his wife in addition to the wives he had.

Jacob is sent to find a wife from among his mother's relatives, a secondary explanation for a flight engineered by Rebekah. Now, without Rebekah's explicit direction, Isaac, like any discerning husband, does what she wants. But differing from his father Abraham who sent a servant to find him a wife (24:1-9), Isaac sends Jacob himself "to Paddan-aram to the house of Bethuel, your mother's father; and take as wife from there one of the daughters of Laban, your mother's brother." Isaac takes the risk that Jacob will never return. Instead of keeping Jacob in the land at all costs as Abraham did with Isaac, Isaac sends Jacob away from the land. The covenant is once more in jeopardy.

As a farewell sendoff to Jacob, Isaac repeats to him "the blessing of Abraham" (12:2-3, 7). Whatever his misgivings were about Jacob's deception, Isaac knows that the blessing belongs irrevocably to his younger son and is compelled to repeat it as they part. Promise and blessing come together as Isaac for the first time designates Jacob the heir of the Abrahamic promise:

> "May God Almighty bless you and make you fruitful and numerous, that you may become a company of peoples. May he give to you the blessing of Abraham, to you and to your offspring with you, so that you may take possession of the land where you now live as an alien—land that God gave to Abraham."

The title "God Almighty" appears for the second time in the Genesis narrative, now on the lips of Isaac. In 17:1 "The LORD appeared to Abram, and said to him, 'I am God Almighty; walk before me, and be blameless. And I will make my covenant between me and you, and will make you exceedingly numerous.'" Apart from its use for emphasis in the patriarchal story, we are able to discern the title's descriptive intent only from its context. The Hebrew title *El Shaddai*, appears in Genesis 17:1; 28:3; 35:11; 48:3; 43:14. *El* is the Semitic generic term for deity. *Shaddai* functions as an adjective.

Although Jacob had ignored his mother's warning, he promptly obeys his father's instruction as he is "sent . . . away to Paddan-aram,"

This image for Jacob builds the contrast with Esau the more sharply as it highlights the contentious character of Esau in the family by setting up Esau's decision that follows. With Jacob's departure, Esau, hit hard by Isaac's blessing and charge that Jacob not "marry one of the Canaanite women," seeks to nullify the impact of his marriages to the Hittite women.

So Esau "went to Ishmael and took Mahalath daughter of Abraham's son Ishmael, and sister of Nebaioth, to be his wife in addition to the wives he had." Esau finally sees that "the Canaanite women did not please his father Isaac." Apparently he gives no thought to his mother's feelings in the matter—the text does not say. One wonders if Isaac failed in not arranging a proper marriage for Esau as he was now setting up for Jacob. Does his quiet patience, a virtue, become a vice?

Jacob is now the son of promise; to him the blessing of Abraham belongs. His mother, doing her part to fulfill the prophetic oracle uttered at his birth, has seen to that. Although all appears to be going Jacob's way, from now on, all his life, Jacob will be both the deceiver and the deceived. As he deceived his father with a kid, his sons will deceive him with a kid (37:31). To what extent will his life be one of blessing or a curse? The patriarchal blessing, which Isaac was unable to retrieve for his older son, remains ultimately in God's hands.

There is a sense in which as Franz Delitzsch observes that "the Divine judgment falls upon [Jacob] and upon every member of the family in proportion as they have been sharers in his transgression"-- Esau for despising his birthright, Rebekah for "her contrivance of the fraud," and Jacob by the manner in which he obtains both birthright and blessing. The life of Jacob will be "one long chain of hardships, disappointments, strifes and anxieties."[82] With the blessing, Jacob gets more than he asks for!

Robert Alter reminds us here that the entire book of Genesis "is about the reversal of the iron law of primogeniture, about the election through some devious twist of destiny of a younger son to carry on the line."[83] Jesus can be viewed as the supreme example of this elder/younger switch. He is everything that the religious culture of his

---

[82] Delitzsch, *Genesis,* II, 158.
[83] Alter, *The Art of Biblical Narrative,* 6.

day, both Greek and Jewish, that a Son of God was thought not to be. Yet, God the Father designates him "heir of all things" (Heb. 1:2) and we are "joint heirs with Christ" (Rom 8:17), for he is destined to "be the firstborn within a large family" (Rom. 8:29)—the family to which we now belong!

As the heir *par excellence,* Jesus is the culmination of all of God's purposes:

> "For God has put all things in subjection under his feet." But when it says, "All things are put in subjection," it is plain that this does not include the one who put all things in subjection under him. When all things are subjected to him, then the Son himself will also be subjected to the one who put all things in subjection under him, so that God may be all in all (1 Cor. 15:27-28).

Jesus the *only* Son possesses both the birthright and the blessing! He is the one who blesses, he is himself the blessing! Thus his followers seek to live and witness in "the fullness of the blessing of Christ" (Rom. 15:29).

But as yet in the story of Jacob, no relationship exists between Jacob and God; God has not become "the God of Jacob" (Psalm 46:7, 11).

4.11 Jacob—Bethel to Peniel

SIX
Jacob at Bethel
(Genesis 28:1-22)

Genesis 28:16-17:   Then Jacob woke from his sleep and said, "Surely the LORD is in this place—and I did not know it!" And he was afraid, and said, "How awesome is this place! This is none other than the house of God, and this is the gate of heaven."

> Yield to me now--for I am weak,
>   But confident in self-despair!
> Speak to my heart, in blessings speak,
>   Be conquered by my instant prayer: Speak, or thou never hence shalt move, And tell me if thy name is LOVE.[84]

The opening lines of Bunyan's *Pilgrim's Progress* reflect the impact of Jacob's dream at Bethel:

> As I walked through the wilderness of this world, I lighted on a certain place where was a den, and laid me down in that place to sleep; and as I slept, I dreamed a dream.[85]

Thomas Merton, as he settled into his life at the Abbey of Gethsemani in Kentucky, found in Jacob's dream the definition of where he was:

---

[84] Hildebrandt, Beckerlegge, and Dale, ed., *A Collection of Hymns for the use of the People called Methodists*, 251

[85] John Bunyan, *The Pilgrim's Progress* (Element Books Limited, 1997), 11.

> This is the land where you have given me roots in eternity, O
> God of heaven and earth, This is the burning promised land, the
> house of God, the gate of heaven, the place of peace, the place of
> silence, the place of wrestling with the angel.[86]

Among the paintings that Jacob's dream has inspired are *Jacob's*

Dream – El sueño de Jacob (1639) by José de Ribera, displayed in the

Museo del Prado in Madrid, *Jacob's Ladder* by William Blake (1800) in

the British Museum, and *Landscape with Jacob's Dream* (1866) in

Gustav Dore's English Bible.

And we do not forget for a moment where Jacob's dream invades

the New Testament on the lips of him who has just been designated the

Lamb of God, the Messiah, the Son of God, and the King of Israel (John

1:36, 41, 49):

> Very truly, I tell you, you will see heaven opened and the angels
> of God ascending and descending upon the Son of Man (John
> 1:51).

Jacob appears by himself for the first time on the Genesis scene in this

account--a new beginning for Jacob. Surely such is needed for the promise of

both progeny and land is at stake. The behaviors of both Esau and Jacob have

kept the prospect of a promised-land and people in jeopardy. Even so, the story

---

[86] Thomas Merton, *The Sign of Jonas* (New York: Harcourt Brace Jovanovich, 1953), 345.

of Jacob remains a "God-Story," a dimension to which Jacob in his utter humanness appears as yet insensitive. But his story is about to open up in ways unexpected.

Jacob is in bad shape; he is "on the run." He is fleeing for his life: "Jacob has filched the blessing from his father and his brother" [87] as J. P. Fokkelman so vividly expresses it. He has deceived his father and robbed his brother Esau who now hates him. Like a dog slinking away with tail between the legs, Jacob has taken off for his uncle Laban's household in a far country. His life is in crisis. Jacob does not have his own relationship with the LORD; the God of Abraham and Isaac is not yet "the God of Jacob" (Psalm 46:7, 11). Isaac is still *the* patriarch. But as Jacob approaches one of his early nights on the road, he finds himself in the picture drawn by Thomas Mann

> standing at a strange door that opens in three directions: behind is his past of failure and alienation; ahead is his future of both hope and uncertainty; and over above, coming down to meet him, is the presence of God.[88]

What happens now in the life of Jacob imports a new perspective into his life; all that has taken place begins to take on some sense to him.

---

[87] Fokkelman, *Narrative Art in Genesis,* 46.

[88] Mann, *The Book of the Torah,* 55.

For now, in a startling dream experience, he receives the patriarchal promise from the LORD himself for the first time, not just from his father Isaac (28:3-4).

Although this carefully structured narrative (vv. 10-22) falls naturally into three paragraphs with Jacob named as the subject of each major action (10-15, 16-17, 18-22), we divide the scene into the five initiatives taken by Jacob: he flees (10-11), he dreams (12-15), he responds (16-17), he commemorates the place (18-19), and he makes a vow (20-22). So first,

Jacob's Flight
(28:10-11)

[10]Jacob left Beer-sheba and went toward Haran. [11]He came to a certain place and stayed there for the night, because the sun had set. Taking one of the stones of the place, he put it under his head and lay down in that place.

Jacob's flight begins at Beer-sheba where Isaac resides.[89] The verb "went" describes him as "on the way." Jacob "sets off" to the northeast via Jerusalem and Shechem for Haran 550 miles and over a month's travel away. The first reason for Jacob's departure for Haran is

---

[89] Genesis 22:19; 26:23, 33, 28:10.

to escape Esau's wrath (27:42-45); the second is for Jacob to find a wife within the clan (27:46—28:2). Both reasons motivate Rebekah's action, but the second reason is Isaac's concern as he sends Jacob away with "the blessing of Abraham" (28:3-4). Isaac's primary motive appears to be ethnic more than spiritual. Jacob must take a wife outside this new land to reduce the risk of cultural and religious assimilation. An appropriate wife for this son of promise is not to be found in the land of Canaan.

After some sixty miles of travel, Jacob "lights" or strikes upon by chance (32:2) "the place" or a "certain place" as the definite article suggests. The threefold mention of "place" in verse 11 hints at the significance of "place" in the narrative, a keyword that anticipates the main theme of the story (vv. 16, 17, 19). This term, literally, "the place," occurs six times in this brief account.

At this "place" Jacob spends the night "because the sun had set." In contrast to the setting sun, the sun will not rise again on Jacob until after his experience at Peniel, another new day in his life (32:24-26). Here at Bethel the setting sun symbolizes the closing of an era in Jacob's life. As Jacob "lay down in that place," the Hebrew text indicates that he took *some* of the stones and placed them around his head, probably for protection. There is no indication as to the size of the stones. Asleep, Jacob comes to a new awareness in an arresting dream that brings a promise with a presence. The apparent wildness, that is, the out of human control nature, of the place is a fitting setting for

Jacob's Dream
(28:12-15)

[12]And he dreamed that there was a ladder set up on the earth, the top of it reaching to heaven; and the angels of God were ascending and descending on it. [13]And the LORD stood beside him and said, "I am the LORD, the God of Abraham your father and the God of Isaac; the land on which you lie I will give to you and to your offspring; [14]and your offspring shall be like the dust of the earth, and you shall spread abroad to the west and to the east and to the north and to the south; and all the families of the earth shall be blessed in you and in your offspring. [15]Know that I am with you and will keep you wherever you go, and will bring you back to this land; for I will not leave you until I have done what I have promised you."

This story raises a significant personal question, "When and where did you and I first sense the presence of God in an unmistakable way?" As you think back on your story, my memory recalls the following scene:

As the child of a devout Methodist mother, I was in church from day one. I was baptized as a baby and have chosen to honor mother's faith and faithfulness. About the age of eight to ten I was sitting after supper one evening at the dining room table around a kerosene lamp with mother's two hired girls. With so many ranch-hands to feed three times a day in the time before tractors, mother needed help in the house. Although they were not faithful attenders of church, the young women's conversation turned to religious matters.

As they talked such a sense or conviction of the reality of God came over me that I soon made my way to my bedroom on the northwest corner, the coldest room in the ranch-house. There I knelt down by my bed, and promised God that I would be a preacher if he wanted me to be.

I date my call to the Christian ministry back to that moment, although my explicit commitment did not come until the second semester of my freshman year in college. But I never could escape the sense of divine imperative that came to me that day. What was put into my heart that evening has held my course steady through "no matter what" all these intervening years.

God's mysterious purpose invades Jacob's self-oriented life as a revelation comes to one of the three patriarchs in a dream for the first time. The dream comes to Jacob at a vulnerable, unexpected time--he has no religious agenda. The dream, as he experiences it, projects three visual images with evocative power, a "ladder . . . angels . . . the LORD." Each image vividly captures our attention by the threefold introductory repetition of *hinnē*, translated as "behold . . . behold . . . behold" (vv. 12-13) by the *New American Standard Bible*. The verbal phrases that follow, "set up . . . ascending and descending . . . stood," all participles in Hebrew, describe each of the three elements as an enduring reality.

First, Jacob sees a "ladder" or stairway "set up on the earth, the top of it reaching to heaven." Those interpreters who see the imagery as reflecting the Mesopotamian temple-towers with their stairways or ramps leading to a summit where divine beings communicated with mortals, prefer to visualize a "stairway." Robert Alter envisions "a vast ramp with terraced landings" after the pattern of the Mesopotamian ziggurat.[90] The picture causes one to stop and wonder at the significance of the place. What is important is that the "ladder" links heaven to the earth, in John Walton's vision—"a sacred portal between realms."[91] The stairway is "set up" on earth where Jacob is and "reaches" to heaven where God is. The two realms are connected as the next line displays.

Second, "the angels of God were ascending and descending on it." The bridge between the divine and the human realms is busy with traffic. The messengers or angels are constantly coming and going.

---

[90] Alter, *Genesis*, 148.
[91] J. Walton, *Genesis,* 571.

Gordon Wenham cites an ancient Jewish interpreter who speculates that the ascending angels are those responsible for Jacob's homeland and the descending angels are responsible for the land to which he is going. The vision of the angels would then assure Jacob of God's protection on him as he leaves home.[92] Anticipated is the verbal assurance of verse 15: "I will . . . keep you wherever you go."

Third, "the LORD stood above it," reading the *New American Standard Bible* as preferable to the *New Revised Standard Version*'s "the LORD stood beside him." The context and the Hebrew preposition both make "above" or "over" the ladder more likely than "beside" Jacob. The twofold movement of the angels invites the gaze to rest on one figure, that of God himself, "the LORD." The messengers, the angelic "sent ones," direct the sight to the "one who sends." Jacob has seen God, if only in a dream, and lived!

The angels are silent, only "the LORD" speaks. The divine speech comes directly to Jacob for the first time as he hears the patriarchal promise: "I am the LORD, the God of Abraham your father

---

[92] Wenham, *Genesis 16–50*, 222, citing Rashi in the Targums.

and the God of Isaac; the land on which you lie I will give to you and to your offspring." An emphatic *hinnē* ("behold") at the beginning of verse 15 becomes "Know that" in *The New Revised Standard Version:* "Know that I am with you and will keep you wherever you go, and will bring you back to this land; for I will not leave you until I have done what I have promised you."

The precise form of the title, "the LORD, the God of Abraham your father and the God of Isaac," occurs uniquely here in the Old Testament. It indicates that Jacob possesses the same relationship to God as did his father Isaac. Yet, essential for the long-range purpose of the patriarchal story, God for Jacob is now designated as "the God of Abraham your father," the patriarch to whom the promise first came. The appearance of "the LORD," the covenant name, with "the God of Abraham," the God the patriarchs know, reveals the same God who will later reveal himself to Moses (Exod. 3:6-17; 6:2-8). The double title, the "God of Abraham . . . God of Isaac," Gordon Wenham reminds us, "recalls the great promises and blessings given to them and anticipates their reaffirmation and reapplication to Jacob."[93]

The covenant God of Israel, the LORD (*YHWH*), having identified himself, now speaks to Jacob as the vision ends and the promise is given:

> the land on which you lie I will give to you and to your offspring; and (*hinnē*) your offspring shall be like the dust of the earth, and you shall spread abroad to the west and to the east and to the north and to the south; and all the families of the earth shall be blessed in you and in your offspring.

The language of the promise, focused now on Jacob, reflects that given both to Abraham (12:2-3; 15:5, 18; 17:1-8; 22:17-18) and to Isaac (26:3-4. 24) as well as the similar words of Isaac to Jacob (28:3-4). The promise speaks of land, offspring, and blessing. Ironically, as Margaret Poteet aptly grasps this moment in Jacob's life, "Jacob is given his promise of land just as he is leaving it."[94]

This first part of the promise, "land . . . offspring," reaches its climax with "all the families of the earth shall be blessed in you and in

---

[93] Wenham, *Genesis 16-50*, 222.

[94] Margaret Ellis Poteet, *Literary Unity in the Patriarchal Narratives*, A Dissertation Submitted to the Graduate Faculty of the University of Oklahoma in partial fulfillment of the requirements for the degree of Doctor of Philosophy (Norman, Oklahoma, 1990), 125.

your offspring." The patriarchal stories suggest that other nations fare in accordance with their relation to the patriarchs. Dietrich Bonhoeffer, of *Letters and Papers from Prison* fame with insight far ahead of most of his peers in the German Church of his day, became disillusioned with Nazi Germany as he observed their persecution of the Jewish people. In the providence of God, can we ask, "How did the holocaust figure into the tremendously costly defeat of Germany?"

But for Jacob personally, the second part of the promise reaches all the way to his fugitive fears:

> now that I am with you and will keep you wherever you go, and will bring you back to this land; for I will not leave you until I have done what I have promised you.

Another "behold" (*hinnēh*) that appears as "now" in the *New Revised Standard Version* highlights the promise to Jacob, a promise capped by "I am with you." This *hinnēh* links the narrative back with the threefold *hinnēh* of Jacob's vision (vv. 12-13a) and fills "I am with you" with awesome content. This promise of divine presence that first appears in 26:3, 24, now characterizes the Jacob story throughout (28:20; 31:3; 46:4).

The intent of the stairway is now stated. The transcendent LORD becomes an immanent God for Jacob! Relationship not place identifies the relation of God to Jacob. Wherever Jacob goes, the God of the patriarchs will both be with and will not leave this man who becomes both *Israel* and the ancestor of the *Israel*ites. Protection, return to Canaan, and divine destiny all belong to him! The plot of Jacob's future is foreshadowed.

The LORD promises to bring Jacob "back to this land"! But when? How long did Jacob think he would be gone from home? Certainly not for the twenty years it took (Gen. 31:41). But God does not hurry. No wonder the Psalmist in Israel's history would cry out from time to time, "O LORD, make haste to help me" (40:13; see 38:22).

We pause a moment to look ahead to a new day and a different vision, but one anticipated by "Jacob at Bethel":

> I saw seven golden lampstands, and in the midst of the lampstands I saw one like the Son of Man, clothed with a long robe and with a golden sash across his chest. His head and his hair were as white as white wool, white as snow; his eyes were like a flame of fire, his feet were like burnished bronze, refined as in a furnace, and his voice was like the sound off many waters. In his right hand he held seven stars, and from his mouth

came a sharp, two-edged sword, and his face was like the sun shining with full force. . . .

"Do not be afraid; I am the first and the last, and the living one, I was dead, and see, I am alive for ever and ever; and I have the keys of Death and Hades." . . .

The seven golden lampstands . . . are the seven churches.[95]

The Risen Lord is present and active in the life and work of his Church on earth! John Calvin, interpreting the "ladder" and in contrast to the "angels," takes a big leap of faith from the Genesis text and concludes that

it is Christ alone, therefore, who connects heaven and earth: he is the only Mediator who reaches from heaven down to earth: he is the medium through which all the fulness of all celestial blessings flow down to us, and through which we, in turn, ascend to God.[96]

Back to Jacob who could not keep silent. We think of Isaiah in Israel's past, "Woe is me! I am lost, . . . yet my eyes have seen the King" (6:5), and of Peter in Israel's future, "Go away from me, Lord, for I am a sinful man!" (Luke 5:8). Like with them, the experience of the holy elicits

---

[95] Revelation 1:12-20.
[96] Calvin, *Genesis,* 113.

Jacob's Response
(28:16-17)

Then Jacob woke from his sleep and said, "Surely the LORD is in this place—and I did not know it!" [17]And he was afraid, and said, "How awesome is this place! This is none other than the house of God, and this is the gate of heaven."

Jacob awakes suddenly from his dream. We are reminded of Moses at "the mountain of God" (Exod. 3:1) where Moses sees the bush that refused to burn up and hears God calling, "Come no closer! Remove the sandals from your feet, for the place on which you are standing is holy ground." In response, "Moses hid his face, for he was afraid to look at God" (Exod. 3:5, 7). With Jacob like with Moses--"the place on which you are standing is holy ground." There too "place" is in the foreground: Jacob exclaims that "Surely the LORD is in this place. . . !" The name of God appears on Jacob's lips for the first time in his story apart from the lie to his father in 27:20.

Jacob is amazed: "I did not know it!" When what he sees sinks in, his amazement turns to fear. He is shaken up. Jacob was awestruck "and said, 'How awesome is this place!'" Jacob's experience was near to the element of "awefulness" in Rudolf Otto's chapter on *Mysterium*

Tremendum where he writes that "the awe or 'dread' *may* indeed be so overwhelmingly great that it seems to penetrate to the very marrow, making the man's hair bristle and his limbs quake"?[97]

Jacob can imagine no better way to describe the place than as "the house of God." Or, in a more daring metaphor, as an entrance into the divine realm—"the gate of heaven"—heaven is open! Jacob can no longer view his world, in N. T. Wright's apt phrase, as a "split-level cosmos."[98] In seeing the LORD in his dream, Jacob has penetrated heaven. We can imagine the impact of that awareness! Jacob utters only a numb "I did not know." J. P. Fokkelman suggests that his exclamation may well indicate that he feels a bit of shame and self-reproach that paves the way for his fear; it is an awe that in turn sharpens his eye for a deeper insight into his dream.[99]

Jacob's discovery that the place where he was sleeping was indeed "the house of God" brings to mind those special places in our lives all of us have--holy places that determine and define who and what

---

[97] Rudolf Otto, *The Idea of the Holy,* trans. John W. Harvey (New York: Oxford University Press, 1923), 16.

[98] N. T. Wright, *Simply Jesus: A New Vision of Who He Was, What He Did, and Why He Matters* (New York: HarperCollins, 2011), 59.

[99] Fokkelman, *Narrative Art in Genesis,* 64.

we are. Jacob's response recalls an early memory of the holy as linked with place:

> There was a small box-like wooden church in Valentine, Nebraska. While still in college, I would attend with my Methodist mother from time to time on Sunday nights. For me, just to walk into that wooden box was to sense the presence of the Holy, it was "the house of God." The catalyst for that "other" atmosphere was a small gray-haired lady, Grandma Horner. She would sit in the second row, lean over the wooden bench in front of her and constantly respond in praise to song and sermon. Somehow, she gave rise to a sense of awe in me. It was "the Presence" that I experienced there that eventually led me into the Church of the Nazarene and its ministry in the good providence of God.

There were other leading influences as well, but the most compelling attraction was an inescapable sense of the holy that met me on occasion in the environment of the Church of the Nazarene—what I thought my Methodist heritage was all about.

Back to Jacob's experience of the holy. He is so profoundly moved that he turns to ritual expression. The narrator transitions from verbal to physical action of necessity, to something concrete, to

Jacob's Stone

(28:18-19)

So Jacob rose early in the morning, and he took the stone that he had put under his head and set it up for a pillar and poured oil on the top of it. [19]He called that place Bethel; but the name of the city was Luz at the first.

We humans require ritual. We find meaning in the repeating of traditional forms of expression, such as the Lord's Prayer. We frequently add to our thoughts posture, hands, and voice. Such is true whether we are singing "Take me out to the ballgame" at the seventh inning stretch or "Praise God from whom all blessings flow" after the offering. We enjoy weddings as the exchanges of vows by those we love touch our emotions. Some take part in walks to raise money for a favorite cause and others gather for protests. Physical action displays the inner experience in outward form. So it is with Jacob's response. Like the baseball umpire with balls and strikes—a pitch is meaningless until the umpire speaks! Physical objects are what we make them; meaning is what we "give" to them! Jacob's object was a stone.

Jacob's first action is to take one of the stones he had placed about his head as he slept "and set it up for a pillar and poured oil on the top of it." Pillars in the world of his day could either be natural or carved, inscribed or plain. Jacob apparently leaves the stone he has erected just as he finds it as a memorial of his now understood sacred dream. He dedicates it to his purpose by anointing the stone with oil that so stains it that those who pass by may recognize it as a sacred symbol.

The "top" of the pillar corresponds to "the top" of the stairway "reaching to heaven" (v. 12). As a cultic pillar the stone could have been quite large requiring near Herculean strength to lift it. This would then anticipate Jacob's feat with a massive weight of stone in the next episode in which he meets Rachel at a well. This is the first of four times that Jacob erects a stone; each time the stone functions with a different significance (28:18; 31:45-49; 35:14, 20).

Jacob's second action is to give the place a name, "Bethel," meaning "the house of God" (v. 17). His action is in essence a name change, for "the name of the city was Luz at the first." The Canaanite town has lost its identity. The character of "that place" is now so changed that a "new name" is required! Name changes are not neutral, whether of places or people—when God is involved! These actions are then brought to a climax with

Jacob's Vow
(28:20-22)

> Then Jacob made a vow, saying, "If God will be with me, and will keep me in this way that I go, and will give me bread to eat and clothing to wear, [21]so that I come again to my father's house in peace, then the LORD shall be my God, [22]and this stone, which I have set up for a pillar, shall be God's house; and of all that you give me I will surely give one tenth to you."

Jacob's encounter with God at Bethel inspires him to make a vow. His experience changes his life as all such experiences often do. Bethel is now a sacred place for him because of what happened there and his resultant vow. Bethel appears in significant ways throughout the Jacob story.[100] When an angel of God instructs Jacob later to leave his father-in-law Laban and return to the land of his birth, the angel speaks to him in a dream saying, "I am the God of Bethel, where you anointed a pillar and made a vow to me. Now leave this land at once and return to the land of your birth" (31:13). Moving on in the story, Bethel appears as again God gives Jacob the command to move on: "Arise, go up to

---

[100]Abraham had built an altar previously at Bethel (Gen. 12:8; 13:3-4). Bethel is mentioned in the Bible more frequently than any other town except Jerusalem. It was destroyed by Josiah (2 Kings 23:15).

155

Bethel, and settle there. Make an altar there to the God who appeared to you when you fled from your brother Esau" (35:1-7).

The *vow* that Jacob *vows,* as the Hebrew reads, repeats language from God's promise to Jacob as it reflects his dream of a stairway with trafficking angels reaching to heaven with the LORD standing above it (v. 15). Jacob adds "bread to eat and clothing to wear" to the previous promise. The mood of Jacob's vow appears conditional, "If God . . . then the LORD shall be my God." Three aspects of God's promise on which Jacob vows to base his future life are repeated. First, "If God will be with me," relies on the promise he has just heard in his dream, words spoken in the biblical record first to Jacob: "I am with you" (v.15). Later Moses (Exod. 3:12), Joshua (1:5), and Gideon (Judg. 6:16) hear the same assuring words that reappear often in the biblical story (Isa. 7:14; Matt. 1:23; 28:20; Heb. 13:5).

Second, "If God . . . will keep me in this way that I go," is a frequent Old Testament promise of protection as in the blessing, "The LORD bless you and keep you" (Num. 6:24; see Pss. 23, 91, 121). The way that Jacob goes is in stark contrast to the way of Abraham's servant

156

in chapter 24 who crossed the desert in grand style with a retinue of camels and underlings to find a bride for Jacob. Jacob flees alone on foot on a most dangerous journey.

The third aspect of God's promise that Jacob repeats, "so that I come again to my father's house in peace," carries with it the full patriarchal promise of land and numerous descendants. It includes the divine assurance that "I will not leave you until I have done what I have promised you" (v.15). Jacob's promised return confirms his future. On these three conditions, the text seems to read, Jacob will confess that first of all "the LORD shall be my God." The LORD of the covenant with Abraham and Isaac will be his God as well. Is Jacob striking a bargain with his vow, is he hedging, bargaining with God to his discredit—"If . . . then"?

But what Jacob now expresses as a condition God has already promised unconditionally. Jacob is claiming the promise as his own; he is holding God to his word as the foundation of his life for the future— and posterity. As Terrence Fretheim concludes, "bargain language does not do justice to the vow."[101] Jacob is only at the beginning of his quest; he is not yet the man of faith who wrestles with a mysterious man of the night (32:24). Yet, his prayer arises authentically from the heart. He is responding humanly to the covenant God offers him; his vow expresses his experience. To what extent, however, does Jacob remain, asks Robert Alter, "the suspicious bargainer—a 'wrestler' with words and conditions just as he is a physical wrestler, a heel-grabber"?[102]

Two more actions flow from Jacob's new affirmation of faith. The stone which he has set up as a pillar "shall be God's house," and of all that God gives him he "will surely give one tenth" to God. The first affects a place and the second, Jacob's material possessions. The tithe appears to be a one-time gift, probably for the care of the newly dedicated place. The stone that Jacob has set up as a monument to bear witness to his awesome experience, both to himself and others, is named as a holy sanctuary. It is a place or area of worship, a "God's house," for it is now a "Bethel" instead of a "Luz"-- the reality of the patriarchal faith in place of an unreal Canaanite religion. As such the stone is more

---

[101] Fretheim, "The Book of Genesis," 542.
[102] Alter, *Genesis*, 150.

than a witness, it is an "object endued with divine power and representing God himself" as described by Gordon Wenham.[103]

Jacob's life and travels are filled with a new sense of vocation. His response to his dream is characterized by awe and a sense of divine presence and his access to it. God has indeed come near to the one who now bears the promise. Jacob's faith depends on this heavenly invasion into his earthly world. Yet, Jacob remains Jacob. We cannot help but ask, what actually happens in Jacob's heart at Bethel? May we call it a conversion? Is Walter Brueggemann stretching it when he writes that Jacob "is prepared to repent and believe"?[104] Is Thomas Mann on target when he writes that "Jacob's vow at Bethel is the beginning of his conversion."?[105]

Let us forget for a moment the scaffolding of the labels we Evangelicals love, and ask to what precisely does the biblical text witness? What is taking place genuinely in Jacob's heart and life? What God is doing is what is important. So what in essence happens?

---

[103] Wenham, *Genesis 16-50,* 224.
[104] Brueggeman, *Genesis,* 246.
[105] Mann, *The Book of the Torah,* 56.

Whatever it was, do we know it in our own journey? We summarize: first, Jacob is in awe, he encounters the holy, the wholly other. Second, he recognizes that it is the God of his fathers, Abraham and Isaac, who is present with him as he sleeps and dreams.

Third, the LORD gives Jacob a promise for his future—"I am with you . . . . and will bring you back to this land." Fourth, Jacob takes steps to encase his experience in ritual action—"Bethel, . . . pillar." Fifth, he makes an authentic commitment, a vow--"the LORD shall be my God, . . . one tenth to you." May we say with Paul that here we have "a new creation" (2 Cor.5:17)? Certainly, "yes" in the presence of a new relationship--"my God." Jacob binds himself to his God as God bound himself to Jacob in the oracle to Rebekah regarding the future of her twins while they were still in the womb (25:23).

A response of life, a commitment, follows an encounter with the "holy." Jacob will walk in a new way. The road he travels is remarkably different as he heads for uncle Laban. Jacob's experience of the awesome impacts his response; the character of a newly revealed God is changing the character of the dreaming Jacob in some measure. But how much and how soon awaits the rest of the story. Jacob will still be Jacob—we never become "not ourselves"! The holy plus the promise, leads to a new commitment for Jacob!

One may compare Jacob's experience of the holy with that of the Apostle Peter. Peter has been fishing all night with no catch when Jesus enters his boat. He complains to Jesus about his "no fish." At Jesus' command, Peter sails the boat out into deep water and lets his nets down one more time. At once the nets in his and a companion boat are so full that the nets are beginning to break. The boats are sinking as they fill up with fish. Peter sees it, falls at Jesus' knees, and cries out, "Go away from me, Lord, for I am a sinful man" (Luke 5:8). Jacob's perception does not yet reach the depth of Peter's call—he is not yet ready to confess his true character.

Even more striking for our faith are Jesus' prophetic words to Nathaniel in the Gospel of John: "Very truly, I tell you, you will see heaven opened and the angels of God ascending and descending upon the Son of Man" (1:51). Jacob's dream invades the New Testament on the lips of Jesus whom John's narrative designates the Lamb of God, the

Messiah, the Son of God, and the King of Israel (1:36-49). How near is the heavenly realm, how close is God to us? God and his heaven are as near as is Jesus--the incarnate Son, the One "close to the Father's heart, who has made him known" (1:18).

Moses once dared to ask God. "Show me your glory, I pray" (Exod. 33:18). The Apostle John declares that

> the Word became flesh and lived among us, and we have seen his glory, the glory as of a father's only son, full of grace and truth" (1:14).

The Apostle Paul thrills us with a "new covenant" in Jesus that penetrates out lives to the core:

> And all of us, with unveiled faces, seeing the glory of the Lord as though reflected in a mirror, are being transformed into the same image from one degree of glory to another; for this comes from the Lord, the Spirit. . . . For it is God who said, "Let light shine out of darkness," who has shone in our hearts to give the light of the knowledge of the glory of God in the face of Jesus Christ (2 Cor. 3:18; 4:6).

Part Two: To Peniel

Genesis 29:1—35:29

I.
Jacob and Laban
(29:1-31:55)

SEVEN
Rachel and Leah
(Genesis 29:1—30)

Genesis 29:11, 17:   "Then Jacob kissed Rachel, and wept aloud. . . . "
Rachel was graceful and beautiful."

'Tis Love! 'Tis Love! Thou diedst for me;
I hear the whisper in my heart.
The morning breaks, the shadows flee,
Pure Universal Love thou art:
To me, to all, thy bowels move--
Thy nature, and thy name, is LOVE.[106]

Herbert Prince entitles his exposition of the account before us

"Chickens Come Home to Roost." [107] The title comes from one of Bud

(Reuben) Robinson's books.[108] In Robinson's opening chapter, also

---

[1] Hildebrandt, Beckerlegge, and Dale, ed., *A Collection of Hymns for the use of the People called Methodists*, 251.

[107] Herbert L. Prince, "The Call of God: Part 17: 'Chickens Come Home to Roost'" (July 22, 2012), on Genesis 29:15-30. As we move into the second part of the narrative, we are in debt to Herbert L. Prince, my co-teacher of the Come and Go Sunday School class at San Diego First Church of the Nazarene who prepared an interpretive path for me as he dealt with Jacob's life from Bethel to his reconciliation with his older brother Esau.

[108] The book was published posthumously by Beacon Hill Press (1958) during the Golden Anniversary year of the Church of the Nazarene. Reuben "Uncle Bud" Robinson (1860-1942) as a ranch hand in Texas in August of 1880 was converted during a camp meeting. With no formal education he began his ministry and in the first year some 300 conversions took place. Subsequently, over sixty years were given to evangelism in the course of which he traveled over 2,000,000 miles, preached over 33,000 sermons, witnessed more than 100,000 conversions, and wrote fourteen books, selling more than 500,000 copies.

entitled *"Chickens Come Home to Roost,"* he mentions a number of biblical figures who were consigned to death but saw the tables turned in their behalf. Those who conspired against them met their grim ends. Similar to the familiar saying "what goes around comes around," "chickens come home to roost" is an old colloquialism meaning that a person often gets back what one hands out. In our story, Jacob is about to learn that he is not the only one who knows how to deceive.

As often in biblical narrative, two characters are prominent. The more important an event is to the narrator, the more apt it is to be presented in dialogue. In Genesis 29:1—31:55 the tensions, even the conflict between Jacob and his father-in-law Laban, permeate the narrative. From scene to scene other family characters move on and off center stage. The opening scene, 29:1-30, features Rachel and Leah in dialogue.

The larger Jacob-Laban episode (29:1—31:55) functions as a centerpiece in Jacob's story. The narrator sandwiches it between Jacob's two life-changing encounters with God at Bethel and at Peniel. Jacob's deceit in obtaining the blessing at Esau's expense leads him

166

into the hands of Laban. Twenty years will elapse. At the very core is

the account of the birth of Jacob's sons, the forefathers of the tribes of

Israel. Our present account begins with the motifs of a well and a

stone, motifs often present in Jacob's story. We saw already a

significant role for stones in the Bethel account.

Jacob arrives at a well
(29:1-8)

[1]Then Jacob went on his journey, and came to the land of the people of the east. [2]As he looked, he saw a well in the field and three flocks of sheep lying there beside it; for out of that well the flocks were watered. The stone on the well's mouth was large, [3]and when all the flocks were gathered there, the shepherds would roll the stone from the mouth of the well, and water the sheep, and put the stone back in its place on the mouth of the well. [4]Jacob said to them, "My brothers, where do you come from?" They said, "We are from Haran." [5]He said to them, "Do you know Laban son of Nahor?" They said, "We do." [6]He said to them, "Is it well with him?" "Yes," they replied, "and here is his daughter Rachel, coming with the sheep." [7]He said, "Look, it is still broad daylight; it is not time for the animals to be gathered together. Water the sheep, and go, pasture them." [8]But they said, "We cannot until all the flocks are gathered together, and the stone is rolled from the mouth of the well; then we water the sheep."

A vivid description opens our narrative in the Hebrew text,

"Jacob lifted up his feet and walked." Most translations ignore this

idiom, Robert Alter suggests is "a general idiom for beginning a

167

particularly arduous journey on foot,"[109] is present only here in these narratives. Was Jacob in a hurry to leave Bethel, perhaps still in fearful haste from Esau's wrath (27:34, 43; 28:5), or does the picture of Jacob's lifting up his feet indicate a buoyant anticipation of his long trek to the east? John Calvin suggests that this emphatic phrase "implies that he travelled on briskly and cheerfully" refreshed by his experience at Bethel.[110] Interestingly, the idiom creates symmetry of phrasing when Jacob discovers Rachel at the end of his journey as he "lifted up his voice and wept" (v. 11).

At his journey's end, Jacob arrives at "the land of the people of the east" in the vicinity of Haran, the home of his mother's people. Employing a twofold *hinnēh* ("behold . . . behold"), the narrator stresses what Jacob sees with his own eyes: "As he looked, (*hinnēh*) he saw a well in the field and (*hinnēh*) three flocks of sheep." Jacob's view takes in first "a well in the field" and second "three flocks of sheep" lying beside the well. The "land" is where he now arrives and will reside is nomadic country with "field" indicating uncultivated or pasture-land.

---

[109] Alter, *Genesis,* 151.
[110] Calvin, *Genesis,* 127.

Watering wells serve as conventional meeting places throughout the patriarchal narratives. Here Jacob's arrival at a "well," with Rachel about to appear in the story, indicates we are entering a betrothal type scene in verses 1-14. These scenes possess similar elements such as the future bridegroom seeking a wife away from home, a meeting at a well, being brought together by drawing water from the well, the future bride running home with the news of the stranger, the latter receiving a warm welcome, and eventually the negotiations that conclude the marriage agreement. [111]

The most fascinating betrothal scent in the Bible is the elaborately told account in Genesis 24:1-67 concerning Isaac and Jacob's mother, Rebekah. The main difference is that in Isaac's case his father Abraham has sent a surrogate, a servant, to find his wife, while here Jacob is a lone stranger on the run in a strange land. The narrator indicates clearly in both instances that divine providence is at work in the lives of the two patriarchs.

---

[111]The brief account of Moses and Zipporah in Exod. 2:15-22 is such a scene..

Jacob opens a dialogue with the shepherds as he arrives at the well with the question, "My brothers, where do you come from?" Contrary to custom, Jacob takes the initiative; this question is usually asked of the new arrival rather than by him. Their dialogue continues with Jacob asking about the welfare of Laban, indicated by a twofold *shalom* (v. 6), recalling Jacob's desire expressed in his oath to God at Bethel to return to his father's house "in peace" (28:21). Meanwhile the "sheep" are waiting to be watered until all the flocks are present. A community fairness issue appears to be at stake. Perhaps there is a "first come, first served" custom accounting for the early arrival of the shepherds with their flocks.

The shepherds announce that Laban's daughter Rachel is about to arrive with her family's sheep, "here (*hinnēh*) is his daughter Rachel, coming with the sheep." At this Jacob requests that they not wait for all the sheep to be gathered. They should at once water the sheep already gathered at the well and return them to pasture for, as Jacob reasons, "Look (*hēn*), it is still broad daylight; it is not time for the animals to be gathered together." The narrator's twofold *hinnēh* . . . *hēn* stresses the minor crisis occasioned in Jacob's mind by the mention of the soon arrival of Rachel. The shepherds, however, object to this brash young man, responding no doubt in a surly tone, "We cannot until all the flocks are gathered together, and the stone is rolled from the mouth of the well."

The "stone on the well's mouth" (vv. 2-3, 8, 10) is prominent in the story. The stone is "large" or great and therefore apparently heavy requiring normally more than one shepherd to remove it. We are reminded of the stones at Jacob's head as he slept (28:11) and of the monument he built at Bethel (28:18, 22). Jacob will erect a stone three times as the narrative develops; each time the action will play a unique role in the story (31:45-49; 35:14, 20). Robert Alter calls the stone "the motif that is [Jacob's] narrative signature."[112] The stone at the well, as Margaret Poteet suggests, is "an obstacle that blocks the giving of life,"[113] anticipating Rachel's future barrenness.

---

[112] Alter, *Genesis*, 152.
[113] Poteet, *Literary Unity in the Patriarchal Narratives,* 127.

The narrator has set the stage for us to see more clearly who Jacob is, now grown up and maturing, and on his own for the first time. What happens now?

Jacob meets Rachel
(29:9-14)

[9]While he was still speaking with them, Rachel came with her father's sheep; for she kept them. [10]Now when Jacob saw Rachel, the daughter of his mother's brother Laban, and the sheep of his mother's brother Laban, Jacob went up and rolled the stone from the well's mouth, and watered the flock of his mother's brother Laban. [11]Then Jacob kissed Rachel, and wept aloud. [12]And Jacob told Rachel that he was her father's kinsman, and that he was Rebekah's son; and she ran and told her father. [13]When Laban heard the news about his sister's son Jacob, he ran to meet him; he embraced him and kissed him, and brought him to his house. Jacob told Laban all these things, [14]and Laban said to him, "Surely you are my bone and my flesh!" And he stayed with him a month.

Rachel is a shepherdess in charge of her father's sheep. Jacob, the premiere shepherd in the scene, ignores the local custom, removes the stone from the top of the well, and waters the sheep that belong to Laban, his mother's brother. A betrothal scene is unfolding with the encounter of a maiden in a foreign land. But unlike his father, Jacob is himself present at the well, and it is he, not the maiden, who draws the water. The actual betrothal is missing.

Where does Jacob get such strength to move such a large stone, a task usually done by several shepherds—the inspiration of beauty, love at first sight? Apparently, even when compared to the outdoorsman Esau, Jacob is a more physically powerful man than we have realized, thus their mother's concern that the twins would kill each other if they came to blows (27:10). Adding to the sight of Rachel, another element could be Jacob's joyful enthusiasm at uniting with blood-relatives that inspires him to summon hero-like strength and enables him to remove the stone, yet surely not without severe physical strain. He waters the sheep primarily because they were Laban's—and in the care of Rachel. Jacob emerges as a confident and decisive leader who acts promptly. He appears on the scene as a person of strength and authority, a man indeed to be reckoned with!

We read that "then Jacob kissed Rachel, and wept aloud," no doubt with joy at finding his mother's family. The kiss is a customary greeting among relatives. The picture is at first one of familial harmony, for Jacob revels who he is and Rachel runs immediately to inform her father. Laban at the news, embraces Jacob, kisses him, and brings him into his home. Then "Jacob told Laban all these things" eliciting Laban's exclamation, "Surely you are my bone and my flesh!" Is "all these things" perhaps a bit vague? Two questions: What does Jacob tell him? What was Laban to think as he encounters his nephew for the first time? The fact that Laban "ran to meet him" suggests that he was remembering the arrival of Abraham's servant with ten heavily laden camels (24:10). Robert Alter wonders if Laban's embrace of Jacob has the secret motive of feeling for gold perhaps secreted on the latter's person?[114]

We are not sure what Jacob divulged of his past, but Laban was certainly sharp enough to discern plenty. He could read between the lines! From what Rachel tells him, Laban sees in Jacob a workman worthy of his hire. Second, he is disappointed when he discovers that Jacob does not bring wealth to the family like what came with Isaac. Laban becomes aware that Jacob is at his mercy, but accepts him because after all, "you are my bone and my flesh." Jacob then

stays with him for a month, apparently working without wages. Laban, in a figure, could easily have put his arm affectionately around Jacob's

---

[114] Alter, *Genesis*, 153.

shoulder while he slips his other hand into his pocket. Franz Delitzsch observes that Laban knows well "how to hide his intentions under the appearance of great unselfishness."[115] At a profound level, Providence provides the scene. Jacob is a paradoxical figure, a man of power, yet powerless. He is at the place where God can work with him—as with us when we are as Jacob! There is therefore a transcendent dimension to this all too human story that informs our faith in God at work. The betrothal scene continues:

Jacob loves Rachel
(29:15-20)

[15]Then Laban said to Jacob, "Because you are my kinsman, should you therefore serve me for nothing? Tell me, what shall your wages be?" [16]Now Laban had two daughters; the name of the elder was Leah, and the name of the younger was Rachel. [7]Leah's eyes were lovely, and Rachel was graceful and beautiful. [18]Jacob loved Rachel; so he said, "I will serve you seven years for your younger daughter Rachel." [19]Laban said, "It is better that I give her to you than that I should give her to any other man; stay with me." [20]So Jacob served seven years for Rachel, and they seemed to him but a few days because of the love he had for her.

A twenty year relationship of love and trickery is under way as

---

[115] Delitzsch, *Genesis,* II. 153.

Laban sets a trap for Jacob with his innocent sounding welcoming words. As the narrative unfolds, the verb "serve" and the noun "wages" reappear significantly.[116] These terms, "laden with the echoes of the exploitation," as Gordon Wenham expresses them, hint at what Jacob will endure at Laban's hands.[117] Laban reduces his relationship with Jacob to the level of negotiation. He changes their blood-relationship, uncle-nephew, into a commercial one, in culture a lord-servant relationship. Laban is now in control. He is well aware of Jacob's negative and positive motives for coming; Jacob is on the run from Esau and he desires a proper wife. What is Laban's attitude at heart toward Jacob?

The depiction of Laban's two daughters, Leah and Rachel, is rife with implications. One is labeled "the elder" and the other "the younger." Jacob was himself the younger sibling and Esau was the elder as the narrator sets up a similar opposition characterized by conflict. Further, Rachel the younger outshines Leah her older sister: "Leah's eyes were lovely, and Rachel was graceful and beautiful." For "lovely"

---

[116] See 29:18, 20, 25, 27, 30; 30:26, 29; 31:6, 41; 30:16, 32, 33; 31:7, 41.
[117] Wenham, *Genesis 16-50,* 234.

other translations have "tender-eyed" (KJV) or "weak" (NASB) suggesting some sort of impairment. Although the precise meaning of the Hebrew adjective is uncertain, Robert Alter suggests that Leah's eyes "are her one asset of appearance, in contrast to her beautiful sister."[118]

Leah, meaning "wild cow, a kind of antelope,"[119] is seen by some interpreters as having eyes that were "soft"[120] or "without lustre,"[121] that is, they did not sparkle. Rachel, in contrast, made a striking impression by the cultural standards of female beauty of that day. She "had a beautiful figure and a lovely face,"[122] as Gordon Wenham translates. But closer to the Hebrew, she was "beautiful of form and beautiful to look at." Understandably, taken in by her beauty, the young virile "Jacob loved Rachel"! Subtly and ironically, Jacob's past is invading his present! In Margaret Poteet's apt phrasing, he will be "victimized by his appetite for Rachel, just as Esau was once victimized

---

[118] Alter, *Genesis,* 153.
[119] Delitzch, *Genesis,* 170.
[120] Wenham, *Genesis 16-50,* 235.
[121] Westermann, *Genesis,* 462.
[122] Wenham, *Genesis 16-50,* 233.

by his momentary physical appetite."[123]

Along with stating Jacob's love for Rachel, the narrator stresses its depth with Jacob's offer: "so he said, 'I will serve you seven years for your younger daughter Rachel." In a legal manner, Jacob gives the daughter's name and the fact that she is the younger as well the length of his service. Seven years of his labor for Rachel was a premium price in that culture. In the Ancient Near East, betrothal was made by the groom's family paying a bride price or marriage present to the bride's family. This was impossible for Jacob, whose life is seemingly always characterized by struggle. It was left to him to devise an alternative. Jacob, as Margaret Poteet succinctly puts it, "courts with empty hands."[124] Laban agrees to Jacob's proposal, but his response is slippery. He cannot be caught in words: "It is better that I give her to you than that I should give her to any other man; stay with me."

Laban's perceptions keep him wary of Jacob. He does not name Rachel, but says only, "I give her to you." Is he playing fast and loose with traditional custom? Jacob, however, clearly has Rachel in mind.

---

[123] Poteet, *Literary Unity in the Patriarchal Narratives,* 131.
[124] Poteet, *Literary Unity in the Patriarchal Narratives,* 130.

Herbert Prince observes that

> the "her" in the larger context appears to be Rachel. However in light of what Laban will do when Jacob's labor is concluded at the end of the seventh year leaves open the question as to whom Laban has in mind here.[125]

For Jacob it is Rachel: "So Jacob served seven years for Rachel, and they seemed to him but a few days because of the love he had for her." What is more, Jacob expects to return home when the seven years of waiting for Rachel to be his wife is completed. When Jacob first fled from Esau, his mother's words were "flee at once to my brother in Haran and stay with him a while ("a few days") . . . until your brother's fury turns away; . . . then I will send and bring you back from there" (26:43-45).

As Jacob completes his seven years for the love of Rachel, the stage is set for the scene in which

Jacob is deceived
(29:21-30)

> [21]Then Jacob said to Laban, "Give me my wife that I may go in to her, for my time is completed." [22]So Laban gathered together all the people of the place, and made a feast. [23]But in the evening he took his daughter Leah and brought her to Jacob; and

---

[125] Prince, "The Call of God: Part 17." on Genesis 29:19.

he went in to her. [24](Laban gave his maid Zilpah to his daughter Leah to be her maid.) [25]When morning came, it was Leah! And Jacob said to Laban, "What is this you have done to me? Did I not serve with you for Rachel? Why then have you deceived me?" [26]Laban said, "This is not done in our country—giving the younger before the firstborn. [27]Complete the week of this one, and we will give you the other also in return for serving me another seven years." [28]Jacob did so, and completed her week; then Laban gave him his daughter Rachel as a wife. [29] (Laban gave his maid Bilhah to his daughter Rachel to be her maid.) [30]So Jacob went in to Rachel also, and he loved Rachel more than Leah. He served Laban for another seven years.

As a classic example of Hebrew narrative art, this brief account allows the reader to experience what is close to reality; only what is absolutely necessary is said. What is unsaid speaks with force giving weight and density to the narrative.[126] What is said drips with irony. Jacob remains true to himself, preferring the younger Rachel to her older sister! Since Laban has apparently kept silent about his agreement with Jacob for his daughter Rachel, Jacob reminds him that the first seven years have gone by. This time Jacob takes the initiative. Having lived within the larger family circle, the apparently so far chaste Jacob eagerly asks to be given his wife "that I may go into her, for my time is completed." The Hebrew text expresses Jacob's understandable sexual

---

[126] Westermann, *Genesis,* 467.

impatience. Without so much as a "Please," Jacob, with a note of desperation, demands his rights. So Laban gathers the clan and gives a feast with an abundance of food and drink. How strong was the drink? How freely did it flow? According to custom, Leah is veiled as was Rachel also throughout the proceedings.

When evening comes, no doubt very late at night, Laban brings Leah to Jacob. Jacob wraps his cloak around his lady and leads her veiled to the nuptial chamber, and the marriage is consummated. But, "when morning came, it was Leah!" The Hebrew is literally, "Behold it was Leah" (NASB). "Behold," *hinnēh,* indicates stunning surprise! How much "joy juice" did Jacob imbibe as the previous evening progressed! One can only imagine!

With his senses now alert by the morning light, Jacob confronts Laban, "What is this you have done to me? Did I not serve with you for Rachel? Why then have you deceived me?" The Hebrew syntax expresses Jacob's astonishment at Laban just as Pharaoh at Abraham (12:18) and Abimelech at Isaac (26:10). With a touch of bitter humor, as Terrence Fretheim observes, through it all "Leah knows what Jacob does not know![127] What kind of a laugh escapes her lips at Jacob's discovery? With poetic justice, darkness for Jacob and blindness for Isaac allow them both to be victims of a misleading sense of touch.

Laban defends his action by an appeal to tradition: "This is not done in our country—giving the younger before the firstborn. Complete the week of this one, and we will give you the other also in return for serving me another seven years." The language he uses is revealing: "our country." The words "younger" and "firstborn" are the precise terms employed earlier to depict the relationship of Jacob and Esau (25:23, 32, 27:19). Laban touches a nerve of guilt in Jacob.

Laban calls on tradition to justify his action--the firstborn precedes the younger. 27:19). Jacob did the opposite. He violated the tradition governing his family by his deceit in dealing with Esau and his father, Isaac. Jacob, being the younger son, usurped the role of the firstborn son. Deception has been matched by deception. Jacob now knows how Esau must have felt, for he has met someone not unlike himself. Why did Laban not mention the marriage custom when Jacob

---

[127] Fretheim, "Book of Genesis," 553.

makes his first deal with him? His use of it now rings hollow. Or why has he not married off Leah during the seven years? The sum of the picture of Jacob is strikingly expressed by Robert Alter as one of "the deceiver deceived."[128]

Laban, now in full control, continues to negotiate: "Complete the week of this one, and we will give you the other also in return for serving me another seven years." Rachel, simply called "the other," is again treated as merchandise. So Jacob, not quite happily we suspect, accepts Leah as his wife, and as Laban requests, completes her week of marriage celebration. Jacob's marriage to Leah is sealed irrevocably. Laban has Jacob fully in his snare, Jacob is to serve or "slave" for Laban another seven years, and will be given Rachel when Leah's week is past. How did he behave with Leah during that week? What did the week contribute to Leah's perception of Jacob's lack of appropriate feeling for her?

Jacob is now seven more years away from freedom to return home. Laban's tactics also deceive Rachel, for he violates Rachel along

---

[128] Alter, *Genesis,* 155.

with Jacob and their love for each other. Laban violates Leah as well; her feelings are not considered as she soon reveals (29:32-35). The wives complain later about their father's use of them (31:15). In a sense, Laban's avarice sets up his two daughters to spend much of their lives as hostile competitors. Sadly, the second seven years for Jacob will not seem as "but a few days" (v. 20) as before!

Finally, we read that "Jacob went in to Rachel also, and he loved Rachel more than Leah." Most interpreters see "loved . . . more than" as Jacob's "preference," describing his love of Rachel. It is more likely, however, that the Hebrew expression (*gam . . . min* ["also . . . from"]) is used rather in an exclusive sense as J. P. Fokkelman translates, "besides, Jacob loved Rachel, and he did not love Leah."[129] This goes with the narrator's coming description of Leah as "unloved" (v. 31) along with her expressed hope that "now my husband will love me" (v. 32) at the birth of Reuben, her firstborn. At the conception of her second son, she exclaims that "the LORD has heard that I am hated" (v.33). Yet to what extent was Leah at fault in her marriage to Jacob? Did she not consent to

---

[129] Fokkelman, *Narrative Art in Genesis,* 129, n. 10.

the deception in order to have a husband? Perhaps she had no choice.

The narrator assigns a high role to the love between a man and a woman. But as Terrence Fretheim notes, such "remains complicated by other issues that make for conflict and rivalry: between Laban and Jacob, Leah and Rachel, and Jacob with each wife."[130] We have come a long way from "peace" (*shālōm*) in verse 6 to tensions that will continue on in the narrative, particularly but not exclusively, the opposition between Jacob and Laban.

Picking up a parenthetical thread with the two maids, Zilpah and Bilhah, Jacob's household is now complete with the two brides and their maids. Leah as well as Rachel are prepared to be the mothers of the patriarchs--most significant for the Genesis story. Human deception does not deter the work of God! As Herbert Prince concludes,

> God's purposes are not stymied by the deceptive acts of people, even if they are God's elect. Jacob had been promised that he would have a multitude of descendants. It will be accomplished through the unloved Leah and her maid Zilpah that eight of the

---

[130] Fretheim, "The Book of Genesis," 553.

twelve tribes can be traced to bring the divine purpose to fulfillment.[131]

Laban is generous with the gift of the maids to his daughters as part of his determination to keep Jacob around, a competent and efficient worker. But with "two" wives, this can hardly be the end of the story. Suffering will often attend the way.

There is a sense in which Laban does the correct thing by conducting himself according to the established legal tradition of his culture. He appears to have initially interpreted it a little creatively—its truth for his time and situation—with regard to Jacob and Rachel. This was no doubt a guise, for now he has turns to the literal form of the tradition. Formally, Laban has some right on his side as he gives Leah first in marriage to Jacob. Yet morally, he is quite suspect. He takes advantage of Jacob's powerless, his impoverished circumstances.

As Jacob earlier deceived a blind man, his father Isaac who could rely only on physical touch, Laban uses the darkness of night as his instrument to eliminate Jacob's sense of sight--equally the victim of a misleading sense of touch! What appears as legally right is been

---

[131] Prince, "The Call of God: Part 17."

employed to justify a moral wrong. To make an action lawful does not necessarily make it moral--ever our temptation to use such a disguise to take advantage of or manipulate others, to piously cover over, Laban-like, our moral wrong!

EIGHT
The Children
(Genesis 29:*31*—30:24)

Genesis 29:31; 30:22:
> "When the LORD saw that Leah was
> unloved, he opened her womb;
> but Rachel was barren. . . . Then God
> remembered Rachel, and God heeded her
> and opened her womb."

> My prayer has power with God; the grace
>   Unspeakable I now receive;
> Through faith I see thee face to face;
>   I see thee face to face, and live!
> In vain I have not wept and strove--
> Thy nature, and thy name, is LOVE.[132]

We come to a tale of two wives, Leah and Rachel, two maids,
Bilhah and Zilpah, a silently present Jacob, and a seemingly absent
Laban. Twelve children, eleven sons, and a daughter will have the
patriarch Jacob as their father. Conflict penetrates the narratives. First
were Jacob and Esau; now Jacob's two wives, Leah and Rachel, are
intense rivals with their consuming passions. Leah longs for Jacob's
love and Rachel craves children. Perhaps they are only human, for the
Genesis narratives vividly teach us that humans always remain human.

---

[132] Hildebrandt, Beckerlegge, and Dale, ed., *A Collection of Hymns for the use
of the People called Methodists,* 251.

188

Jacob's competitive wives now command the center stage as an old theme of the unloved and the firstborn continues to characterize the narrative.

This short, compact story at first glance appears as a low point in the Jacob narratives. Two wives are at war over husband and children. Jacob's story is built around two highpoints, his visionary experience at Bethel (28:10-22) and his encounter with the stranger at Peniel (32:22-32). Yet, a case can be made for seeing 29:31—30:24 as at least a secondary high point in-between. With this text we arrive at the center both of the whole Jacob cycle and of the more immediate Laban-Jacob narrative (29:1—31:55). A chiastic analysis, abcd*cba,* of the latter's structure places our story (**d**) neatly as the centerpiece. The birth of the children, future Israel, at this structural center makes, as Walter Brueggemann asserts, "a deliberate theological statement."[133] What goes before in 29:1-30 is preparation as it sets the stage, introduces the characters and hints at the coming conflict. The birth of Joseph rounds out the story, for Jacob takes his cue from this event as

---

[133] Brueggemann, *Genesis,* 249-250.

the time to return home.

The birth of Jacob's children speaks to what the book of Genesis is all about. A few chapters after the creation narratives (1:1--3:24) come the birth and formation of a called out-people—Israel--through whom God will carry out his sovereign and redemptive purposes in the world (12:1ff.). God is mentioned in the Laban-Jacob account for the first time by Leah on the birth of her first son, Reuben (29:32). She involves God four times more (29:33, 35; 30:18, 20), her younger sister Rachel three times (30:6, 23, 24), Jacob once (30:2), and the narrator three times (29:31; 30:17, 22)—thirteen times in all. God is the decisive initiator as the divine and human roles weave their way through our story.

In classic prose style, our story falls into two groups (29:31—30:13 and 30:14-24) of three scenes each. The LORD opens Leah's womb in the first scene as we begin with

Leah's First Sons
(29:31-35)

[31]When the LORD saw that Leah was unloved, he opened her womb; but Rachel was barren. [32]Leah conceived and bore a son, and she named him Reuben; for she said, "Because the

LORD has looked on my affliction; surely now my husband will love me." [33]She conceived again and bore a son, and said, "Because the LORD has heard that I am hated, he has given me this son also"; and she named him Simeon. [34]Again she conceived and bore a son, and said, "Now this time my husband will be joined to me, because I have borne him three sons"; therefore he was named Levi. [35]She conceived again and bore a son, and said, "This time I will praise the LORD"; therefore she named him Judah; then she ceased bearing.

Laban, Jacob's father-in-law, does not appear in the narrative. His influence, however, poisons the inner circle with envy and hatred by giving Jacob the elder daughter before the younger. The character of Jacob is present only "sexually." Although Jacob undoubtedly resents Leah's consent to Laban's duplicity, Jacob does not totally neglect his "unloved" wife! Jacob certainly knows how to increase! To what extent is his productivity due to his knowledge that Leah is fertile and Rachel is "barren"? One suspects that she was not physically unattractive to a virile young man! Yet certainly, in Jacob's time and culture the need for offspring trumps everything! To have an heir was all-important.

Apart from "the LORD" who both *sees* "that Leah was unloved" and *acts* as "he opened her womb," Leah is the sole speaker and actor in this scene. She tells the story from her perspective. Central to her story as Gordon Wenham reminds us is that "when the LORD sees, he intends to act decisively in defense of the weak and oppressed"[134] (6:5; Exod. 2:25; 4:31)—here for the "unloved" Leah. Thus "the LORD" graces Leah with fertility. In her time and culture she perceives motherhood as her crowning joy and her lack of children as a calamitous failure. Ironically the LORD makes Leah equal to Rachel in the sense that the "unloved" has children before the "loved" (v. 18): "he opened her womb, but Rachel was barren."

Leah, as her firstborn, Reuben, arrives, hopes that Jacob will now love her. She explains the name with the exclamation that "the LORD has looked on my affliction." The name "Reuben" can be associated with the verb "to see, "See, a son," and the noun "my affliction." Herbert Prince concludes that "what is clear is that the hand of God is seen at work initially through the "unloved Leah." Since God spoke to Jacob at Bethel (28:10-22) the narrative does not involve the divine in subsequent

---

[134] Wenham, *Genesis 16-50,* 243.

events. Now, "some seven years later, God's caring and loving activity is seen in the opening of the womb of Leah."[135]

Leah soon conceives again and bears Jacob a second son, Simeon. She explains his name in two ways. Leah does this first with "the LORD has heard"; the verb for "hear" (*shm'*) has the same Hebrew consonants as the name "Simeon" (*sim'ōn*). Second, there is also a slight consonantal similarity between the Hebrew of "I am hated" (*snû'āh*) and the name she has given her second son. It should be noted too that the Hebrew word "hated" in this verse is the same word in Hebrew as "unloved" in verse 31. The names Leah gives to her sons speak to her situation, and significantly four of them, Reuben, Simeon, Judah, and Joseph are all explained with reference to "the LORD." Children are supremely the gift of God throughout the narrative.

Leah produces two more sons for Jacob before she ceases bearing, completing the first of three sets of four offspring in the narrative. She names this third son "Levi" with the possible meaning of "attached" or "joined." Leah is expressing her hope of renewed contact

---

[135] Prince, "The Call of God: Part 18: Chicanery is Bound to Follow" (August 5, 2012) on Genesis 29:31—30:43.

with Jacob because she has now given him three sons. Her desire for Jacob's love remains desperate.

Another conception and birth brings a fourth son whom Leah names Judah. As with Reuben and Simeon, she acknowledges the LORD's mercy to her and decides to count her blessings: "This time I will praise the LORD." Leah no longer gives expression to hope as lament turns to praise; she is simply thankful for her four sons. The name "Judah" is related to "praise," but just how is uncertain. Margaret Poteet looks ahead, commenting that "the bitter irony of Leah's life will be answered in future generations; . . . it will be through her son Judah that the favored line of David will spring."[136] But we wonder, Why not through the loved and lovely Rachel? Would not that be a more providentially blessed route?

Why Leah "ceased bearing," the reader can only speculate. Was she temporarily infertile or has Jacob's nocturnal visitations ceased? If the latter, who is to blame, Jacob or Leah? Has the emotional climate become worse between them, and Jacob ceases to show? Or is Leah

---

[136] Poteet, *Literary Unity in the Patriarchal Narratives,* 132.

tired of loveless sexual activity and unappreciated child-bearing? So, Jacob, you go to Rachel! With this question unanswered, our narrative moves on to a new development in the conflict between the two ladies, that concerning

Rachel/Bilhah's Sons
(30:1-8)

[1]When Rachel saw that she bore Jacob no children, she envied her sister; and she said to Jacob, "Give me children, or I shall die!" [2]Jacob became very angry with Rachel and said, "Am I in the place of God, who has withheld from you the fruit of the womb?" [3]Then she said, "Here is my maid Bilhah; go in to her, that she may bear upon my knees and that I too may have children through her." [4]So she gave him her maid Bilhah as a wife; and Jacob went in to her. [5]And Bilhah conceived and bore Jacob a son. [6]Then Rachel said, "God has judged me, and has also heard my voice and given me a son"; therefore she named him Dan. [7]Rachel's maid Bilhah conceived again and bore Jacob a second son. [8]Then Rachel said, "With mighty wrestlings I have wrestled with my sister, and have prevailed"; so she named him Naphtali.

As with Leah, when "the LORD saw" that she "was unloved" (29:31) and gave her children, it is now Rachel who *sees* that she has no children. The envy of her sister overtakes her and she speaks for the first time in the narrative. In biblical narrative a character's first speech defines the speaker's character. Rachel's sudden speech reveals her as simmering with frustration. With a vehement outburst, "vexed to death that she had no children"[137] as Franz Delitzsch describes her, Rachel lays the blame for her barrenness on Jacob: "Give me children, or I shall die!"

Rachel's words foreshadow her early death even as she desires "sons." She wants "sons" (*banim*) not just "a son" (*bēn*). She will have two sons, but she dies giving birth to the second son. But now, not even Jacob who loves her and whom she loves can help her barren state. Jacob in turn becomes angry at the impiety of Rachel, for children are uniquely God's gifts in the patriarchal culture (16:2; 25:21): "Am I in the place of God, who has withheld from you the fruit of the womb?" Only God can help her! Rachel protests when she should pray! The "beautiful, gentle love story of 29:1-20," writes Claus Westermann, has become an angry exchange, "our first and only experience of their marriage,"[138] is now seemingly marred.

Rachel, determined one way or another to have children, ignores Jacob's rebuke. She resorts to carnal scheming, and tells Jacob, "Here

---

[137] Delitzsch, *Genesis,* II, 174.
[138] Westermann, *Genesis 12-36*, 474.

(*hinnēh*) is my maid Bilhah; go in to her, that she may bear upon my knees and that I too may have children through her." To "bear upon my knees" (52:23) signifies the ancient custom of adoption. To "have children" is literally in Hebrew as with Sarah in 16:2 "to be built up," expressing the importance of children for wives in that day.

And like Abraham with Hagar, Jacob proceeded to please his wife as he complied willingly no doubt with Rachel's request, and in due time, a son was born to Bilhah. Rachel, delighted, named her new son "Dan" (*dān*), because "God has judged me (*dānnî*), and has also heard my voice." The derivation of the name "Dan" from the verb "has judged me," suggests in legal terms that God has vindicated her. It appears that Rachel has been praying, prayers all mixed quite humanly with her scapegoating anger at Jacob, and with ambition—like some of our prayers!

Jacob continues his liking for Bilhah's tent, and another son is born for Rachel. This one she names "Naphtali" (*naftālî*) for "with mighty wrestlings (*naftûlê*) I have wrestled (*niftaltî*) with my sister, and have prevailed." One senses a correspondence with the struggle of the twins in Rebekah's womb, the younger with the older brother. Rachel's expression, "mighty wrestlings," is literally "a wrestling of God (*naftûlê *ᵉlōhîm*)." Scholars differ as to which translation is more accurate. Is *ᵉlōhîm* meant as an adjective as in our text, "mighty wrestlings," or was Rachel's struggle with Leah in some way also a "divine" struggle, one in which God was involved, or even a wrestling with God Himself?

It was a difficult time for Rachel, certainly, whose perception is that it was God who closes her womb and opens Leah's. J. P. Fokkelman sees Rachel's struggle with Leah as in "reality a struggle for God's favor."[139] Or, could it have been like with Job, a struggle to understand the ways of God in her life? If the struggle is with God, the phrase anticipates Jacob's own wrestling with the stranger at the ford of the Jabbok until daybreak (32:24) and was told, "you have striven with God, and have prevailed" (32:28).

In this manner one lady's maid, Bilhah, entered the conflict. What is next?

Leah/Zilpah's Sons
(30:9-13)

---

[139] Fokkelman, *Narrative Art in Genesis,* 135-136.

> [9]When Leah saw that she had ceased bearing children, she took her maid Zilpah and gave her to Jacob as a wife. [10]Then Leah's maid Zilpah bore Jacob a son. [11]And Leah said, "Good fortune!" so she named him Gad. [12]Leah's maid Zilpah bore Jacob a second son. [13]And Leah said, "Happy am I! For the women will call me happy"; so she named him Asher.

Leah now does Rachel one better, and Jacob continues on the move, hopping between tents! When for whatever reason Leah "ceased bearing children, she took her maid Zilpah and gave her to Jacob as a wife." Somehow, although Leah already has four sons, they are not sufficient. Without recourse to the God whom she has just recently praised (29:35), but out of sibling rivalry, she follows Rachel's compromising example and gains two more sons by her maid, a total of six! Leah names her first son from Zilpah "Gad" (*gād*) meaning "Good Luck" (*bāggād*) or "Good Fortune!" The name is meant either as a wish or as an observation. Here as with Bilhah it is the wife not the maid who names the maid's child. Are the maids then mere ciphers in the story?

As with Rachel's Bilhah, Leah's maid Zilpah again conceived and gave Jacob another son. This son Leah names Asher (*'ssēr*) and exclaims "Happy am I! (*b'ssrî*). For the women will call me happy (*'issss^erûnî*)." The term Leah uses for women is literally "daughters" hinting perhaps of the birth of Dinah to come in verse 21. A second group of four children is now on hand, eight sons in all to Jacob. The twelve sons are not yet in the picture as we anticipate the founding of a nation—a chosen people from whom the Christ will come..

The struggle between the two wives, however, rages on with the passing of the years. The tension intensifies with their confrontation becoming public as the narrative moves on to

Rachel's Bargain
(30:14-15)

[14]In the days of wheat harvest Reuben went and found mandrakes in the field, and brought them to his mother Leah. Then Rachel said to Leah, "Please give me some of your son's mandrakes." [15]But she said to her, "Is it a small matter that you have taken away my husband? Would you take away my son's mandrakes also?" Rachel said, "Then he may lie with you tonight for your son's mandrakes."

Two wives are extremely frustrated; Leah is unloved and Rachel is barren. Both have stooped to underhanded tactics in their resort to surrogate motherhood, a practice that was unacceptable to the narrator in

Sarah's case (16:1-14). Their conflict bursts out into the open. Leah's son Reuben finds mandrakes in the field. With her son's mandrakes, Leah has the upper hand on fertility. Rachel, with her now exclusive access to Jacob, proposes a deal. With five brothers born after him Reuben is now at least six or more years old.

Both wives desire the mandrakes, thought to be a fertility drug; Rachel has never conceived and Leah has become infertile. John Walton describes the mandrake as "a stemless, perennial root in the potato family . . . that has narcotic and purgative properties which explain its medicinal use. Its shape and pungent fragrance may be the origin of its use in fertility rites and as an aphrodisiac (see Song 7:12-13)."[140] Claus Westermann writes that the mandrakes' purple flowers tend toward dark blue and at harvest time become yellowish green apples, nutmeg-size, with a particularly piercing odor. In our story, he observes, "love-apples" become "apples of discord"[141] as Rachel makes her request of Leah, politely put, "Please give me some of your son's mandrakes."

---

[140] J. Walton, *Genesis*, 588.
[141] Westermann, *Genesis*, 475.

Leah, in this first dialogue between the wives, responds bitterly to jealous Rachel's request. She stresses her slighted rights as she names Jacob "my husband" to her sister-wife: "Is it a small matter that you have taken away my husband? Would you take away my son's mandrakes also?" Leah's infertility is due in part obviously to the absence of Jacob—he spends his after-work leisure with Rachel rather than Leah! So Rachel, sensing the justice of Leah's grievance, proposes a creative, perhaps reconciling, compromise from which both women will benefit. She bargains with Leah: "Then he may lie with you tonight for your son's mandrakes." So once again, we have a scene regarding

Leah's Children
(30:16-21)

[16]When Jacob came from the field in the evening, Leah went out to meet him, and said, "You must come in to me; for I have hired you with my son's mandrakes." So he lay with her that night. [17]And God heeded Leah, and she conceived and bore Jacob a fifth son. [18]Leah said, "God has given me my hire because I gave my maid to my husband"; so she named him Issachar. [19]And Leah conceived again, and she bore Jacob a sixth son. [20]Then Leah said, "God has endowed me with a good dowry; now my husband will honor me, because I have borne him six sons"; so she named him Zebulun. [21]Afterwards she bore a daughter, and named her Dinah.

What an embarrassing and depressing scene! A wife goes out to meet her husband, sweaty, dusty, and tired from all day in the field, announcing in a triumphal tone that she has "hired" his sexual services for the night—what a lamentable way to go! When Leah says to Jacob, "You must come in to me," Jacob has probably been sexually boycotting Leah. Is this the reason Leah has not been bearing children? What are Jacob's feelings about all this; has he any sensitivity at all? What *is* his true attitude toward his wives? All we are told is that Jacob assents to Rachel's proposal and does as Leah asks. Or does the narrator with his rhetoric subtly tell us a lot more?

Leah's language becomes commercial as she employs the key word-root for "hire" (*skr*), the word that Laban uses when Jacob first begins to work with him (29:15). The "service-wages" terminology throughout the Laban/Jacob account (30:28, 32, 33; 31:7, 8, 41) degrades their blood-relationship o the level of a business-contract that Jacob and Laban never overcome. Now with Rachel's offer and Leah's emphatic response, "I have surely hired you," and Jacob's compliance-- "So he lay with her that night"—Jacob's marriage is contaminated by the same object-oriented bargain-ethos as his relationship with Laban. Even how he relates to his wives is a matter of rent. Jacob, the hireling of Laban for the sake of Rachel, is now a hireling of Rachel. Jacob is contracted out to Leah!

Rachel's bargain, "tonight," becomes three years or more as Jacob returns to Leah after each son is born. Not one, but two children result from the swap—mandrakes for Jacob's services! Why? Is it just because she is fertile? The two sons born to Leah now make her and Jacob six sons, with Leah dreaming that "now my husband will honor me." And then, as a bonus, a daughter, Dinah, is born. Leah got the better of the deal, for ironically; the one night that Rachel trades for the mandrakes brings years of renewed fertility to Leah, rather than a child to Rachel. Rachel even possessing the mandrakes remains barren while Leah bears two more children! "It is again shown," writes Franz Delitzsch, "that an incalculable power resides over the history of the patriarchs."[142]

---

[142] Delitzsch, *Genesis*, II, 168.

Although it is a result of Jacob's visit that Leah conceives and bears two sons, it is God who alone is responsible for the births in Jacob's family. God listened to or "heeded Leah and she conceived." Leah named her fifth son "Issachar" (*yissāskār*) for she said, "God has given me my hire (*sᵉkārî*) because I gave my maid to my husband." This son's name, meaning "May God be gracious," may indicate that she sees Issachar's birth as a reward for giving Zilpah to Jacob. Leah names the second son from the mandrake-exchange, Zebulun, a name obscure in meaning. Her response, however, is doubly upbeat: "God has endowed me with a good dowry; now my husband will honor me, because I have borne him six sons." Six sons, half of the future tribal twelve, constitute a "a good dowry" and Leah expresses a hope that "my husband will honor me." Leah is indulging in illusory optimism!

When Leah's daughter is born, she names her Dinah with a note of joyful vindication. To mention her name alone without explanation is sufficient, for the name (*dînāh*) speaks of judgment or vindication (*dîn*). Normally, the birth of a daughter is not mentioned in such narratives; Dinah will not found a tribe. Her arrival is noted probably because of her future tragic role in the story (ch. 34). Leah's family is now complete with nine children, seven of which are born to her--Reuben, Simeon, Levi, Judah, Issachar, Zebulun, and Dinah, and two born to her maid Zilpah—Gad and Asher—one child for each of the seven years that Jacob served for his love of Rachel!

We come now to the turning point in the Jacob story, the birth of

Rachel's Son
(30:22-24)

> Then God remembered Rachel, and God heeded her and opened her womb. ²³She conceived and bore a son, and said, "God has taken away my reproach"; ²⁴and she named him Joseph, saying, "May the LORD add to me another son!"

To climax the birth stories the narrator strikes a happy note: "God remembered Rachel, . . .God heeded her . . . God opened her womb." The phrase that opens the section about the children, "the LORD . . . opened [Leah's] womb" (29:31), now ends it, forming an *inclusio,* an obvious frame. God hears Rachel's prayers and her first son, Joseph, is born. Of note is that the text relates that God first "remembered Rachel" and second he "heeded" or listened to her rather than the natural reverse order. Biblical divine "remembrance" always precedes and leads to action as with Noah (8:1) and Abraham (19:29)

and now with Rachel who thought the LORD had forgotten her.

Gordon Wenham observes that "the present order stresses the

priority of God's grace" citing Isaiah 65:24:[143]

> Before they call I will answer,
>   While they are yet speaking I will hear.

Bernard of Clairvaux (1090-1153) once reminded his fellow monks that

"every soul among you that is seeking God should know that it has been

anticipated by [God], and has been sought by [God] before it began to

seek [God]."[144] How else could it happen? Jesus said, "No one can come

to me unless drawn by the Father who sent me" (John 6:44).

Why does God open Rachel's womb at this time? Rachel has

waited seven years since her marriage to Jacob (29:18, 27). The

mandrakes Rachel obtained from Leah are not mentioned; they are

insignificant and are not even the means that God uses to open her

womb. J. P. Fokkelman comments that "God reacts mercifully to

---

[143] Wenham, *Genesis 16-50*, 248.

[144] Bernard of Clairvaux, "*Sermon LXXXIV on the Song of Songs, 2;*" *Late Medieval Mysticism,* The Library of Christian Classics, Volume XIII, ed. Ray C. Petry (Philadelphia: The Westminster Press), 74-75.

Rachel's actions and because of their profound meaning he is now willing to recognize her."[145] What profound meaning?

Rachel possesses a special treasure; she is the wife who is loved, not Leah. In one sense, it is the mandrakes after all. In her desperation, Rachel asks Leah for her son Reuben's mandrakes and in exchange gives Jacob to Leah for a night. She temporarily surrenders her position of being "first" to Leah--the most profound exchange in a story of four exchanges.[146] J. P. Fokkelman notes that Rachel "gives up the only thing that that shows her precedence, the access to Jacob, and after that God shows mercy."[147] As Scripture stresses, "God opposes the proud, but gives grace to the humble."[148] God acts graciously on Rachel's behalf!

Rachel has a twofold explanation for the name that she chooses for her son, "Joseph." First, like the lamentation language of the Psalms, she says, "God has taken away my reproach."[149] Rachel suffered for years the same sense of inferiority as Sarah (Gen. 16.4). Now, naming

---

[145] Fokkelman ,*Narrative Art in Genesis*, 139.
[146] The other three are 25:29-34; 27:1-36; 29:16-25.
[147] Fokkelman ,*Narrative Art in Genesis*, 140-141.
[148] James 4:6 and I Peter 5:5 quoting the Greek (LXX) of Proverbs 3:34.
[149] For example, Psalm 69:7: "It is for your sake that I have borne reproach, that shame has covered my face."

her firstborn "Joseph," she adds, "May the LORD add to me another son!" Another birth is anticipated. Earlier, Rachel in desperation had asked for "sons" (30:1). The name Joseph is an abbreviated form of "May El (God) add [another son]" (*yôsēf-'ēl*). This etymology of this son of Jacob is clearer than most since the name Joseph (*yôsaf*) and the verb in "May the LORD add" employ the same root form (y*sf*).

This account of Jacob's two wives at war ends on a happy note. It begins in the same vein with the birth of Leah's first four sons. With the birth of Levi, Leah exclaims, "This time I will praise the LORD" (29:35). But as the alienations intensify, the covenantal and more personal name, "LORD," leaves off and the generic word, "God," indicates a change in emotional tone. This use of the more distant term "God" for the deity continues until Rachel gives birth to Joseph in answer to her prayer. At that point she returns to the patriarch's more intimate term with the happy wish, "May the LORD add to me another son!"

The beginning of the covenant people, God's "treasured possession out of all the peoples" (Exod. 19:5), is before our eyes. Even the use of the divine names expresses the irony of Israel's dysfunctional beginning. Are the people of God characteristically an ironic people? At this point in the longer Jacob narrative, Jacob turns the story in a new direction; he is ready to go home!

These birth stories (29:31—30:24) are at the center of the whole Jacob cycle.. Everything revolves around them. The birth of the children in its long-range perspective takes on theological significance for the biblical story of salvation as God forms a people. Herbert Prince points out that one purpose of our story is "to introduce briefly the initial background for the eventual rise of the twelve tribes of Israel that figure so prominently in the Old Testament."[150]

At the end of his lesson on divine providence as the story "speaks realistically of Jacob and the practices of his family in 'the ongoing rhythms of life and death, joy and sorrow, family conflict and unity,'" Here Herb Prince asks, "Where can God be in all this?"[151] Gordon Wenham answers:

---

[150] Prince, "The Call of God: Part 18."

[151] Herbert L. Prince, "The Call Of God: Part 25: Bringing Good Out Of Wrongdoing" (February 3, 2013).

It is into this bitterly divided family that the forefathers of the twelve tribes were born. Fathered by a lying trickster and mothered by sharp-tongued shrews, the patriarchs grew up to be less than perfect themselves. Yet through them the promises to Abraham took a great step toward their fulfillment, showing that it is divine grace not human merit that gives mankind hope of salvation."[152]

God is not canceled out by human perversity and conflict; he remains present and at work in the midst of even a dysfunctional family. This is shown by the verbs that have God as their subject—"saw . . . opened . . . has looked . . . has heard . . . heeded , , , given . . .endowed . . . remembered . . . heeded . . . opened . . . taken away . . . added": "the presence of God is no guarantee of harmony"[153] observes Kevin Walton. The witness of the biblical narrator is that God's activity is initiatory and decisive in the story. So what does this biblical text (29:31—30:24) reveal to us about God and how he is at work in every aspect and circumstance of our lives? Can we so believe in divine providence that with the late Lewis T. Corlett we can lift up our hearts and say, "thank God and take courage"?[154]

---

[152] Wenham, *Genesis 16-50*, 250

[153] K. Walton, *Thou Traveller Unknown*, 148.

[154] Lewis T. Corlett (1896-1992) was a pastor, teacher, college president, and the president of Nazarene Theological Seminary. See Lewis T. Corlett, *Thank God and*

These birth stories of Jacob's offspring speak to the question of why we frequent regularly a place called the Christian Church. They speaks to us as to why we sit together in Bible study and reflect on an ancient document from a world so far from ours. We do these things because like the rest of Scripture, this story of envy, strife, and divine presence defines who we are as the people of God. Leah, Rachel, and Jacob help us understand what we are about as we seek to live our lives of faith—of prayer, reflection, worship, and service to others in the name of Jesus the Christ.

When Rachel had borne Joseph, Jacob said to Laban,
"Send me away, that I may go to my own home and country" (30:25).

Take Courage: How the Holy Spirit Worked in My Life (San Diego: Point Loma Press, 1992).

NINE
Jacob Prospers
(Genesis 30:25-43)

Genesis 30:43:   "Thus the man grew exceedingly rich, and had large flocks, and male and
female slaves, and camels and donkeys."

> I know thee, Saviour, who thou art—
>   Jesus, the feeble sinner's friend;
> Nor wilt thou with the night depart,
>   But stay and love me to the end:
> Thy mercies never shall remove:
> Thy nature, and thy name, is LOVE.[155]

Jacob is ready to go home. Only Laban presents an obstacle.

Jacob needs his permission to leave: "Send me away, that I may go to

my own home and country" (30:25). We return to the familiar tension

between father-in-law and son-in-law that characterizes the Jacob-Laban

narrative. Even when the two finally part ways, the benediction (31:49)

Laban's pronouncement to Jacob indicates not a resolution to their

conflict, but only a truce:

> The LORD watch between you and me, when we are absent one
> from the other.

---

[155] Hildebrandt, Beckerlegge, and, ed., *A Collection of Hymns for the use of the People called Methodists,* 251.

213

Growing up as a child, I attended Sunday School at the Methodist Church in the small town near our Nebraska ranch. Faye Farber, the local baker's wife, was in charge of the children's area in the church basement. It was a single large room with the furnace in the center. Her quotations of Scripture verses belonged to the era of the King James Version. For example, she would often quote Psalm 121:1 which ended with a period: "I will lift up my eyes unto the hills, from whence cometh my help." She assumed she was lifting her eyes up to the Lord. The NRSV, however, with attention to the context, ends it with a question: "I lift my eyes to the hills—from where will my help come?" The answer comes in verse 2: "My help comes from the LORD, who made heaven and earth." The hills were where the apostate Israelites sacrificed to the heathen Baals!

In similar manner, Mrs. Farber would quote Laban's last words to Jacob, "The LORD watch between you and me, when we are absent one from the other" (31:49), as a benediction to the children. These words rang in our ears as the Sunday School session ended and we went happily on our separate ways. She did not notice that Laban followed his benediction with a warning to Jacob: "If you ill-treat my daughters, though no one else is with us, remember that God is a witness between you and me" (31:50). Yet Scripture and its relevance to our lives was indelibly impressed upon us!

Laban's benediction serves as an acknowledgment of an unresolved conflict--such is often a part of real life. We let the matter rest and keep on loving one another. With Laban's words we leave the end and return to the beginning of this final narrative of the battle of wits between these two wily characters in conflict. Before us is a narrative that traditionally has presented exegetes with extreme difficulty--the negotiations between Jacob and Laban, how the animals are described, and the breeding techniques used. We will, of course, solve all its problems!

The narrative begins with

Jacob's Request
(30:25-28)

> [25]When Rachel had borne Joseph, Jacob said to Laban, "Send me away, that I may go to my own home and country. [26]Give me my wives and my children for whom I have served you, and let me go; for you know very well the service I have given you." [27]But Laban said to him, "If you will allow me to say so, I have learned by divination that the LORD has blessed me because of you; [28]name your wages, and I will give it."

Jacob has long been waiting for a son by the wife he loves. Now with the birth of Rachel's son Joseph, Jacob considers time is up in Laban's service and decides to return home. He wants go before the light of the promise goes out, to see the land once more: "Send me away, that I may go to my own home and country." The theme of return takes over in the Jacob story with verse 25. The verse functions as a conclusion to what proceeds as well as an introduction to what follows, structurally a pivot sentence. A new event is at hand—Jacob prospers materially at Laban's expense as the latter well knows!

Rachel was vulnerable without a child. Apart from the protection of her father's family, her husband could discard her (31:50). With the birth of Joseph, the risk to Rachel in Jacob's leaving no longer exists. She is Jacob's first love. He is no doubt especially sensitive to Rachel's position--her giving birth to Joseph is Jacob's signal that it is time for him to go home. So without as much as a "please," Jacob, in an aggressive tone, requests that he be given leave to return to his "own home and country." It is not only his "own home and the country" of his birth but it is literally "to my place and to my land." "Place" is a significant term as we saw in the Bethel account, and the "land," according to the promise at Bethel, belonged to Jacob (28:4, 13). Naturally, he requests to take his wives and children with him.

Jacob is fully aware of his father-in-law's *modus-operandi* as he makes this new request of Laban. He senses that he has met a worthy foe in deceit. But Jacob now needs Laban's permission; he is a hired servant and is not free to leave until Laban releases him. Jacob was a stranger, a dependent, hardly a full member of the legal community. As Laban puts it later in the narrative, "the daughters are my daughters, the children are my children, the flocks are my flocks, and all that you see is mine" (31:43). Jacob's request is a bold one; he did not possess the right to decide to be independent with regard to his wives and children.

Jacob's stresses how he has he has served Laban; three times he uses the Hebrew root '*bd* ("served," "service," "have given") in verse

217

26. Having served the agreed fourteen years of bride-price, Jacob is asking, at least indirectly, if the terms of the arrangement with Laban have been fulfilled. Laban's response is gracious, "a model of oriental courtesy and cunning" in the words of Gordon Wenham.[156]. Laban's "If you will allow me to say so" can also be translated as "If I have found pleasure in your eyes, please stay" (v. 27 NIV). Laban, unusual for him, recognizes that the LORD has blessed him with material prosperity because of Jacob: "the LORD has blessed me because of you." Is it superstition—"by divination"—or is he now a believer? Does Laban recognize that it is the blessing of Abraham that on Jacob? How aware is he that he is affirming the God of Abraham, Isaac, and Jacob?

Laban knows that Jacob's departure would only harm him. But since in Laban's eyes Jacob may only be maneuvering for better wages, Laban diplomatically says, "name your wages, and I will give it." The repetition of the verb "said" (v. 27)—omitted by NRSV—may indicate an urgent attempt to think of a way to keep Jacob. So Laban subtly tosses the ball into Jacob's court. Jacob, with equal cunning, rejects any

---

[156] Wenham, *Genesis 16-50*, 225.

wages. Is Jacob seeking to change the very nature of his relationship to

Laban? Can he succeed?

Jacob and Laban Bargain
(30:29-36)

[29]Jacob said to him, "You yourself know how I have served you, and how your cattle have fared with me. [30]For you had little before I came, and it has increased abundantly; and the Lord has blessed you wherever I turned. But now when shall I provide for my own household also?" [31]He said, "What shall I give you?" Jacob said, "You shall not give me anything; if you will do this for me, I will again feed your flock and keep it: [32]let me pass through all your flock today, removing from it every speckled and spotted sheep and every black lamb, and the spotted and speckled among the goats; and such shall be my wages. [33]So my honesty will answer for me later, when you come to look into my wages with you. Every one that is not speckled and spotted among the goats and black among the lambs, if found with me, shall be counted stolen." [34]Laban said, "Good! Let it be as you have said." [35]But that day Laban removed the male goats that were striped and spotted, and all the female goats that were speckled and spotted, every one that had white on it, and every lamb that was black, and put them in charge of his sons; [36]and he set a distance of three days' journey between himself and Jacob, while Jacob was pasturing the rest of Laban's flock.

When Laban generously, as it seems, makes Jacob an open-

ended offer, "name your wages, and I will give it" (v. 28), he is in fact

rejecting Jacob's request to leave Laban's employ and household. In

response, Jacob stresses his service and Laban's resultant prosperity for he knows, and Laban knows, that it is Jacob's labors alone that have made something out of Laban's property:

> "You yourself know how I have served you, and how your cattle have fared with me. For you had little before I came, and it has increased abundantly; and the Lord has blessed you wherever I turned. But now when shall I provide for my own household also?"

Jacob apparently would have been content to leave with very little in the way of livestock when he first made his request to leave. But now his worth to Laban is established: "the Lord has blessed you wherever I turned." Jacob creates prosperity wherever he appears for God has kept his promise made at Bethel. Laban, aware that he is dependent on Jacob for God's blessing, now knows Jacob's continued service will come at a high price. So he appears to give Jacob the advantage: "What shall I give you?" But to Laban's surprise and confusion, Jacob rejects Laban's offer of higher wages: "You shall not give me anything." He will no longer in any way be obligated to Laban. With faith and bold self-confidence Jacob is ready to go into business on his own: "when shall I provide for my own household?" He expects to flourish under Laban's oppression, and dealing with him according to his own disposition, Laban walks blissfully into Jacob's trap.

Jacob makes a proposal that again gives Laban the advantage, or so Laban thinks: "'Good! Let it be as you have said." Jacob's offer appears straightforward. He will continue to care for Laban's flock with his wages being the limited number of abnormally colored sheep and goats. The precise scenario at this point is difficult to picture. We take it that Jacob is talking about future offspring from Laban's flock as his wages. He offers to receive from Laban much less than the 20 percent of newborn lambs or kids that ancient shepherds normally received for their labors.[157]

Jacob offers to separate all such animals now in the flock so that the number multicolored offspring will not be unduly influenced by their presence. He stakes his loyalty--literally, "righteousness" on the accuracy of what he does: "So my honesty will answer for me later, when you come to look into my wages with you." Is there a touch of reproof couched in Jacob's words? Jacob goes on to tell Laban that any

---

[157] Wenham, *Genesis 16-50s,* 256.

time Laban is free to go through Jacob's flock and count as stolen any animal that does not fit their agreement. Laban accepts Jacob's offer enthusiastically with his exclamation, "Good![158] Let it be as you have said." But Laban is thinking!

Always wary of Jacob—a cheat sees others in his own image—Laban hedges his bets. He takes no chances that Jacob might pull a fast one on him down the road. Laban separates the multicolored animals himself from the flocks that Jacob will keep for him and puts them under the care of his sons." In Laban's thinking he has substantially reduced Jacob's chances of acquiring any significant number of livestock.

Further, to be on the safe side, lest Jacob somehow find a way to acquire some of the oddly colored animals, "while Jacob was pasturing the rest of Laban's flock," Laban sets "a distance of three days' journey between himself and Jacob." Laban has apparently stolen what he had previously agreed was Jacob's before Jacob could take possession of them. Perhaps Laban wants Jacob to think that there are no such animals

---

[158] "Good" is the Hebrew *hēn* normally translated as "Behold" or "See."

in the flock. Jacob, however, who trusts in the patriarchal blessing, is

also thinking!

Jacob's Cunning Strategy
(30:37-43)

[37]Then Jacob took fresh rods of poplar and almond and plane, and peeled white streaks in them, exposing the white of the rods. [38]He set the rods that he had peeled in front of the flocks in the troughs, that is, the watering places, where the flocks came to drink. And since they bred when they came to drink, [39]the flocks bred in front of the rods, and so the flocks produced young that were striped, speckled, and spotted. [40]Jacob separated the lambs, and set the faces of the flocks toward the striped and the completely black animals in the flock of Laban; and he put his own droves apart, and did not put them with Laban's flock. [41]Whenever the stronger of the flock were breeding, Jacob laid the rods in the troughs before the eyes of the flock, that they might breed among the rods, [42]but for the feebler of the flock he did not lay them there; so the feebler were Laban's, and the stronger Jacob's. [43]Thus the man grew exceedingly rich, and had large flocks, and male and female slaves, and camels and donkeys.

We make no attempt to understand fully this paragraph in detail; it describes a series of actions beyond our explanation. The point the actions make, however, is clear, as Jacob shrewdly applies the science of his day. Jacob's cunning in this context is positive; Laban and his sons are providentially three days journey away. Jacob is able to carry out his "strange" breeding techniques in relative privacy without being checked or spied upon by Laban's camp. If Jacob is to increase his flock, he faces the challenge of getting Laban's all white animals to produce spotted or dark young. White" in Hebrew is *laban;* it is the *laban* or white sheep that belong to Laban! Walter Brueggemann suggests that "the narrator intends the Israelite listener to enjoy and celebrate this odd man, Jacob, for whom there are strange, positive powers at work."[159]

Jacob puts his plan into operation. He believes that putting spotted or striped objects in front of the animals at their drinking troughs during mating would produce spotted or speckled animals. The concept is not modern, but is probably in line with the folk traditions of Jacob's time. Making more sense to us is his second breeding principle. Jacob knew from his own experience that the stronger animals were able to reproduce much better than the weaker and that the stronger animals reproduced earlier than the weaker. So he made sure that that the weaker animals bred for Laban and the stronger for himself.

Jacob then "put his own droves apart, and did not put them with Laban's flock." He ended up eventually, it appears, with a flock of

---

[159] Brueggemann, *Genesis,* 251.

4.11 Jacob—Bethel to Peniel

multicolored sheep and goats both more numerous and vigorous than Laban's, a cause for complaint later by Laban's sons (31:1). Jacob is able to outmaneuver Laban by his cunning; but as he does so, he keeps within the terms of an agreement freely entered into between them.

The narrative concludes on a high note: "Thus the man grew exceedingly rich, and had large flocks, and male and female slaves, and camels and donkeys." Although Jacob's ingenious efforts are clearly involved, the story implies that the seemingly extravagant success— literally he "prospered greatly greatly"--that Jacob enjoys in the process is attributable only to God. As Laban said, "the LORD has blessed me because of you," which Jacob himself affirmed: "the LORD has blessed you wherever I turned" (vv. 27, 30). How fully aware Jacob was of the true nature of his own success at this point in the story as he acknowledged later (31:6-9) is another question.

Jacob's desire to return to his own land at the birth of Joseph began this account when he asked Laban to allow him and his family members to leave. But now, near the end of his sojourn with Laban, Jacob is now differently situated. He had arrived at Laban's house alone and penniless, now he has two wives and twelve children--a prosperous Jacob "exceedingly rich, with large flocks, and male and female slaves, and camels and donkeys." Jacob will soon be off to the land of promise!

In its own unique way, this story shows the promises of God being fulfilled. We can take heart that the promise of God is being fulfilled precisely in this doubtful character. God does not wait for perfect instruments through whom to fulfill his purposes. All of his human instruments, save One, were and are flawed!

The great King David, out of whose line the Messiah was to come, had a roving eye and made his own contribution to a dysfunctional family. The reformer Martin Luther was intemperate in speech and sometimes coarse, even vulgar in language; the brilliant prophetic figure Kierkegaard was most eccentric; the poet and songwriter Charles Wesley ruined his brother John's best chance for a happy marriage; and our spiritual father John Wesley himself was not exactly a wisdom sage when dealing with the opposite sex. So there is plenty of room for you and I to be used of God in all our peculiar humanness and with all our flaws. It is divine grace, at times even in its hiddenness, both from ourselves and others, that gives us hope for the land of promise in our lives now and in the life to come.

TEN
Jacob Leaves for Home: Part One
(Genesis 31:1-21)

Genesis 31:5: "I see that your father does not regard me as favorably as he did before. But the God of my father has been with me."

> The Sun of Righteousness on me
> > Hath rose with healing in his wings;
> Withered my nature's strength; from thee
> > My soul its life and succor brings;
> My help is all laid up above;
> Thy nature, and thy name, is LOVE.[160]

As we reflect on the narrative of the life of Jacob, we can view it in terms of the progress of deceit. Jacob has revealed himself as a "deceiver" in relation to his brother and his father. When he flees to the household of his uncle Laban, he joins up with one who shows himself as "a deceiver of a deceiver." Jacob proves himself to be "a deceiver of a deceiver of a deceiver" in this episode. Jacob deceives, he is deceived by a deceiver, and now he deceives one who has deceived a deceiver! As J. P. Fokkelman interprets their story,

whenever people like Jacob and Laban mix with each other,

---

[160] Hildebrandt, Beckerlegge, and Dale, ed., *A Collection of Hymns for the use of the People called Methodists*, 251.

there is no end to it. How is this to go on? Will the two take to an escalation of deceit, will they continue *ad infinitum*? What a prospect! [161]

Moving on in Genesis 31, we see how Laban and Jacob begin to bring their relationship to a revealing close. Terence Fretheim speaks of "a watershed period in the life of this family."[162] Ever since Rachel gave birth to Joseph there has been a desire on Jacob's part to return to Canaan (30:22-25). A measure of distance has developed between Jacob and his father-in-law, Laban. In tune with his character, Jacob finds it necessary to deceive Laban one more time before Jacob and his family can actually leave. The break is twofold between the two families as the story progresses. Chapter 31 presents the theological and personal justifications for Jacob to return to his homeland.

Genesis 31 is an episode within the broader (Gen. 27-33) and narrower (Gen. 29-31) contexts of what is taking place with regard to Jacob and Esau. Jacob fled from Esau in chapter 27, setting forth what some term the Jacob-Laban cycle. The cycle began with a flight and will end with a flight as Jacob returns to his homeland (32:1). In chapter 31

---

[161] Fokkelman, *Narrative Art in Genesis*, 151.
[162] Fretheim, "The Book of Genesis," 558.

the tension between Laban and Jacob moves from suspicion to confrontation to a final resolve in a negotiated covenant between the two men. Thus far God has at times been more indirectly than directly involved in what transpires between Jacob and Laban. And yet, God is not entirely absent as the text at hand indicates. God's presence becomes more obvious as the chapter develops from episode to episode.

Since the biblical text of this episode with fifty-five verses is longer than we usually consider in one chapter, but comprises one conceptual unit, we forego quoting it up front. Rather, we make use of it all as we work through the chapter. We begin with

Jacob and His Wives
(31: 1-16)

J. P. Fokkelman aptly notes that the "thunder-clouds are gathering"[163] with Jacob's acquisition of wealth at Laban's expense. The narrative moves on to the reasons for Jacob's decision to leave for home (vv. 1-3):

,

---

[163] Fokkelman, *Narrative Art in Genesis,* 151.

First, Jacob heard that Laban's sons were complaining, "Jacob has taken all that was our father's." The sons' own self-interests have come into play since the less their father has, the less they will have! In their avarice, they did not consider whether Jacob acquired his wealth justly or unjustly. Second, Jacob saw that Laban was not as favorably disposed toward as before. Avarice runs in the family. The Hebrew words afford a vivid picture, literally, "Jacob saw Laban's face and, behold, it was not with him as formerly." The important factor is that the situation is seen through Jacob's eyes, he "noticed" it as the presence of *hinēh* (behold) stresses. Jacob has become *persona non grata* to both his father-in-law and his brothers-in-law. With no other family around, he is vulnerable; he is now aware of the weakness of his position. But Jacob was not the only one who took note of the situation:

> ³Then the LORD said to Jacob, "Return to the land of your ancestors and to your kindred, and I will be with you."

In the face of developments, God tells Jacob to return home to his own kindred, thereby in effect re-enforcing Jacob's earlier request of Laban (Gen. 30:25). At the same time, God promises his own presence: "I will be with you" (31:3). Leah, Rachel and the children will go with him. More importantly, God's presence will be with him, just as God promised earlier at Bethel when Jacob was fleeing Canaan (28:15a). Jacob now thinks it wise to share with his wives his recent perceptions about Laban.

> ⁴So Jacob sent and called Rachel and Leah into the field where his flock was, ⁵and said to them, "I see that your father does not regard me as favorably as he did before. But the God of my father has been with me. ⁶You know that I have served your father with all my strength; ⁷yet your father has cheated me and changed my wages ten times, but God did not permit him to harm me. ⁸If he said, 'The speckled shall be your wages,' then all the flock bore speckled; and if he said, 'The striped shall be your wages,' then all the flock bore striped. ⁹Thus God has taken away the livestock of your father, and given them to me.

Jacob calls his two wives to come "into the field" where his flock was. Although dedicated to his work and busy, as Robert Alter suggests, Jacob wants "a safe location beyond the earshot of Jacob and his sons."[164] Jacob speaks to his two wives together about their father's change of attitude or "face" toward him; he values their opinion as strong independent women. The rare Hebrew pronoun "You" in Jacob's "You know" to his wives emphasizes their role. They are united as a family unit in this new situation. Apparently their rivalry in child-

---

[164] Alter, *Genesis,* 167.

bearing has ceased, with only Benjamin left to be born later on the journey home (35:16-18). Regardless of his affection for Rachel, for she is named ahead of Leah; Jacob honors equally their status as wives in relation to their father. They are now more than mothers in the story.

The speeches of Jacob and his two wives are longer than normal in biblical narrative (31:5-16). Their unusual length indicates their rhetorical importance as Jacob makes sure his wives support him in relation to their father. Jacob describes Laban's action toward him but does not name him!

As Jacob expresses his basic grievance in the situation that prevailed during the last six years, he wisely leaves out his previous fourteen years of service for Laban's daughters in seeking to persuade them. He omits both the embarrassing substitution of Leah for Rachel on his wedding night and Esau's deadly hatred causing him to flee from home. Such would possibly discourage Leah and Rachel from coming with him. Also, the sisters are not told what Laban's sons were saying about Jacob, only about the father's change of heart: "your father does not regard me as favorably as he did before." Jacob stresses instead God's protection of him and his interests--a theological explanation.

Jacob thus openly alludes three times to the leadership of God in his service to their father (vv. 5, 7, 9). In contrast to Laban's behavior, "the God of my father has been with me." Jacob could well be remembering God's promise to him many years earlier at Bethel (31:13):

> Know that I am with you and will keep you wherever you go, and will bring you back to this land; for I will not leave you until I have done what I promised you" (28:15).

God is *with* Jacob as Laban is not! As Jacob says, "God did not permit him to harm me" when your father "cheated me and changed my wages ten times. Such is the painful irony for Laban as his intentions are thwarted--Jacob's flocks multiplying regardless. It is "frustrating enough to make someone gnash his teeth in rage"[165] in J. P. Fokkelman's vivid depiction. Laban's cleverness did not work. Jacob credits God for the third time in his favor against Laban. His summary reflects what Laban's sons were saying with a rhetorical flourish, "thus God has taken

---

[165] Fokkelman, *Narrative Art in Genesis,* 154

away the livestock of your father, and given them to me." Jacob reports a seeming miracle that could not help but impact his wives; they would be able to connect it to the blessing given to Jacob.

Jacob's explanation of the size of his own flocks does not contradict any agreement that he has made with Laban. Jacob's assessment of his activity over recent years reflects his own crafty efforts that are consistent with his commitments to Laban. Wwith hindsight, he is able to put the increase of his flocks in proper perspective. And yet, evidently, the account thus far is not enough. The biblical story adds to what has been shared as Jacob appeals to revelation in the form of a dream:

> [10]During the mating of the flock I once had a dream in which I looked up and saw that the male goats that leaped upon the flock were striped, speckled, and mottled. [11]Then the angel of God said to me in the dream, 'Jacob,' and I said, 'Here I am!' [12]And he said, 'Look up and see that all the goats that leap on the flock are striped, speckled, and mottled; for I have seen all that Laban is doing to you. [13]I am the God of Bethel, where you anointed a pillar and made a vow to me. Now leave this land at once and return to the land of your birth.'

The use of *hinēnî* that we have highlighted all along appears as Jacob's name is called by the angel of God in a dream: "'Jacob,' and I said, 'Here I am!'" His duel with Laban gives way to a dialogue with the God of Bethel prominent in Jacob's consciousness: "I am the God of Bethel, where you anointed a pillar and made a vow to me." As Jacob dreams, the messenger of God interprets, "I have seen all that Laban is doing to you." God appears to Jacob reminding him of the vow he made at Bethel, and orders Jacob to return to the land of his birth. Jacob had vowed that if God will be with him and protect him and bring him back to his father's house in peace, "then the LORD shall be my God" (28:22). God has obviously protected him away from home and Jacob is thus obligated to return. The divine order, reinforced by the reference to the God of Bethel, leads Jacob to put persuasive pressure on his wives.

Jacob's wives, convinced by his appeal, acting in concert, respond with their own words of trust: "Now then, do whatever God has said to you." They base their case, however, upon their father's abuse of them rather than on Jacob's experience:

> [14]Then Rachel and Leah answered him, "Is there any portion or inheritance left to us in our father's house? [15]Are we not regarded by him as foreigners? For he has sold us, and he has been using up the money given for us. [16]All the property that God has taken away from our father belongs to us and to our children; now then, do whatever God has said to you."

236

Laban has engaged in false dealings, misusing their dowry. He has kept all the fruits of Jacob's fourteen years of labor; Laban has shortchanged his own daughters! Financially the daughters are abandoned. Laban has undermined their loyalty to him. The sisters agree.Jacob's wealth is properly theirs, not because Jacob has stolen it, but because God has given it.

The overtones of the sisters' response are both negative and positive. They are negative in the sense that they are content to leave their father's house (vv.14b-15a), giving as their reason an accusation that they lay against their father (vv.15b). They are positive in that they agree that Jacob is following the call of God. Implied is the belief that God and Jacob acted justly and properly.

On hearing his wives' response, Jacob moves promptly to return to his homeland with all the family's possessions. J. P. Fokkelman concludes in Jacob's favor:

> Now God keeps the promise made there [Bethel] and again Jacob is the keen observer and genuine believer and grateful proclaimer of God's help; his interpretation is profound and authoritative.[166]

---

[166] Fokkelman, *Narrative Art in Genesis,* 162.

The flight from Laban
(31: 17-21)

[17]So Jacob arose, and set his children and his wives on camels; [18]and he drove away all his livestock, all the property that he had gained, the livestock in his possession that he had acquired in Paddan-aram, to go to his father Isaac in the land of Canaan. [19]Now Laban had gone to shear his sheep, and Rachel stole her father's household gods. [20]And Jacob deceived Laban the Aramean, in that he did not tell him that he intended to flee.[21] So he fled with all that he had; starting out he crossed the Euphrates , and set his face toward the hill country of Gilead.

Jacob departs in haste on the authority of God with his wives' full support. They are willing to break with family and father. Jacob again "arose . . . and fled" (vv. 17, 21) just as his mother said at the wrath of Esau: "arise, flee" (27:43, NASB). Jacob is going "to his father Isaac in the land of Canaan," that is, not only to his home country, but also to his family. He will re-establish his relationship with his father, but what about Esau who will not be afar off?

The flight back to his homeland will be much more difficult than his flight from his homeland years before. First, Jacob's possessions are extensive, so to get all his acquired wealth across the River (Hebrew), the Euphrates, is no small endeavor. The crossing was, however, decisive, allowing no turning-back, giving him his first sense of security: Jacob "set his face toward the hill country of Gilead," east of the Jordan, a little south of Lake Tiberias. Second, it was difficult because he had to deceive Laban to do it. Jacob is able to leave without telling him because Laban is away shearing sheep—Jacob's deception is literally "stole the heart" of Laban: as John Calvin translates, "he stole away unawares to Laban."[167].

But unknown to Jacob, "Rachel stole her father's household gods"—a most serious offense. Who is Rachel like? But what these apparently small, perhaps even ugly, human shaped images stood for and why she took them are difficult to discern. Terrence Fretheim suggests that they were "symbols of Laban's authority over his household, perhaps tokens of inheritance."[168] Their function for Laban and the family piety could certainly represent for Rachel a link to her family. Was she quite as sure about leaving home as she had previously sounded? Is she seeking protection for their long travels? Perhaps she

---

[167] Calvin, *Genesis*, 170.
[168] Fretheim, "The Book of Genesis," 557.

fears that if Jacob should meet Esau face to face, the wronged brother would kill her husband?

Delay and disappointment could be said to mark Jacob's time here in Paddan-Aram. He had originally planned, in his mother Rebekah's words, to spend a few days there (27:44). This short stay grew to seven years as he worked for Rachel's hand in marriage. Then, cheated by his father-in-law, he worked another seven years until Rachel bore her first son, Joseph. At the time Jacob asked Laban to release him, but Laban refused. So Jacob worked another six years to acquire enough wealth of his own in order to make a break and return to his homeland. Though one may doubt the complete candor of Jacob's defense for wanting to leave (31:1-9), it is apparent that he stresses God's overall protection.[169] Looking back at our story with human eyes, as with Jacob, so with us,

The best-laid schemes o' mice an' men
Gang aft' agley.[170]

---

[169] Prince, "Part 19A: Getting out of Dodge."

[170] Robert Burns (1759-1796), "To A Mouse," *The Poetical Works of Robert Burns* (London and New York: Collins' Clear-Type Press), 92. "To a Mouse" is subtitled "On turning her up in her nest with the plough, November 1785." "Gang aft' agley" is "go oft astray."

for

Nae man can tether time nor tide.[171]

---

[171] Inscribed in the flyleaf of the above book by Scotsman John Hogg who gave it to me sometime in 1959-61 while studying at New College, Edinburg, Scotland.

ELEVEN
Jacob Leaves for Home: Part Two
(Genesis 31:22-55)

Genesis 31:49:   "The LORD watch between you and me, when we
are absent one from the other."

The Sun of Righteousness on me
Hath rose with healing in his wings;
Withered my nature's strength; from thee
My soul its life and succor brings;
My help is all laid up above;
Thy nature, and thy name, is LOVE.[172]

Jacob, with his wives, children, and all his acquired possessions,
livestock and servants, has fled and that secretly. Laban is unaware of
the flight for he is out of town. With this deception, in J. P. Fokkelman's
vivid characterization, the "deceiver of a deceiver of a deceiver"[173] has
fled in haste from Laban whom he has served for twenty years. Thus
far Jacob has stressed God's overall protection in Paddan-Aram.
Providence has been Jacob's guide, often unknown to him but faithful
none-the-less. We go to Herbert Prince for an understanding of

---

[172] Hildebrandt, Beckerlegge, and Dale, ed., *A Collection of Hymns for the use
of the People called Methodists*, 251.
[173] Fokkelman, *Narrative Art in Genesis*, 151.

providence.[174]

Herbert Prince points out that the term "providence," literally, can be a "seeing-for" (caring for), comes from the Latin *providentia*, Quoting Millard Erickson, he defines providence as "the continuing action of God by which he preserves in existence the creation which he has brought into being, and guides it to his intended purposes for it."[175] Although providence is not a biblical term, the biblical record is clear on a divine purpose at work within creation. Jacob takes matters a step farther when he confesses that "the God of my father has been with me" (Gen. 31:7). What may have appeared impersonal earlier in Jacob's theology is revealed as a personal conviction. The God of his father, Isaac, is also the God of Abraham (26:23-4) and the God of Bethel (31:13)!

Jacob's wealth in terms of his herds and number of slaves and family members will make for a slow return to Canaan and his homeland. The setting for story is already fraught with tension and

---

[174] Herbert L. Prince, "The Call Of God: Part 19B: Getting' Out of 'Dodge'" (August 2, 2012).

[175]Millard Erickson, *Christian Theology.* Volume 3 (Grand Rapids: Baker Book House, 1983).

uncertainty before Jacob can get beyond Laban's reach. Laban is three days away, tending his own flock. Jacob may be well on his way, but he is still close enough to be caught if Laban discovers that Jacob and his wives are gone. We will soon see what happens once the discovery occurs.[176]

Laban Overtakes Jacob
(31: 22-35)

We begin with Laban's delayed discovery of Jacob's absence:

> [22]On the third day Laban was told that Jacob had fled. [23]So he took his kinsfolk with him and pursued him for seven days until he caught up with him in the hill country of Gilead.

It takes Laban only seven days to overtake Jacob. The three hundred miles, however, from the Euphrates to Gilead would be difficult for Jacob's herds to cover in ten days; interpreters suggest that the number seven may be idiomatic or approximate. Normally whenever the Hebrew text refers to a journey, the number is one, three, or seven. What is significant is Laban's dream in the midst of his pursuit:

---

[176] We continue in part two as in part one to forego quoting the biblical text upfront, but will utilize it all as we work through the chapter.

²⁴But God came to Laban the Aramean in a dream by night, and said to him, "Take heed that you say not a word to Jacob, either good or bad.

Laban's divinely inspired dream confirms that God has been indeed watching over Jacob; the dream prompts the leniency Laban will show to Jacob. Gordon Wenham sees the last phrase of the verse as idiomatic; he translates it as "Take care lest you contradict Jacob in any way."[177] Laban and his wife used the same expression in 24:50 when they gave consent to Abraham's servant to take his sister Rebekah to be Isaac's wife. Despite what is said here, Laban's diatribe (31:26-30) that follows is one of the longest and fiercest in the entire book of Genesis. The narrator composes the scene around this speech like the dialogue in the previous scene (vv. 1-21).

Laban proceeds to arraign Jacob as one still under his authority. His charges are twofold: first, Jacob has not observed the proper formalities for leaving his father-in-law's household, and second, that Jacob has stolen from him. We read that

---

[177] Wenham, *Genesis 16-50*, 274.

²⁵Laban overtook Jacob. Now Jacob had pitched his tent in the hill country, and Laban with his kinsfolk camped in the hill country of Gilead.

With his tents pitched opposite Jacob's, Laban presses his charges with passion. His opening words, "What have you done?" are precisely the words spoken by Jacob when he confronted Laban the morning of his wedding after discovering Leah as his wife instead of Rachel. Irony comes home to roost! Laban's questions here are a mix of indignation, anger, pure hypocrisy, sweet words, denunciation, and a threat, concluding with a blunt question: "Why did you steal my gods?" We listen to Laban's speech:

> ²⁶Laban said to Jacob, "What have you done? You have deceived me, and carried away my daughters like captives of the sword. ²⁷Why did you flee secretly and deceive me and not tell me? I would have sent you away with mirth and songs, with tambourine and lyre. ²⁸And why did you not permit me to kiss my sons and my daughters farewell? What you have done is foolish. ²⁹It is in my power to do you harm; but the God of your father spoke to me last night, saying, 'Take heed that you speak to Jacob neither good nor bad.' ³⁰Even though you had to go because you longed greatly for your father's house, why did you steal my gods?"

Laban's "You have deceived me" to Jacob is literally "You have stolen my heart."

Laban understands why Jacob wants to return to his homeland, recognizing that Jacob is homesick after twenty years: "you longed greatly." Laban's talk, however, about a festive send-off is sheer hypocrisy. But he does not or pretends not to understand why Jacob would take off with the household gods, called "gods" first by Laban and then repeated by Jacob as "your gods." This is the more serious charge; Jacob has stolen what Laban worships. Laban respects Jacob's God, "the God of your father," but Jacob has no respect for Laban's gods. Apparently the household gods are images of either the ancestors or the patron gods of the ancestors important for family piety. They were thought to bring prosperity and to provide protection.

Laban's accusation contains an inner contradiction; he accuses Jacob of carrying away his daughters "like captives of the sword." The verb "carried away," associated usually with the driving of animals and the phrase "captives of the sword" has ominous military implications. Laban suggests that Jacob like a marauding army has seized the young women to serve as sexual and domestic slaves. Ironically, the daughters had spoken of their father's treating them like foreigners, selling them and using up the profit (31:15). And Jacob is aware that Laban is leading a group of armed men. "It is in my power to do you harm."[178]

Laban had detained Leah and Rachel as well as Jacob in similar manner for an extra seven years by his deception at Jacob's wedding (29:25). One wonders, what were Rachel's thoughts that night? By his deception, Laban set hatred and jealousy loose to work their devastating effect upon their family-life. He has accused Jacob of what he, Laban, would have liked to do, but has to refrain from doing—take his daughters from Jacob by force. So Jacob answers Laban with words that heighten the suspense:

> "Because I was afraid, for I thought that you would take your daughters from me by force. [32]But anyone with whom you find your gods shall not live. In the presence of our kinsfolk, point out what I have that is yours, and take it." Now Jacob did not know that Rachel had stolen the gods.

Jacob does not contest that his flight was a breach of etiquette; instead, he launches a counterattack. He accuses Laban of wanting to "rob" him or "steal" his wives by force. Jacob is so convinced of the innocence of everyone in his party that he pronounces death on anyone

---

[178] The suggestions of Alter, *Genesis*, 170, inform this paragraph.

found guilty of the theft. Jacob was unaware that Rachel took them and thereby condemns her to death if the gods are found on her. His unknowing words foreshadow her premature death in childbirth. Suspense brings the story to a dramatic high point.

In a comic picture, Laban is left to search on his own for what has been stolen from him as he proceeds to examine the tents of Jacob and his two wives:

> [33]So Laban went into Jacob's tent, and into Leah's tent, and into the tent of the two maids, but he did not find them. And he went out of Leah's tent, and entered Rachel's. [34]Now Rachel had taken the household gods and put them in the camel's saddle, and sat on them. Laban felt all about in the tent, but did not find them. [35]And she said to her father, "Let not my lord be angry that I cannot rise before you, for the way of women is upon me." So he searched, but did not find the household gods.

Rachel, treating the gods as unclean, sits on them pleading "the way of women" to her father. She deceives him as she was deceived on her supposed wedding night. Just as Isaac felt of Jacob dressed in animal skins enabling Jacob to receive his irrevocable blessing, so here Jacob's uncle is feeling, frisking, house-searching, and now a Jacoba's trick renders this search vain. Jacob thus retains the blessing and leave with his most precious asset, Rachel. As J. P. Fokkelman describes him,

Laban is now nowhere, he is "the great loser, for he cuts a foolish figure." [179]

By this time Jacob is incensed and rejects Laban's charge, so he vents his anger.

Jacob's Rebuttal
(31: 36-42)

Jacob's speech brings us to the climax of the narrative; he gives witness to a God who stands by him in his affliction. While Laban, now on the defense, is still gasping for breath, Jacob, up for the encounter, rejects Laban's charge against him:

> [36]Then Jacob became angry, and upbraided Laban. Jacob said to Laban, "What is my offense? What is my sin, that you have hotly pursued me? [37]Although you have felt about through all my goods, what have you found of all your household goods? Set it here before my kinsfolk and your kinsfolk, so that they may decide between us two.

Jacob begins a rhetorically devised formal plea of defense against a false accusation in poetic form. He stresses stressing the role of their common "kinfolk," For with Laban's fruitless search for the household gods, Jacob has had it, and mounts his challenge: "Set it

---

[179] Fokkelman, *Narrative Art in Genesis,* 170, to whom this paragraph is in debt.

here." Significantly, the Hebrew verb for "upraided" is a legal term with the accompanying picture of a court of law as he voices his grievance.[180] With this, Jacob leaves his defensive stance and takes the offensive with a hard-hitting frontal attack. Continuing his rhetorical prose, Jacob makes short work of Laban as he hits back with his own list of grievances.

> [38]These twenty years I have been with you; your ewes and your female goats have not miscarried, and I have not eaten the rams of your flocks.[39]That which was torn by wild beasts I did not bring to you; I bore the loss of it myself; of my hand you required it, whether stolen by day or stolen by night.[40]It was like this with me: by day the heat consumed me, and the cold by night, and my sleep fled from my eyes. [41]These twenty years I have been in your house; I served you fourteen years for your two daughters, and six years for your flock, and you have changed my wages ten times.

Jacob's grievances reveal how obsessed Laban was with property and how cheated Jacob feels. With his list of grievances, Jacob reminds Laban that he has gone way beyond what is expected of a shepherd. He has made himself responsible for Laban's flocks. When a lion would kill a lamb Jacob would accept its loss. He does not allow it to be counted against Laban as he had a right to do. Jacob the shepherd took the loss;

---

[180] Alter, *Genesis,* 172, again informs this paragraph.

Laban as owner suffered no loss at all. In addition, the demands of the field and the hardships of weather took their toil on him so that "sleep fled from my eyes." Jacob's loyalty, his "twenty years" with Laban, has its ironic repayment; Jacob has prospered. Laban had changed Jacob's wages ten times, cheating him by doing so (31:7)!

But that is not all that Jacob has to lay upon Laban. The crucial or highpoint of his charge, Jacob saves until the end:

> [42]If the God of my father, the God of Abraham and the Fear of Isaac, had not been on my side, surely now you would have sent me away empty-handed. God saw my affliction and the labor of my hands, and rebuked you last night."

God, rather than Laban, is *with* Jacob, the God he knows as the God of his "father, the God of Abraham and the Fear of Isaac" has been "on [his] side" all along. As Jacob told his wives earlier, "God did not permit him to harm me" (31:7). God saw Jacob's situation and ensured that he was not overwhelmed: "the Fear [Terror] of Isaac" describes the deity's presence as one who has scared Laban, protected Jacob, and discouraged him from wreaking revenge on Laban. The title "Fear of Isaac" occurs only here and in verse 31:53 in Genesis.

252

The table is fully turned as Jacob becomes the prosecutor; judgment is at hand: "you would have . . . but God saw . . . and rebuked you" (31:24). Jacob's final words to Laban are more than a climax for Jacob's self-justification. They are a summary, even the solution, of the twenty years of Jacob's life in Harran. Jacob acknowledges that his life and wealth are due to God's power that overrides the dastardly attempts of Laban to control him. Jacob's God enriches people even under oppressive conditions.

The Watch
(31:43-55)

Laban answers Jacob with a whining complaint. Four times he stresses what is supposedly his: "My daughters," "my children," "my flocks," "all you see is mine." But what can Laban do? Nothing! Laban's legal position has been undercut. He must let go of the women, children, and flocks that he claims as his. He must surrender them all into the hands of a foreigner:

> ⁴³Then Laban answered and said to Jacob, "The daughters are my daughters, the children are my children, the flocks are my flocks, and all that you see is mine. But what can I do today about these daughters of mine, or about their children whom they have borne?

Laban no doubt fears to use force against Jacob after the divine warning. He is left to protect himself from the blessing that is obviously on Jacob in the only way he knows how--by making a deal with Jacob. He proposes a covenant between them:

> [44]Come now, let us make a covenant, you and I; and let it be a witness between you and me."

Gordon Wenham points out that in the Genesis narrative "when foreigners seek to make covenants or oaths with the patriarchs, it is an acknowledgement of the latter's' superiority."[181] As it is customary in such matters to call for witnesses (Deut. 9:15), Laban proposes two witnesses who are to give the covenant binding authority. The first is the covenant itself, and the second is the heap and pillar.

> [45]So Jacob took a stone, and set it up as a pillar. [46]And Jacob said to his kinsfolk, "Gather stones," and they took stones, and made a heap; and they ate there by the heap. [47]Laban called it Jegar-sahadutha: but Jacob called it Gilead. [48]Laban said, "This heap is a witness between you and me today." Therefore he called it Gilead, [49]and the pillar Mizpah, for he said, "The LORD watch between you and me, when we are absent one from the other. [50]If you ill-treat my daughters, or if you take wives in addition to my daughters, though no one else is with us, remember that God is witness between you and me."

---

[181] Wenham, *Genesis 16-50*, 279. See 21:22-24; 26:26-31.

Not only does Laban take the initiative in word and action, his voice is the dominant voice throughout the "negotiations." Jacob responds to Laban in action rather than vocally. Jacob says only two words—"Gather stones"—and these are directed to his kinsmen. Is Jacob giving Laban the silent treatment? For Jacob, the building of a heap is a way of memorializing God's goodness to him as he did earlier at Bethel (28:18) and later for Rachel (35:14, 20). Laban names the site of several stones in his own Aramaic language, Jegar-sahadutha, but Jacob names it Gilead in Hebrew. Both names mean "mound" or "cairn" of witness.

. A benediction familiar to us defines the final meeting between Laban and Jacob in one brief sentence:

"The Lord watch between you and me, when we are absent one from the other."

These words are called the "Mizpah benediction." Contrary to the way it is sometimes used, this benediction expresses suspicion. Since Laban does not trust Jacob, and Jacob does not trust Laban, the benediction means that we do not trust each other out of each other's sight.

Following the benediction, Laban lays down the conditions for peace between he and Jacob in terms of the latter's treatment of Laban's daughters. Jacob is neither to ill-treat them nor take additional wives, far from what he would likelywant to do. Whatever else one might say, the benediction testifies to the work of God in the two men's lives. Even Laban, probably a polytheist (31:53), came to the point of recognizing Jacob's God. Now Jacob is "on the road again." But it means that Esau looms on the horizon!

The "heap" and the "pillar" are set up to designate the territory of each; they constitute political boundary markers that neither Jacob nor Laban are to cross with hostile intentions. The stones serve as witnesses to their agreement. For Laban they mean that God is the guarantor of their treaty; for Jacob, they speak of the God who actively intervenes in his life with blessing:

> [51]Then Laban said to Jacob, "See this heap and see the pillar, which I have set between you and me. [52]This heap is a witness, and the pillar is a witness, that I will not pass beyond this heap to you, and you will not pass beyond this heap and this pillar to me, for harm. [53]May the God of Abraham and the God of Nahor" — the God of their father—"judge between us." So Jacob swore by the Fear of his father Isaac, [54]and Jacob offered a sacrifice on the

height and called his kinsfolk to eat bread; and they ate bread and tarried all night in the hill country.

As customary in the ancient world, the covenant was confirmed by the offering of sacrifice and a communal meal. The farewell blessing indicates that the agreement is sealed and that the dispute has ended in a truce (31:43-54). Blessing and peace go together.

With a heightened recognition, Laban now appeals to Jacob's God as the judge between them: "May the God of Abraham . . .'judge between us.'" But until "Jacob swore by the Fear of his father Isaac," he has not said a word. Jacob has been silent. He consents to the covenant proceedings only by taking part in the closing ceremony. Plainly put, he is fed up with uncle Laban. He does not fear him, for as God's protégé he is victorious and unassailable and knows it. For Jacob such a pact is unnecessary, he is safe under the shelter of God's wings. But ironically, it is now Laban who demands security. Jacob is blessed, Laban is simply inferior.[182]

---

[182]We are in debt here to Fokkelman, *Narrative Art in Genesis,* 188.

Laban's angry chase is now over. Its end has come in a guarantee for peace between the families and territory in the future. All that is left is the traditional parting.

> [55]Early in the morning Laban rose up, and kissed his grandchildren and his
> daughters and blessed them; then he departed and returned home.

Laban's departure brings us to the close of the Jacob/Laban cycle of stories (chapters 29-31). We will hear from Laban no more. But before leaving Laban and his fascinating relationship with Jacob, it is time to sum up the nature of their relationship. What began with an embrace and kiss by Laban welcoming Jacob (29:13) has been marked since then by deceptions, cunning and intrigue. Now at the end Laban has negotiated a covenant with Jacob and departs the next morning paying no attention or giving any embrace to Jacob: "Laban rose up, and kissed his grandchildren and his daughters and . . . returned home." But Jacob is off to a fresh, God-given start. But again, there is yet Esau!

How easy it would have been for the narrator to paint a rosy, idyllic picture of Israel's origins, a Garden of Eden sort of beginning. But with a realistic understanding of the human condition, the storyteller knew that this would not be realistic. Thus the more deeply we probe into the past history of Israel, the more our present time looks like more of the same.

Yet, precisely because of the continuity at the level of both human and divine action, we can see ourselves as in a mirror and gain new levels of self-understanding and be assured of God's continuing involvement in our troubled lives. The community of faith is fortunate. It has a God who does not wait for or insist on perfection before working in and through it. Like Israel, we have a God who blesses the family of Jacob, Rachel, Leah, and their children in the very midst of its conflicts. God makes life possible even within a dysfunctional system.[183]

---

[183] This paragraph is in debt to Fretheim, "The Book of Genesis," 558-560.

II.
Jacob and Esau
(32:1—33:17)

TWELVE
Esau is Coming
(Genesis 32:1-21)

Genesis 32:11: "Deliver me, please, from the hand of my brother, from the hand of Esau, for I am afraid of him; he may come and kill us all, the mothers with the children."

> Contented now upon my thigh
> I halt, till life's short journey end;
> All helplessness, all weakness, I
> On thee alone for strength depend;
> Nor have I power from thee to move:
> Thy nature, and thy name is LOVE.[184]

Introduction

Laban is now off Jacob's back, but Esau is not! After being repressed for twenty years, Jacob's past has returned to haunt him! An encounter with brother Esau is at hand (33:1-20). Jacob cannot go home again without facing his brother. Jacob has changed, has Esau as well? As Jacob approaches Esau's territory, he sends messengers ahead, only to hear that Esau is on his way with four hundred men to meet the estranged brother who fled from his wrath. But immediately

---

[184] Hildebrandt, Beckerlegge, and Dale, ed., *A Collection of Hymns for the use of the People called Methodists,* 251.

ahead for Jacob is a strange encounter with a mysterious figure in the darkness of the night (32:23-32). The narrative centers on the prayer of Jacob (vv. 9-12) in preparation for the two meetings ahead—with the unknown figure and with the known Esau.

The now prosperous Jacob is under God's command to leave Haran that has ceased to be his home. No longer a fugitive, he is to return to his homeland. Heading for home territory, Jacob is met by the angels of God (vv. 1-2). Is he about to enter new, even dangerous, human and spiritual territory—one and the same? Jacob's facing both Esau and the figure of the night appearing so close together unites them in some mysterious way. The coming of Esau in 32:1-22 combines with the meeting with Esau in 33:1-20 to enclose Jacob's other-worldly experience in 32:22-32. With the specter of Esau on both sides of the encounter in vv. 22-32, these verses function as the centerpiece of chapters 32-33. No wonder Jacob resorts to prayer.

What is going through Jacob's mind is quite evident as he moves closer and closer to the country he fled twenty years before. Back then Esau was threatening to kill Jacob due to the latter's deceptions that cost

Esau his birthright. Now, as Jacob heads for home, he cannot forget how

he deceived his brother. Is Esau still out to kill him? Jacob has to assume

that Esau has revenge on his mind, so Jacob, "afraid and distressed" (v.

7), prepares with a series of steps in mind..

We begin with

The Angels of God
(32:1-2)

¹Jacob went on his way and the angels of God met him; ²and
when Jacob saw them he said, "This is God's camp!" So he
called that place Mahanaim.
At Bethel Jacob dreamed that he saw "the angels of God . . .

ascending and descending" (28:12). Later in the midst of his conflict

with Laban, again in a dream, "the angel of God" spoke to him (31:11).

At Mahanaim there is no dream, simply, "the angels of God met him."

In the dreams, there was a word of revelation, but here is only Jacob's

response: "This is God's camp!" Jacob appears to perceive no hostile

intent in the encounter with the angels. Rather, linked to the divine

promise, his response conveys his clear sense of God's ongoing

protection and presence. We are reminded of Jacob's exclamation at

Bethel, "Surely the LORD is in this place—and I did not know it!" (28:16).

For Jacob this experience anticipates his coming encounter with Esau. Is he receiving renewed courage for the dangerous journey ahead? The meeting is somewhat of an enigma. J. P. Fokkelman notes the text as narrative art is "full of ambiguity and suspense." Is there a "unique, of great 'historic' moment," even foreboding, event just ahead? [185]

An element of dread appears to be present. Robert Alter renders "met him" as "accosted him."[186] The literary structure makes it clear that the incidents involving the angels in Genesis 32 is parallel to the incident at Bethel in chapter 28 in balance and contrast. In both instances, angels encounter Jacob, and in both chapters the verb *pāga* is used that means "strike upon," "fall upon," "assail," "attack," as well as "meet" or "encounter." It is unclear whether the presence of the angels is indicative of God's help for Jacob, or whether it points toward an impending battle between Jacob and Esau. Or?

---

[185] Fokkelman, *Narrative Art in Genesis,* 198-199.
[186] Alter, *Genesis*, 177.

More is going on than meets the eye in this implicitly theological preface to our story. The themes present in Genesis remind one of Psalm 34:4-8:

> [4]I sought the Lord, and he answered me,
>   and delivered me from all my fears.
> [5]Look to him, and be radiant;
>   so your faces shall never be ashamed.
> [6]This poor soul cried, and was heard by the Lord,
>   and was saved from every trouble.
> [7]The angel of the Lord encamps around those who fear him,
>   and delivers them.
> [8]O taste and see that the Lord is good;
>   happy are those who take refuge in him.

The language of the Genesis account is parallel to that of the Psalm where the "angel encamps . . . and delivers." Like Jacob's prayer ahead (32:9-12), the Psalm speaks of a poor man, his prayer for deliverance, the promise of good, and the assertion that no good is lacking. In this brief paragraph, Jacob is reassured that God is at work as he goes on his way.

As his dream twenty years earlier led Jacob to name the place Bethel meaning the "the house of God" (Gen. 28:17-19), just so this second encounter with God's messengers produces the name Mahanaim meaning "Two Camps." The dual reference may be either to Jacob's

camp and God's camp, or to Jacob's camp and Esau's camp. The
following paragraph that introduces Esau would favor the camps of the
two brothers. But does the narrator really want us to separate the two—
God's camp and Esau's camp? The ambiguity of this brief notice
introduces tension into the narrative: is Jacob to be encouraged? Perhaps
the account reflects uncertainty on his part. Jacob does not yet know
Esau's intent—has his attitude towards Jacob changed? We keep that
question in mind as Jacob sends

Messengers to Esau
(32:3-8)

[3]Jacob sent messengers before him to his brother Esau in
the land of Seir, the country of Edom, [4]instructing them, "Thus
you shall say to my lord Esau: Thus says your servant Jacob, 'I
have lived with Laban as an alien, and stayed until now; [5]and I
have oxen, donkeys, flocks, male and female slaves; and I have
sent to tell my lord, in order that I may find favor in your sight.'"
[6]The messengers returned to Jacob, saying, "We came to your
brother Esau, and he is coming to meet you, and four hundred
men are with him." [7]Then Jacob was greatly afraid and
distressed; and he divided the people that were with him, and the
flocks and herds and camels, into two companies, [8]thinking, "If
Esau comes to the one company and destroys it, then the
company that is left will escape."

Hoping to make a good first impression on Esau and find out his
intentions, Jacob prepares to meet his brother by sending "messengers"

ahead. At this point, Jacob is hiding behind his messengers rather than see Esau face to face. Jacob's language to his twin is what one uses to speak to a superior: "my lord Esau . . . your servant Jacob." Is he silently acknowledging his guilt as he subordinates himself to his brother Esau? Sending messengers in an age when writing was scarce enabled people at a distance from one another to communicate just as if the sender were present in person. The classic messenger formula is used: "Thus says."

The term "messengers" as the same Hebrew word as "angels" (*mal'ākîm*) sets up the intermingling of the human and the divine in this chapter. Thus "messengers" links this episode with the immediately preceding one. Is Jacob to be seen as doing what God is doing? Jacob's intent is to mollify Esau since the brothers have not met for two decades and Jacob surely assumes that Esau has neither forgotten nor forgiven him. The messengers are sent to "the land of Seir, the country of Edom." Three words--"Seir . . . country . . . Edom" recall the three sources of tension between the brothers—birth, birthright, and blessing. These Hebrew terms were used earlier in Genesis, each with reference to some feature associated with Esau. "Seir" refers to Esau's being "hairy" (25:25); "country" references Esau as a "man of the field" (25:27); and "Edom" speaks of Esau's redness at birth (25:25) and his attraction to the "red stuff" (25:30).

Jacob's message is threefold. First, "I have lived with Laban as an alien, and stayed until now," that is, I have not been hiding from you. Second, "I have oxen, donkeys, flocks, male and female slaves"–I have plenty so I am not planning to take anything from you. And third, "I have sent . . . that I may find favor in your sight," "Let us put the past behind us and start over." Jacob summarizes the twenty years he has been delayed or detained in returning with no hint as to why he left in the first place.

Jacob names his possessions in the singular rather than in the plural as the English translates. It is perhaps a subtle move to give Esau enough information to arouse his attention without Jacob giving his hand away. Further, Jacob's use of the "servant" and "lord" language with its reversal of "the elder shall serve the younger" (25:23) comes across as one who wants reconciliation. Is he also, as Terence Fretheim wonders, in going beyond the norms of oriental courtesy willing to reverse the blessing gained by deceiving Esau?[187] Certainly Jacob is appealing to the generosity of Esau in hopes that the rift between them can be healed. Esau's forgiveness is the only way out left for Jacob.

Jacob's "Please accept my gift"; "my gift" is literally, "my blessing" in 33:11. His return to the language of blessing in 33:4, 8, and 13-14 shows his seriousness about reconciliation with his estranged brother. The designation of Esau as "brother" on the lips of the messengers (v. 6), suggests to Robert Alter that "an elaborate irony of terms underlies the entire reunion of the twins."[188] Jacob, however, is distressed and frightened at the report he receives and uncertain about its meaning. "[Esau] is coming to meet you, and four hundred men are with him" is ambiguous at best. Did not Isaac say that Esau would live by sword (27:40)?

Is Esau coming to harm Jacob or not? What is clear is that Esau with the standard number for a raiding party, four hundred men, appears to contradict Jacob's hopes for a healing meeting. Jacob is fearful and

---

[187] Fretheim, "The Book of Genesis," 563.
[188] Alter, *Genesis,* 178.

prepares for the worst; he devises a survival plan. As in the past when the narrative presented twin brothers struggling over a blessing, two sisters competing for a husband's love, and flocks divided into two groups according to color, Jacob now divides his company into "two companies," literally, "two camps." Should Esau attack, at least one group might be saved: "thinking, 'If Esau comes to the one company and destroys it, then the company that is left will escape'"—a degrading stratagem. But if Esau intends to attack Jacob, why have the messengers been allowed to return? Is this a psychological ploy, a cat and mouse game, on Esau's part? Suspense intensifies. No wonder

Jacob Prays
(32:9-12)

[9]And Jacob said, "O God of my father Abraham and God of my father Isaac, O Lord who said to me, 'Return to your country and to your kindred, and I will do you good,' [10] I am not worthy of the least of all the steadfast love and all the faithfulness that you have shown to your servant, for with only my staff I crossed this Jordan; and now I have become two companies. [11]Deliver me, please, from the hand of my brother, from the hand of Esau, for I am afraid of him; he may come and kill us all, the mothers with the children. [12]Yet you have said, 'I will surely do you good, and make your offspring as the sand of the sea, which cannot be counted because of their number.'"

Jacob acts, then he prays as he did at Bethel (28:20-22); his approach, though not all it could be, is quite different in tone (28:20-22). There Jacob's prayer or more precisely his vow took the form of a bargain: "*If* God will be with me . . . , *then* the LORD shall be my God."[189] Here, Jacob shifts the focus from himself to God. In the only extended prayer in the book of Genesis, Jacob's prayer opens as he quotes God after his initial address: "who said to me" (v. 9); he closes on a note of "you have said" (v. 12). His appeal to God's faithfulness rather than his own worthiness begins with the promises God made to him and ends with the promises of God to Abraham.

As he prays, Jacob believes he has some claim upon God. First, the God he invokes is the God who blessed his patriarchal family: "O God of my father Abraham and God of my father Isaac." Second, Jacob is only doing what God told him to do—return to his homeland. Third, Jacob has the promise from God that he would treat him well and prosper him. Jacob revises the earlier promise, "I will be with you" (31:3), one of divine presence, to "I will do you good" (vv. 19, 12).

---

[189] The Italics are mine.

Jacob's double appeal God's "I will do you good" frames the prayer and summarizes the divine promises; the very structure of the prayer grounds his plea in the faithfulness of God to the promises he has made.

A fourth reason for Jacob's belief that he has a claim upon God is found in his own unworthiness. Here Jacob prays at his best, "I am not worthy of the least of all the steadfast love and all the faithfulness that you have shown to your servant." Jacob does not deserve God's kindness, yet he asks that whatever kindnesses God has bestowed upon him continue. Franz Delitzsch wrote over a century ago that "to keep to His word the God who keeps His word, is the way of all true prayer. Upon what else can Jacob rely but upon the promise of God, and how else can he do so but by praying?"[190]

All these reasons surround Jacob's basic petition: "Deliver me, please, from the hand of my brother, from the hand of Esau, for I am afraid of him; he may come and kill us all, the mothers with the children." Stressing his fear with an emphatic "I," Jacob, according to promise, dearly wants his "offspring [to be] as the sand of the sea, which

---

[190] Delitzsch, *Genesis*, II, 202.

cannot be counted because of their number." With Jacob's prayer, the scene arrives at a profound climax. He is now reasdy to put his plan into operation as

Jacob Prepares to Move on
(32:13-21)

[13]So he spent that night there, and from what he had with him he took a present for his brother Esau, [14]two hundred female goats and twenty male goats, two hundred ewes and twenty rams, [15]thirty milch camels and their colts, forty cows and ten bulls, twenty female donkeys and ten male donkeys. [16]These he delivered into the hand of his servants, every drove by itself, and said to his servants, "Pass on ahead of me, and put a space between drove and drove." [17]He instructed the foremost, "When Esau my brother meets you, and asks you, 'To whom do you belong? Where are you going? And whose are these ahead of you?' [18]then you shall say, 'They belong to your servant Jacob; they are a present sent to my lord Esau; and moreover he is behind us.'"

[19]He likewise instructed the second and the third and all who followed the droves, "You shall say the same thing to Esau when you meet him, [20]and you shall say, 'Moreover your servant Jacob is behind us.'" For he thought, "I may appease him with the present that goes ahead of me, and afterwards I shall see his face; perhaps he will accept me." [21]So the present passed on ahead of him; and he himself spent that night in the camp.[191]

Whether from doubt, fear, cunning, or faith, or a mixture of them all, Jacob puts feet to his prayers: John Calvin commends him: "he takes

---

[191] The "moreover" in vv. 18 and 20 translates our attention-calling word *hinnēh,* translated by NASB as "Behold."

confidence and meets the danger."[192] As he goes about to spend the longest night in his life, Jacob sends ahead of him a "present" or a "tribute"--over 550 animals. He does not pretend that it is a love-gift. Yet the "present," prominent in this account (vv. 13, 18, 20, 21), indicates a step toward the grace that he seeks.

Jacob cleverly sends the gift of livestock in three stages putting "a space between drove and drove." The strategy is to separate Esau's forces, to encumber them with all the animals, and to mix Jacob's servants with Esau's men. The result would be less room for Esau to move and more difficult for him to do harm to Jacob, not to speak of the psychological effect of the presentation. Is Jacob declaring himself to be Esau's vassal with his tribute or is he symbolically returning the blessing he had stolen from Esau? Regardless, Jacob's great hope is that Esau "will accept me."

Jacob remains "behind" the droves as he instructs his servants to tell Esau, "Moreover your servant Jacob is behind us (v. 20). Later in the account we read that "the present passed on ahead of him." J. P.

---

[192] Calvin, *Genesis,* 194.

Fokkelman suggests insightfully that now "Jacob has betrayed his moral and psychological position in a revealing way." That is, "now that the place has become too hot for him, the man of 'I first!' is eager to come last, to shelter behind the work of other people, . . . who are innocent."[193] The one who led the way at birth, who came first to Isaac to make himself the blessed first born, and who wanted to marry first and only Rachel of Laban's daughters, now places himself last. Does the "present" that he sent ahead constitute a buffer-zone between Jacob and his brother as well as a delay of an actual meeting?

The heart of the account is Jacob thinking, "I may appease him with the present that goes ahead of me, and afterwards I shall see his face; perhaps he will accept me." Without any ambiguity, the approach he takes to his problem is in tune with his character; Jacob's dependence on God as he prays is only partial. Most fascinating, even significant is the particular play on the word "face" in verse twenty; "the most radiant key word in the story of Jacob" according to J. P. Fokkelman.[194] My mind leaps ahead to the great key verse in in 2 Corinthians 4:6: "For it is

---

[193] Fokkelman, *Narrative Art in Genesis,* 205,
[194] Fokkelman, *Narrative Art in Genesis,* 206.

the God who said, 'Let light shine out of darkness,' who has shone in our hearts to give the light of the glory of God in the face of Jesus Christ." As we move on in the story of Jacob and Esau, the appropriateness of the note of fulfillment in this verse will become all the more fascinating.

The Hebrew word often translated literally as "face" (*pānāh*) occurs seven times in verses 13-21. Four times it appears idiomatically as "ahead" (vv. 16, 17, 20, 21). Of the most interest, however, is its use three times in verse 20 in the three expressions "I may appease him . . . I shall see his face . . . perhaps he will accept me." Robert Alter writes that the term is being used as a posture of one unworthy to look upon the face of the other as before royalty. [195] The phrase, "I may appease him," literally, "cover his face," heightens the scene with its cultic ring suggesting the meaning of "make atonement." The Hebrew verb "cover" (*kāfār*) appears often in the Old Testament in atonement contexts.

This thought allows Jacob, as he meets his brother Esau, to say that "afterwards I shall see his face" with the result that "he will accept

---

[195] Alter, *Genesis*, 177, 180.

me." Jacob hopes that Esau, now the stronger party, will look kindly upon him with acceptance, literally, "lift up my face" in recognition and well-being. The gravity of the situation is apparent. Jacob has done all he knows to play upon the sympathies of his brother. But there is a dimension beyond his efforts.

Jacob's presents have gone on ahead and he spends the "night in the camp." The two camps, "Mahanaim," are now obviously Jacob's and Esau's, still opposites. Jacob is not yet free of suspicion and fear. Yet, he prefers to sleep—in the darkness! More danger is coming than Jacob is aware of, although with his encounter with the angels he may have sensed an eerie time ahead. Thus, prior to Jacob's encounter with Esau, the narrative pauses to describe a much different encounter. Or are they really that separate or different?

Jacob's prayer (vv. 9-12) as the climax of the scene affords us a fresh insight into the development of Jacob's character. He is growing, and his growth is that of becoming smaller! Jacob has exhausted all of his resources, yet feels exposed to Esau's attack if Esau so desires. Jacob is where God wants him to be. At ninety-seven years old, he is totally vulnerable with no recourse left but to rely upon God.

As Herb Prince challenges us, "Jacob is not alone on that score. How often have we found ourselves in a circumstance where our only recourse is an appeal to God?" We, too, have rivers to cross with the unknown on the other side. What will our struggles be? They may not be merely human! Prince closes his lesson with an appropriate Moravian prayer:

> Gracious God, we do not know what tomorrow may bring. Grant us the comfort of your presence, and the faith that you are with us unfailingly. In the name of your precious Son we pray. Amen.[196]

---

[196] Prince, "Part 20: Chasing After Some Finer Day."

Eugene Delacroix (1861): French Romantic Painter (1798-1863)

THIRTEEN

Jacob at Peniel
(Genesis 32:22-32)

Genesis 32:29: "You shall no longer be called Jacob, but Israel, for you have striven with God and with humans, and have prevailed."

> Lame as I am, I take the prey,
> Hell, earth, and sin with ease
> o'ercome;
> I leap for joy, pursue my way,
> And as a bounding hart fly home,
> Through all eternity to prove,
> The nature, and thy name, is LOVE.[197]

"Wrestling Jacob" has all along been the overshadowing theme and underlying goal of our study of Jacob. We did not plan and are indeed surprised that the final verse of Charles Wesley's hymn, "Wrestling Jacob," appears appropriately the day we arrive at "Jacob at Peniel." Peniel, Jacob's great encounter with God, is where we have been heading, the account we have been anticipating from the start—the lens through which we approach the entire Jacob story.

We first met Jacob struggling in the womb with his elder brother; he was born "with his hand gripping Esau's heel, so he was named

---

[197] Hildebrandt, Beckerlegge, and Dale, ed., *A Collection of Hymns for the use of the People called Methodists,* 251.

Jacob" (25:26). The twins were quite literally born wrestling as the prophet Hosea centuries later links the two accounts:

> In the womb he took his brother by the heel,
>   And in his maturity he contended with God.
> Yes, he wrestled with the angel and prevailed;
> He wept and sought his favor.
> He found him at Bethel,
> And there he spoke with us (12:3-4). [198]

Who is Jacob's antagonist? Who is this mysterious "man" of the night? To what extent does the struggle foreshadow that central confrontation of the Jacob story--Jacob's meeting with Esau?

Has Jacob's past caught up with him? Will our past, like with Jacob, eventually catch up with us? What happens then? What do we do? What about the divine dimension, how is God present with us when this happens? What is it like for us when inevitable invades? Who are we when the sun goes down (32:21) in our lives, when the dark night arrives, and we are left alone (32:24) in our anxiety? And then when the sun does come up (32:24, 26, 31)? The sunrise *does* follow the sunset just as surlye as the sunset follows the sunrise.

---

[198] We quote the NASB that stays with the Hebrew text reading as ":us."

With "Jacob at Peniel" we enter the most extensively interpreted narrative in the patriarchal stories, yet notes Kevin Walton, one "notoriously difficult to interpret."[199] Walter Brueggemann goes so far as to call it a narrative "that does not want us to know too much."[200] According to Edward Curtis, Martin Luther designated it "one of the most obscure in the Old Testament"; Luther described it as "one of the most enigmatic incidents in all of Scripture."[201] We need to keep our natural desire to make sense" of a difficult passage in check—a little! Yet the account is here *to read*; we do seek to understand. We do not presume to give the correct and final interpretation, but with relative confidence and the help of others, we present *our* understanding of the meaning of this account.

The Peniel story places a decisive stamp on the whole Jacob narrative as do the distinctive themes of the surrounding two accounts of God's appearances to Jacob at Bethel (28:10-22; 35:1-15). Gerhard Von Rad reminds us that in the Bethel accounts "the paradoxical character of

---

[199] K. Walton, *Thou Travellor Unkown*, 66.

[200] Brueggemann, *Genesis*, 267.

[201] Edward Curtis, "Structure, Style and Context as a Key to Interpreting Jacob's Encounter at Peniel," 3, 8. Unpublished paper read at the 1983 meeting of the Evangelical Theological Society.

the divine action is as sharp as can be imagined."[202] At Peniel especially, the narrator seeks to reproduce for the reader some of the same suspense that Jacob experiences in this event.

Our present account is placed purposely in this precise location within the larger Jacob story as it has a special function. What happens here gives shape to Jacob's final encounter with Esau. After Jacob sends his family and possessions ahead of him across the river Jabbok in "the crossing" (vv. 22-23), the scene of Jacob alone at the Jabbok is narrated in three parts. First, in 32:24-25, we focus on "the description of the wrestling match;" second, 32:26-30 gives voice to "the dialogue between the wrestlers"; and third, 32:31-32 contains the "departure and closing comment."

The dialogue that follows "the description of the wrestling match" is composed of two "namings"--that of "Israel" (vv. 26-28) and "Peniel" (vv. 29-30). The emphasis of the account lies on these two significant names. Jacob is not asleep on the river bank dreaming nor is the narrator giving us a spiritualized account of an inner struggle; he is

---

[202] Gerhard Von Rad, *Biblical Interpretations in Preaching*, trans. John E. Steely (Nashville: Abingdon, 1977 [German 1973, *Predigt-Meditationen*]), 40.

reporting a real flesh and blood fight. Yet as Gordon Wenham interprets, "the nature of the experience still remains mysterious, as all encounters with God must necessarily be."[203]

The narrative in chapter 32 resumes the story of the Jacob-Esau conflict that the narrator has left unresolved since 27:4. As Jacob fearfully, to put the matter mildly, prepares to meet Esau, he does not know that God has two meetings in mind! Jacob's meeting with Esau will be far different than he anticipates. We begin our entry into this top-of-the-iceberg account with

The Crossing
(Genesis 32:22-23)

[22]The same night [Jacob] got up and took his two wives, his two maids, and his eleven children, and crossed the ford of the Jabbok. [23]He took them and sent them across the stream, and likewise everything that he had.

Darkness surrounds the events throughout chapter 32 (vv. 13, 21). Apparently Jacob could not or did not want to sleep for he "got up"

---

[203] Wenham, *Genesis 16-50*, 295

in the "night." Is his mind disturbed with worry, conscience-stricken, eager to make amends with Esau, or does he just want time to reflect in the quiet of the night alone? Does he want to pray? Perhaps with new insight into his divided heart Jacob is devising a new plan. Once again he acts (v. 14): in the "same night" Jacob "got up and took his two wives, his two maids, and his eleven children, and crossed the ford of the Jabbok." We recall that it was during the night at Bethel that God was first made known to Jacob (28:10-22).

The Jabbok River is a fast-flowing tributary of the Jordan River that flows into the Jordan River about 25 miles north of the Dead Sea. The river is about 50 miles long, descending from about 1900 feet above sea level to about 115 feet below sea level. This marked descent accounts for the deep-cut canyons, but it also makes possible places where it is shallow to ford.

Jacob first sends his family across to the other side of the river and then everything he possesses. Why he apparently does not cross the Jabbok Jacob does not say. Does he even know why? In sending his people across--all his men, however, he does surrender his line of

285

defense. Any fighting plans are now obsolete. Jacob is defenseless, vulnerable, and left alone in the darkness of night, but not for long. As the confrontation with Esau is looming, the crossing introduces the coming scene. Jacob, poised on the brink of a new life, must face what he has been before he can enter the land of his birthright as who he is to be .[204] We are now prepared for the

The Wrestling Match
(Genesis 32:24-25)

[24]Jacob was left alone; and a man wrestled with him until daybreak. [25]When the man saw that he did not prevail against Jacob, he struck him on the hip socket; and Jacob's hip was put out of joint as he wrestled with him.

Utterly vulnerable, "Jacob was left alone." Yet the fight itself just ahead is but a preamble to the most significant part of the scene, the dialogue between the antagonists (vv. 26-29). Not only was Jacob "left alone," but "a man wrestled with him until daybreak." In Jacob's eyes, his assailant is simply an unidentifiable male, "a man," with whom he has to fight for his life. All he knows is what he sees. Does he suspect that the man may be Esau? For Jacob to be certain of the man's

---

[204] We are in debt here to the wording of Poteet, *Literary Unity in the Patriarchal Narratives,* 146.

identification would reduce the dread inherent in the narration of the story. The wrestling match is hardly described; how can one describe a mystery--what one does not and cannot understand?

The play on words in the narrative between the river Jabbok (*yabboq*), the name Jacob (*ya'ᵃqob*), and the verb "wrestled" (*yē'ābēq*) reminds us that the "wrestling" motif is implicit throughout the Jacob story. We see it all the way from Jacob's grabbing Esau's heel as he emerges from the womb, to his striving with Esau for the birthright and blessing, to his rolling the stone away from the mouth of the well, and to his multiple contentions with Laban. Jacob's wrestling now becomes physical and explicit. He had manifested the strength to roll away the large stone twenty years earlier (29:2-10). Here at ninety seven, Jacob is apparently still a person of considerable strength!

As the two wrestled, "the man saw that he did not prevail against Jacob." The fight appears to end in a draw—an even match? Is it Jacob's strength or his determined unwillingness to yield? Yet the man merely touched Jacob "on the hip socket; and Jacob's hip was put out of joint." Was it superhuman power that dislocated Jacob's hip? Was it a sacred touch, "the tip of the veil of the mystery" as J. P. Fokkelman puts it?[205]

Jacob does not yet know for the man is nameless and faceless. Perhaps

the touch may have given Jacob even more determination to struggle on.

Thus, the struggle between the two antagonists begins

The Dialogue
(Genesis 32:26-30)

[26]Then he said, "Let me go, for the day is breaking." But Jacob said, "I will not let you go, unless you bless me." [27]So he said to him, "What is your name?" And he said, "Jacob." [28]Then the man said, "You shall no longer be called Jacob, but Israel, for you have striven with God and with humans, and have prevailed." [29]Then Jacob asked him, "Please tell me your name." But he said, "Why is it that you ask my name?" And there he blessed him. [30]So Jacob called the place Peniel, saying, "For I have seen God face to face, and yet my life is preserved."

If there is an interpretive "in" to this unusual story, it is here in

the dialogue where the narrator highlights the names "Jacob . . . Israel . .

. Peniel." The real struggle takes place in the verbal exchange between

the wrestlers. First, Jacob forces his opponent to speak. The two parties,

instead of continuing to wrestle, are reduced in the text to speech in

---

[205] Fokkelman, *Narrative Art in Genesis*, 214.

three exchanges. Jacob takes the initiative only in the third exchange—so the man, the man, then Jacob.

In the first exchange the man says, "Let me go, for the day is breaking." Does he want to conceal his identity? Is the man hinting at the concern that no one can see God and live (Exod. 33:20) and thus indicating a supernatural character? Instead, Jacob hangs on as he refuses the man's request, "I will not let you go, unless you bless me." Jacob at this point appears as the stronger party. He exploits the situation to seek a blessing. Jacob as a man supremely interested in blessing insists on one here, otherwise he will not let go. He wants to emerge an enriched man. But for the moment, the man ignores Jacob's request.

The second exchange gives "the man" the stronger part as he asks Jacob, "What is your name?" Jacob's name has embodied his character all along. Now he must confess his true moral nature and spiritual character as a "trickster" and "supplanter": "Is he not rightly named Jacob? For he has supplanted me these two times?" (27:36). Then instead of blessing Jacob, "the man" gives Jacob a new name and declares a new character and destiny for him: "You shall no longer be

289

called Jacob, but Israel, for you have striven with God and with humans, and have prevailed."

"Israel," is literally "El (God) fights"[206] according to Gordon Wenham as the Jacob story becomes the story of Israel. Something new appears in the world. Wenham adds, indeed, Jacob's renaming becomes "itself a valuable gift, a blessing."[207] With the re-naming, Jacob is thrust into a transforming process; he is one in whom a new nation is being born. Could we say that Jacob at heart is undergoing more of a moral redemption than a merely ethical reform? Jacob has yet to work out the latter in his life. As he deals with what and who is to this point, especially in relation to Esau, Jacob is encountering a Person! The new name "Israel" does not replace the old name "Jacob" as the occurrence of the two names in the parallelism of Old Testament poetry indicates; Israel will always be Jacob. Jacob is a part of who Israel is!

Jacob, now Israel, has prevailed with God, as we shall see--no small matter indeed. Has Jacob successfully confronted his "Jacob"--and his Esau? The crux is that you, Jacob, "have striven with God and with

---

[206] Wenham, *Genesis 16-50*, 296.
[207] Wenham, *Genesis 16-50*, 297.

humans, and have prevailed." This is Israel, as characteristically present in its entire history with God. God is indeed gracious as Jacob is brought to a major turning point in his life.

With the third exchange--an act of incredible boldness, Jacob seeks control of the situation. He senses that he is dealing with someone as he asks, yet with respect, "Please tell me your name." Jacob's desire to know the name of his adversary reflects the ancient view that to know the name of a divinity is to be able to summon or manipulate it. The "man," however, evades the question and returns to Jacob's request for a blessing: "Why is it that you ask my name?" At this point, Jacob is apparently again left alone. Did Jacob permit the man's departure, or did he in freedom disappear in the darkness as suddenly as he came? As the stranger leaves he maintains his inscrutable role; he does not reveal his name.

Jacob, however, does receive the blessing he has so long craved: "there he blessed him." With the blessing, Jacob comes to a startling realization, he "called the place Peniel, saying, 'For I have seen God face to face, and yet my life is preserved.'" Jacob could appropriately name the place even if he could not name his adversary. Who all has Jacob been wrestling with? With Esau? With his own life-long actions and character? With God, for this struggle brought a lifetime of battling and groping to a head? Could his experience be three-in-one—God, Esau, himself--as a unified profound spiritual reality? What really is the blessing? How is the God of mystery at work as Jacob prepares for his looming encounter with Esau? How is God at work with us in our desire for reconciliation with those from whom we are estranged? Having met again the God whose hiddenness remains intact, Jacob is ready to face his Esau. He is no longer only Jacob--he is also Israel!

Jacob is blessed; he has determined not to let the stranger go until his request is granted. At Bethel Jacob simply received the promises, here at Peniel he is forced to beg for a blessing. God's response is positive: "And there he blessed him." The blessing spoken by God enables the promises put in place by Isaac to be realized in Jacob's life. With the blessing, God binds his own self afresh to Jacob. For Jacob, the promises given at Bethel (28:10-22) are here renewed with spiritual force. At Bethel the LORD stood beside Jacob and said,

"I am the LORD, the God of Abraham your father and the God of Isaac; the land on which you lie I will give to you and to your offspring; and your offspring shall be like the dust of the earth, and you shall spread abroad to the west and to the east and to the north and to the south; and all the families of the earth shall be blessed in you and in your offspring. Know that I am with you and will keep you wherever you go, and will bring you back to this land; for I will not leave you until I have done what I have promised you" (28:13-15).

God takes Jacob seriously enough to initiate and engage him in a struggle, yet God does not fully reveal himself to Jacob. Why so? First, it was commonplace that to see God's face is dangerous: "no one shall see me and live" (Exod. 33:20).[208] This is a concern, not for God, but for the life of the one who sees. In today's story, God is not the endangered one. To see God in the full light of day would have meant death for Jacob. At the same time the continued grasp of "the man" by Jacob says something about Jacob and that not only physically. He is willing to risk death for the sake of the divine blessing. He is again *tām*. (25:27), a single-minded man who knew what was of value, As Terrence Fretheim

---

[208] See also Deut. 5:25-26, Isaiah 6:5, and John 1:18. But see Exod. 33:11: "the LORD used to speak to Moses face to face, as one speaks to a friend"!

observes, "Jacob's action suggests that he will risk seeing the face of Esau, too."[209]

Significant changes can be discerned in the process of this encounter. Jacob's change of name has implications for God as well as for Jacob. Struggling, the two are caught up in a mutual relationship. God's promise to Jacob from Bethel on involves not a passive, but an active, engaged relationship. The narrator explains the name change only in the positive terms of Jacob's strength and capacity for struggling on with the stranger. Nothing appears with respect to Jacob's earlier acts of deception. The name change suggests that if Jacob can hold his own with God, he most assuredly can hold his own with Esau.

With Jacob's naming of the place "Peniel" as "the face of God," he now knows that God is mysteriously, yet essentially, involved in his possibly dangerous meeting with his brother Esau: "For I have seen God face to face, and yet my life is preserved." That Jacob has lived to tell of his experience assures him that will not be alone as he meets Esau. God is with Jacob in this crucial event of his life—"face to face"! God and

---

[209] Fretheim, "The Book of Genesis," 566.

Esau are intertwined in Jacob's experience, for God is at the heart of all reconciliation; reconciliation is the business God is in. God is the Reconciler!

With the verbal exchange, the account of Jacob at Peniel moves quickly to an end as the narrator reports that

Jacob Departs
(Genesis 32:31-32)

[31]The sun rose upon him as he passed Penuel, limping because of his hip. [32]Therefore to this day the Israelites do not eat the thigh muscle that is on the hip socket, because he struck Jacob on the hip socket at the thigh muscle.

The sun, which had gone down on Jacob earlier (v. 13, 22, 24), now literally "comes up" as "the day is breaking" (v. 26). Darkness is gradually giving way to light as the narrative progresses. A new day is before Jacob with a radiant sun in his face. Elsewhere the name Penuel appears instead of Peniel (Judg. 8:8-9, 17; I Kgs 12:25). Since how words sound in Hebrew is as important as to what they mean in some situations, the narrator may have used Peniel here since it sounds more like "face of God."

"Israelites" is literally "the sons of Israel," a designation appearing here as such for the first time. A family is changing into a people. This custom of not eating the thigh muscle that is on the hip socket appears nowhere else in the Old Testament or in later Jewish law. Gordon Wenham suggests that this dietary practice as observed by the children of Israel would function for them as a reminder of their nation's election as well as a remembrance of "Jacob's meeting with God, and the promise of ultimate victory and blessing he wrung from God then."[210]

Jacob limps because God "struck Jacob on the hip socket at the thigh muscle." If, as Margaret Poteet suggests, that "thigh" as with Abraham and his servant (24:2-3) represents the source of Jacob's productivity, Jacob is attacked at the center of his fruitfulness that touches the source of all that he values. The main point, however, is that Jacob not only has a new name, Israel, but also a crippling limp. Is his limp a mark of defeat or of victory? Or both? Walter Brueggemann observes that only now is Jacob able to understand that his exclamation

---

[210] Wenham, *Genesis,* 297-298.

of 28:16, "God is in this place," cannot be made lightly: "It is cause for dread as well as exultation."[211]

The new name involves a new crippling. There may be a costly mystery in drawing too near and claiming too much. We can appreciate why it was considered death to see God face to face. Jacob emerges from his wrestling with "a man who was no man" as a cripple but with a blessing. The life of Jacob points to the nature of the emerging Israel. Thus is Israel, the people of God crippled among the nations! Are we here anticipating the gospel of the cross; is it possible that Jacob's struggle with the Holy One hints of the coming of the Crucified One? As a church triumphant does the Church limp with Jacob *only* at the cross? Are the Christian folk and the Christian way marked by a crippling in the midst of the world and its value-structures?

No ordinary story is this account in Jacob's journey for it reflects some of the nation of Israel's most sophisticated theology, a theology fully applicable to the Church in any day. On the one hand, Jacob/Israel soars to new heights, yet there is a wounding aspect. Both are essential

---

[211] Brueggemann, *Genesis*, 270.

for the story's theological witness—and for us in our world. Jacob is coming to terms with his past, beginning with the changes in his own life. No longer is Jacob a supplanter to be identified with the stigma of heel (25:26). Only God can truly help us deal with the reality and consequences of our past as we face an open future.

Jacob from here on is a marked man, Israel a marked nation, and the Church a marked people. All are never to be fully accounted for or understood: "The reason the world does not know us is that it did not know him" (1 John 3:2). Israel, the Church, and the Christian as such, cannot be properly understood by the secular mind except by looking to the God of Israel whom we know in the crucified and risen One. Jacob is now characterized by his limp in the present text, thereby acknowledging that only God is God—never his people. The people of Israel and the Church must ponder how it is that blessings are given and at what cost.

All this leads us to the theology of weakness in power and power in weakness as the New Testament's gospel of the cross is turned toward daily living:

"My grace is sufficient for you, for power is made perfect in weakness." So I [Paul] will boast all the more gladly of my weaknesses, so that the power of Christ may dwell in me (2 Cor. 12:9).

The Swiss minister and scholar Eduard Schweizer concludes his sermon on Jacob at Peniel with the admonition, "My dear friends, this is the way we live, between the Israel-struggle, fought through to the end in Gethsemane and at Golgotha, and the final consummation in which Peniel will be fulfilled and we shall see God as he is."[212]

Jacob had his dark night where he was gripped by what he did not understand, what he could not see through. Yet, the night brought a marked change. Does the grace of God have its dark aspect? In the tradition of John of the Cross, whose writings she fully enjoyed, Mother Teresa, during the last years of her amazing ministry became fully aware of what she designated as darkness. Darkness became an essential element of her vocation and the source of the attractive force that drew so many people to her. Mother Teresa came to understand that her mysterious suffering was an essential part of living out her mission for it

---

[212]Eduard Schweizer, *God's Inescapable Nearness* (Waco, Texas: Word Books, 1971).
104.

was an imprint of Christ's Passion on her life, which she loved so dearly.

As a result, Mother Teresa radiated remarkable joy and love for she had built the edifice of her life on pure faith. She came in fact to love the darkness. Like Jacob she hung on and would not let go. But the answer to her unquenched thirst for God was not the consolation of a personal awareness of God's presence; rather it was the blessing of a radiant and fruitful ministry. In traditional terms, Mother Teresa's darkness then appears not as the purification of past sins and faults, but clearly reparatory, that is, it gave her a unique power in mission. She knew with the apostle Paul that "death is at work in us, but life in you" (2 Cor. 4:12).[213]

With Jacob at Peniel, set within the full story of Jacob to this point, we are entering into the biblical paradigm of repentance and forgiveness--repentance on Jacob's part, forgiveness on Esau's. It is a moving picture of reconciliation. This biblical witness to how

---

[213] These two paragraphs are dependent on Brian Kolodiejchuk, ed., etc., *Mother Teresa: Come Be My Light,* The Private Writings of the "Saint of Calcutta" (New York: Doubleday, 2007), 220-226, and note 59 on page 380.

reconciliation can happen will be fully evident when Jacob finally meets Esau (33:1-15). But on the way Jacob has to first deal head-on with the God to whom he has already made intercession (32:9-12). God is inherently at the heart of any fully effective reconciliation. This Jacob story of reconciliation prepares us for the Joseph story (37:1—45:28) that takes us deeper into the process of forgiveness. The two stories together give us a probing picture of reconciliation in its full biblical sense—as a truly spiritual process![214]

We now anticipate Jacob's encounter with the one who stands between him and his entry into the land of promise, his brother, Esau, whom he has severely wronged. *The Torah* delightfully remarks that "Esau expected to meet the old Jacob," but "it is Israel, not Jacob, whom Esau meets."[215]

---

[214] We refer here to Herbert L Prince in the Come and God class in his series of studies on the Joseph story.
[215] *The Torah: A Modern Commentary*, 325.

FOURTEEN
The Face of God
(Genesis 33:1-17)

Genesis 33:10   "Jacob said, "No, please; if I find favor with you, then accept my present from my hand; for truly to see your face is like seeing the face of God—since you have received me with such favor.

The time has come for Jacob and Esau to meet. Tension and anticipation permeated the atmosphere in chapter 32. Jacob was uneasy, even fearful, as he contemplated what Esau might do when they meet. He anticipates the worst. As for Esau, deceptive acts can rob a man of both birthright and blessing and produce extreme measures of retaliation: "I will kill my brother Jacob" (27:41). As Jacob nears his homeland, he takes steps to ready a gift in the hope that his brother may be placated (32:13-21). He sends messengers ahead to prepare for the meeting with the estranged brother from whose wrath he has fled (32:3-8). Their report back drives him to his knees in prayer (32:9-12). Then, surprisingly, the text takes an abrupt turn as Jacob wrestles with a mystery "man" all night until daybreak (32:22-32).

302

Jacob has been wrestling with "a man who was no man"! No small feat: "I have seen God face to face" (32:30). Jacob now limps (32:31). But the wrestling match has not changed the threatening situation as far as Jacob knows. Esau is still coming with four hundred men! Only reconciliation with his brother can make possible Jacob's return to his homeland. How will Jacob's encounter with God affect the situation—even Jacob? With the exception of the burial of their father, Isaac (35:28-29), we come to the last episode in the Jacob-Esau accounts, Jacob's

Final Preparation
(Genesis 33:1-3)

[1]Now Jacob looked up and saw Esau coming, and four hundred men with him. So he divided the children among Leah and Rachel and the two maids. [2]He put the maids with their children in front, then Leah with her children, and Rachel and Joseph last of all. [3]He himself went on ahead of them, bowing himself to the ground seven times, until he came near his brother.

The sudden resumption of the coming encounter between the brothers gives us no time to re-evaluate Jacob. The narrative is characterized by an underlying irony, perhaps even reservations. The first question, however, is, who now is our Jacob? This momentous moment is fraught with uncertainty as Jacob lifts up his eyes and looks and "behold" (*hinnēh*) Esau is approaching with his four hundred men. Jacob acts quickly. Without hesitation he divides his household into two groups, the children with their mothers:

> He put the maids with their children in front, then Leah with her children, and Rachel and Joseph last of all.

Jacob's attachments and intent are obvious to all as well as his fear of assault. The two maids and their children are placed in front, with Rachel and Joseph, the most cherished and the ones to be protected above all, put safely in the rear. What are their feelings? Robert Alter suggests, however, that the order is not for defense, but for display.[216] Defense may no longer make any sense.

More significant in contrast to his earlier ordering of family and property, Jacob now places himself "ahead of them," literally, "before their faces." The personal pronoun "he himself" placed before the verb accentuates a change of stance for Jacob. Gordon Wenham suggests that

---

[216] Alter, *Genesis*, 184.

the new Israel is "triumphing over the old fear-dominated Jacob."[217] The earlier Jacob had other people pass on before him (32:17, 21).

As Jacob proceeds to meet Esau he bows "himself to the ground seven times, until he came near his brother." His actions indicate in ancient culture a vassal's respect to his overlord as shown in the 14thcentury BC Egyptian Amarna letters. Earlier in the story, Isaac's blessing of Jacob was quite different:

> Let peoples serve you,
>> and nations bow down to you.
> Be lord over your brothers,
> and may your mother's sons bow down to you (27:29).

A reversal occurs, Jacob bows down before Esau the ancestor of the Edomites, not once, but seven times until he reaches his brother. Is Jacob seeking to counter the stolen blessing? Is he trying to undo that great act of deception by which he cheated Esau out of his blessing?

The lord who has now made himself a servant is ready for

The Meeting
(Genesis 33:4-11)

[4]But Esau ran to meet him, and embraced him, and fell on his neck and kissed him, and they wept. [5]When Esau looked up and

---

[217] Wenham, *Genesis 16-50,* 298.

saw the women and children, he said, "Who are these with you?" Jacob said, "The children whom God has graciously given your servant." [6]Then the maids drew near, they and their children, and bowed down; [7]Leah likewise and her children drew near and bowed down; and finally Joseph and Rachel drew near, and they bowed down. [8]Esau said, "What do you mean by all this company that I met?" Jacob answered, "To find favor with my lord." [9]But Esau said, "I have enough, my brother; keep what you have for yourself." [10]Jacob said, "No, please; if I find favor with you, then accept my present from my hand; for truly to see your face is like seeing the face of God—since you have received me with such favor. [11]Please accept my gift that is brought to you, because God has dealt graciously with me, and because I have everything I want." So he urged him, and he took it.

Esau's behavior, in contrast to Jacob's ceremonial manner, surprises Jacob: "Esau ran to meet him, and embraced him, and fell on his neck and kissed him." Although the embrace and the kiss were normal biblical greetings among relatives, who could have foreseen these actions on Esau's part with Jacob! Instead of a drawn-out affair over who did what and what difference it makes, we get an apparent reconciliation without a word being spoken. At first, no confession is given, no forgiveness asked, no remorse expressed. A modest restraint is at work in the silence that speaks of their profound awareness of each other.

Jacob limps and bows, Esau runs. Is it possible as Franz Delitzsch suggests that Esau's "brotherly affection, which was never extinct, is rekindled at the sight of Jacob"?[218] Esau, the wounded party, is the initiator. Terrence Fretheim notes that "this impressive list of welcoming activities, he 'ran. . . embraced. . . fell. . . kissed his brother,' is unparalleled in Genesis." [219] In that culture Esau's actions may well have expressed forgiveness. Regardless, the result of this first encounter is plainly and simply, "they wept." How deeply the twins must have felt their estrangement.

The narrator calls attention to how the brothers first see each other. Esau "looked up" at Jacob's family just as Jacob "looked up" at Esau earlier (v. 1). They "lift up their eyes" at one another is the Hebrew metaphor. Esau continues as the initiator; he asks who is it that is accompanying Jacob? Jacob answers: "The children whom God has graciously given your servant." One wonders why Jacob did not employ the more appropriate verb "blessed" for the gift of children instead of "graciously given." No doubt Jacob wants to say that the children God's

---

[218] Delitzsch, *Genesis,* II, 208,
[219] Fretheim, "The Book of Genesis," 572.

favor has given him are the result of a long and harsh history; the Hebrew verb for "graciously given" (*chnh*) includes forgiving grace while the verb for bless (*brk*) does not. Gordon Wenham suggests that Jacob wants to avoid any reference "to that unhappy day when he cheated Esau out of his blessing."[220]

For the first time, Jacob witnesses publicly to God's graciousness or undeserved favor concerning the growth of his family (33:5, 11). Jacob's "graciously given" (*chānan*) is the verb form corresponding to the noun for "grace" or "graciousness" (*chēn*) that appears seventeen times in Genesis, five of them here in chapters 32-33 (32:5; 33:5, 8, 10, 11). Jacob's use of this "grace" language is closely related to his earlier prayer in which he confessed to God that he was not worthy of "the steadfast love and all the faithfulness that you have shown to your servant" (32:10). Here in chapter 33, Jacob attests to the grace displayed previously in the lives of his wives, Leah and Rachel (29:31-30:24). In opening their wombs, God makes possible children that Jacob now acknowledges were gracious gifts of God.

---

[220] Wenham, *Genesis 16-50*, 299.

At Jacob's response to Esau, the maids and the two wives each with their own children draw near and bow down respectfully before Esau. The dialogue in verses 8-11 brings us to the core of story both stylistically and theologically. At the heart is Jacob's declaration to Esau in verse 10b: "for truly to see your face is like seeing the face of God—since you have received me with such favor." Jacob sees a parallel between the positions of Esau and God with his use of the "grace" terminology. "Grace" explicitly equates Jacob's relationship to his brother with his relationship to God for the first time in the story.

The dialogue begins as Esau turns his attention to the gift or tribute that Jacob had sent earlier (32:14-15). Esau asks, "What do you mean by all this company that I met?" The idiom behind Esau's use of the verb "mean" is "what is to you?" Jacob answers Esau with the language of grace, "To find favor (c*ḥēn*) with my lord," literally, "in the eyes of my lord." Earlier he had sent the same message when with his messengers instructing them to say to Esau, "To find favor in your sight" (32:5). Esau, however, refuses the gift: "I have enough, my brother; keep what you have for yourself." With this, Jacob recognizes that Esau has already accepted him.

Esau's use of "my brother" indicates that reconciliation has been accomplished even though Jacob continues to call Esau "my lord." Yet, as we have seen, the presence in the narrative of the "grace" words (32:5; 33:8, 10, 11) has put Jacob's relationship with Esau on a level with his relationship to God:

> Jacob said, "No, please; if I find favor with you, then accept my present from my hand; for truly to see your face is like seeing the face of God—since you have received me with such favor. [11]Please accept my gift that is brought to you, because God has dealt graciously with me, and because I have everything I want." So he urged him, and he took it.

Jacob changes his gift from one of appeasement to that of gratitude. With "accept my gift" (bir^{e}kātî) he moves into "blessing" language. Jacob's gift intended for Esau has turned out to be also a gift of gratitude to God: "because I have everything I want." Jacob is bearing witness to God's blessing at work in his life.

Jacob comes to an inspired awareness through seeing Esau's face: "truly to see your face is like seeing the face of God—since you have received me with such favor." The blessing Jacob has received has been so bountiful that it flows out through him to Esau: "God has dealt graciously with me." The Hebrew verb for "dealt graciously" is a sacrificial term, so some translate "my gift" in the next verse as "my offering." The text says that Jacob "urged" Esau with the subtext or underlying implication according to Gordon Wenham that "you must receive back the blessing I stole from you."[221] Esau gave in and accepted the *birᵉkātî*, the blessing/gift, ironically expressed. Jacob has attempted restitution, but as Esau is as wealthy as Jacob and more powerful, it is irrelevant in Esau's mind.

Verses 9-11 stress the parallel between the positions of Esau and God; Esau's behavior is coupled with God's behavior. Jacob's encounter with God and his meeting with Esau are viewed in single perspective; there is a sense in which the two meetings are *one* meeting. When Jacob asks Esau to accept his present, he is asking Esau to confirm the forgiveness implied in verse 4. The reason Jacob dares ask him to accept it is that now Esau is to him like God: "to see your face is like seeing the

---

[221] Wenham, *Genesis 16-50*, 299,

face of God." The Hebrew idiom to "see one's face" is to be in a right relationship with that person. J. P. Fokkelman concludes:

> Esau is the lord of the servant Jacob as God is. Esau is the wronged and critical authority which alone, by his mercy, can absolve Jacob's guilt and which can lend a new integrity to Jacob.[222]

By granting his mercy to Jacob, Esau confirms the renewal of Jacob on the Jabbok at Peniel. The contrast is deliberate. The two relationships, with God and brother, are now *one* relationship. Jacob wants to achieve the destiny assigned to him by God, but his deception of Esau rose up as a barrier. So Jacob depicts his deliverance as from "God-and-Esau in one" [223] as J. P. Fokkelman captures it. Jacob's two exclamations, "I have seen God face to face, and yet my life has been preserved" (32:30) and "truly to see your face is like seeing the face of God" are one in Jacob's experience—and in a spiritual sense, also ours in any reconciliation! Is it really true that all human reconciliation takes the presence and action of God?

The stage is now set for

---

[222] Fokkelman, *Narrative Art in Genesis,* 227
[223] Fokkelman, *Narrative Art in Genesis,* 226-227.

The Parting
(Genesis 33:12-17)

[12]Then Esau said, "Let us journey on our way, and I will go alongside you." [13]But Jacob said to him, "My lord knows that the children are frail and that the flocks and herds, which are nursing, are a care to me; and if they are overdriven for one day, all the flocks will die. [14]Let my lord pass on ahead of his servant, and I will lead on slowly, according to the pace of the cattle that are before me and according to the pace of the children, until I come to my lord in Seir." [15]So Esau said, "Let me leave with you some of the people who are with me." But he said, "Why should my lord be so kind to me?" [16]So Esau returned that day on his way to Seir. [17]But Jacob journeyed to Succoth, and built himself a house, and made booths for his cattle; therefore the place is called Succoth.

Esau's response to Jacob's gift of herds is an invitation to come with him to Seir, the homeland of the Edomites: "Let us journey on our way, and I will go alongside you." Esau wants to depart in good faith and offers Jacob his companionship by traveling together. But Jacob declines Esau's offer in a courteous manner: "Let my lord pass on ahead of his servant." His stated reasons are the frailty of his children and the fact that his flocks and herds are nursing. So Jacob must as he says, "lead on slowly, according to the pace of the cattle that are before me and according to the pace of the children, until I come to my lord in Seir."

There has been, however, no previous mention of such frailness. Is Jacob suspicious of Esau, mistrusting the one whom he has twice deceived? Is he returning to his old ways? The question bothers us. Peniel has marked a change. Esau certainly has changed but one is left to wonder how much Jacob's character has changed. His attitude toward his brother shows a certain ambivalence.

Esau even offers to send a protective escort with Jacob—"some of the people who are with me." But Jacob says, "Why should my lord be so kind to me?" Or, closer to the Hebrew: "Let me find favor in the eyes of my lord?" (NASB). Jacob's last spoken word to Esau is "my Lord." Jacob continues his deferential Lord/servant stance although Esau affirms him as "my brother" (v. 9). Esau's offer may be an attempt on his part to develop a more solid familial relationship with his brother. Jacob, however, appears to be saying in essence that our relationship ought not to result in the merging of our families. We are reconciled, but our families and our futures are to remain separate. As Jacob separated from Laban, he now separates from Esau. But no treaty is needed as with his duplicitous father-in-law. Jacob and Esau will not meet again until the passing of their father Isaac (35:29).

The reason for the parting of the ways, however, is more profound. Jacob is not just "Jacob," he is also "Israel"! He is on his way to Canaan, the land of the ancestral promise to Abraham, Isaac, and Jacob to possess his destined heritage. Jacob is ready to receive it. His entire life has been characterized by his determination to seize the promise and the blessing for himself. Jacob now sees the difference between receiving the inheritance as a gift and gaining the it through his own manipulative powers.[224] Esau of Edom, like Laban, leaves the stage of promise! As the narrator reports,

> Esau returned that day on his way to Seir. But Jacob journeyed to Succoth and built himself a house, and made booths for his cattle; therefore the place is called Succoth."

The long-time exile and traveler is finally settling down to a sedentary life. Jacob builds a house for himself and a shelter for his cattle. The wanderings of the patriarchs have come to an end in Canaan.

---

[224] Curtis, "Structure, Style and Context as a Key to Interpreting Jacob's Encounter at Peniel," 11.

In this "reconciliation classic," the paradigm of biblical reconciliation before us is now complete. Reconciliation is a three-dimensional spiritually profound process. Here it is Jacob-God-Esau. In the present moment of time the three are you and I with the God whom we know in Jesus Christ—our flesh and blood sisters and brothers, ourselves, and God. The transforming presence of God is indispensable to the formula. To experience true reconciliation God must do his work front and center in the hearts of all parties. In truth we are never more near the Holy heart of God than in reconciliation, for we are "at the cross"! Chapters 32-33 frame this picture of biblical reconciliation, "Jacob went on his way" (32:1)—"Jacob journeyed" (33:17).

As we read on, "Jacob came safely to . . . the land of Canaan" (v. 18), indicating that Jacob is now in his promised homeland. But how will the new Jacob conduct his life? Did Jacob's experience at Peniel obliterate the past and to what extent does it change his character? Or does the new Israel continue with some features of the old Jacob? No doubt, like most of us "sanctified" folk in our day, much of the time he will perform very well, and at other times, well that is another story! As

Gordon Wenham observes, "this seems the right place to end the story of Jacob, but as so often in Genesis, what promises to be the ultimate resolution proves to be the making of another crisis."[225]

A Thought

A question remains. Where does the story of Jacob intersect with our lives? As one example, we revisit the story of one woman whom we met in our first lesson in this series who found healing with Jacob at Peniel. We speak again of the British theologian, Frances M. Young (b. 1939), who in her *Brokenness and Blessing* uses the account of "Jacob at Peniel" as an inspirational source. An undercurrent in her book is her life with her first-born son, Arthur who failed to develop in his prenatal stage. She and her husband have been supporting him in their home for over forty years. Arthur requires total care as he has no self-help skills, no independent mobility, and no language.[226]

In her book, Frances Young sketches how the Genesis account was understood in the Church Fathers including Augustine (354-430)

---

[225] Wenham, *Genesis 16-50*, 304.
[226] Frances Young, "Suffering and the Holy Life," *Wesleyan Theological Journal,* Volume 43, Number 1 (Spring 2008), 7-21. See also Young *,Brokenness and Blessing,* 31.

and concluding with Gregory Nazianzen (329-389). The Fathers approached the biblical text with interpretive freedom. She sees Charles Wesley with his hymn "Wrestling Jacob" following in the patristic tradition as he gave evangelical meaning to the story. With his poetic lines in verse after verse Charles Wesley related the biblical text to his own soul and the story of its salvation. Like Jacob, Charles Wesley sees himself

> left alone to wrestle (v. 1), demanding to know who is the stranger with whom he struggles (vv. 2-4). Like Jacob, he knows himself a sinner (v. 2) and wrestles for release, wanting to know the name and nature of God in Christ. To see God face to face is to receive God's grace, to know that God is love (vv. 5-8). The soul limps on life's journey as a result (v 9), and yet is empowered, because it is dependent on God alone (vv. 9-10).[227]

The opening and closing verses of Charles Wesley's hymn are

> Come, O thou Traveller unknown,
>   Whom still I hold but cannot see!
> My company before is gone,
>   And I am left alone with thee;
> With thee all night I mean to stay,
> And wrestle till the break of day. . . /
>
> Lame as I am, I take the prey,
>   Hell, earth, and sin with ease

---

[227] Young, *Brokenness and Blessing,* 42. The numbers in parentheses are those of Wesley's verses.

> o'ercome;
> I leap for joy, pursue my way,
> And as a bounding hart fly home,
> Through all eternity to prove,
> The nature, and thy name, is LOVE.[228]

As Frances Young applies the biblical "Jacob at Peniel and Wesley's "Wresting Jacob" to her own life she bears a powerful witness for our time in human global culture:

> for some, including myself, wrestling with God has been a desperate plea for blessing, hanging in there like Jacob, and getting lamed in the process. The struggle centered on my severely disabled son, largely because he became the symbol of all the "gonewrongedness" that modernity has identified as a good reason for calling God into question. . . . Peace is hardly found when wrestling with God, and one can end up wounded and disabled; yet the wound of love is exactly what heals us. . . . The rediscovery that God is beyond us, yet reaches out in Christ to grasp our hands in the midst of the struggle, even wound us with his arrow of love, might enable us, both individually and as the body of Christ on earth, to live the way of love and true humility in following Jesus.[229]

Have we, have you, have I, ever been with Jacob at Peniel?

I have seen God face to face, and yet my life is preserved.

---

[228] Hildebrandt, Beckerlegge, and Dale, ed., *A Collection of Hymns for the use of the People called Methodists*, 250, 252.

[229] Young, *Brokenness and Blessing: Towards a Biblical Spirituality,* 49-50, 121-122.

Epilogue: Jacob in Canaan
(Genesis 33:18—50:14)

Genesis 35:11-12:   "I am God Almighty: be fruitful and multiply; a nation and a company of nations shall come from you, and kings shall spring from you. The land I gave to Abraham and Isaac I will give to you, and I will give the land to your offspring after you."

Jacob is home; he has returned to the land promised to Abraham, Isaac, and now to him. He is now 147 (47:28) and will live many more years and be gathered to his ancestors. How does he fare after his experience at Peniel and his reconciliation with his brother Esau? What about the continuing effect of his change of character in the realities of living on in Canaan? To what extent has Jacob really changed? How much of the old Jacob still resides in the new Israel? As the Genesis narrative proceeds, we read of the Israelite ancestor both by his old name, Jacob, and by his new name, Israel. We proceed to wrap up our story of Jacob, and set the stage for the appearance of Israel as a people and a nation. We begin as

Jacob Arrives in Canaan

(Genesis 33:18-20)[230]

As both a conclusion to chapters 32-33 and a prelude to chapter 34, these verses open with the announcement that "Jacob came safely to the city of Shechem, which is in the land of Canaan." "Schechem" was the "son of Hamor the Hivete, the prince of the region" (34:2). "Safely," literally "in peace (*shālēm*)," recalls Jacob's vow at Bethel where a condition of his trust in God's promise was "that I come again to my father's house in peace." Jacob's goal has been reached with his return to Canaan from Paddan-aram; the promises to the patriarchs are coming to fulfillment.[231] Jacob is no longer associated with the land of Laban.

At peace, Jacob "camped before the city" and proceeds to buy "the plot of land on which he had pitched his tent" from " the sons of Hamor, Shechem's father." On this plot "he erected an altar and called it El-Elohe-Israel," that is, "God, the God of Israel." Jacob, a true patriarch at worship, is following the practice of his grandfather, Abraham (12:7, 8; 13:18; 22:9), and his father, Isaac (26:25).

---

[230] In the Epilogue we will reproduce the biblical text only as necessary..
[231] Gen. 28:2, 5-6, 15; 30:25; 31:3, 13, 18; 32:9.

But now, a crisis:

Jacob and Sons at Shechem
(Genesis 34:1-31)

Jacob "held his peace." About what and why? Shechem had raped Dinah--"he seized her and lay with her by force." This daughter of Jacob, unwisely at best, "went out to visit the women of the region"—her curiosity was fraught with danger as an immigrant's daughter rather than a daughter of the land. After the rape, Schechem, falls sincerely in love with her and wants her for his wife: "he loved the girl and spoke tenderly to her." Did she respond in kind—she did go to live in Shechem's house (v. 26)?

Jacob, cautious however, keeps in check whatever emotions he has--Dinah was Leah's daughter! He is silent until his sons return from the field, his response conspicuous by its absence--he fails both to act and to react. The narrator subtly introduced an opposition between Jacob and his sons that by degrees covertly will occupy the dramatic center of the story.[232]

When the sons hear of the rape they are outraged "because

---

[232] Sternberg, *Poetics*, 448.

[Shechem] has defiled their sister Dinah," Deceitfully, they allow the marriage arrangements proposed by Hamor the father of Shechem to proceed (vv. 13-17). The soft-spoken Hamor is negotiating from a strong position unfairly obtained--Dinah has been violated and is being held in their home (v.26). Shechem's father, realizing that "the heart of my son Shechem longs for your daughter," likes the prospect of becoming "one people" with Jacob and his sons. Hamor appears enticed by economic advantage: "Will not their livestock, their property, and all their animals be ours? Only let us agree with them, and they will live among us." They conceal their thinking from Jacob and his sons.

Hamor and Shechem agree to the demand by Jacob's sons that "you will become as we are and every male among you be circumcised." Since Shechem, "the most honored of all his family," is "delighted with Jacob's daughter," he is eager to comply without delay. Following the circumcision we read that "while they were still in pain, two of the sons of Jacob, Simeon and Levi, Dinah's brothers [by Leah], take their swords and come against the city unawares, and kill all the males."

After killing Hamor and his son Shechem, Simeon and Levi took Dinah from Shechem's house and went away. The other sons of Jacob, "because their sister had been defiled," plunder all their wealth and "captured and made their prey all their little ones and their wives, all that was in the houses."

For the first time Jacob finally speaks saying to Simeon and Levi:

> "you have brought trouble on me by making me odious to the inhabitants of the land, the Canaanites and the Perizites; my numbers are few, and if they gather themselves together against me and attack me, I shall be destroyed, both I and my household."

Jacob shows himself as the story's least sympathetic character. His concern is selfish. He does not protest against the moral offenses of Dinah's two brothers, neither their abuse of the rite of circumcision nor even the massacre. Simeon and Levi with some justification respond to their father, "Should our sister be treated like a whore?" Their passion appears to flow from "our sister" as opposed to the "daughter of Jacob"! So now who is Jacob?

For Walter Brueggemann, Jacob is the "seasoned voice of maturity." He has lived a long time, and has never drawn back from the conflicts he has encountered. Jacob remains in the background as he recognizes that he occupies a marginal position in the city of Shechem. His response to his sons' actions is that of a "clear-headed pragmatism." They have brought "trouble," or even "ruin," upon him with the peoples near whom he lives.[233] Is the rift deepening between Jacob and his sons by Leah and her maid Zilpah?

Gordon Wenham sees Jacob's silence as parental irresponsibility and Jacob as too willing to accept intermarriage with the Shechemites. Jacob is unconcerned over the killing and plundering by his sons until he sees their actions as threatening his ruin at the hands of their neighbors. He appears to care only for his own skin. Simeon and Levi respond to their father in crude terms, "Should our sister be treated like a whore?" Robert Alter concludes that although Jacob will soon return to Bethel and reconfirm the covenant," from this point on he "will lose much of his paternal power and will be seen repeatedly at the mercy of his sons, more the master of self-dramatizing sorrow than of his own family."[234]

---

[233] Brueggemann, *Genesis*, 278.
[234] Alter, *Genesis,* 194.

With relief we see the story of Jacob taking a turn for the better as

Jacob Returns to Bethel
(Genesis 35:1-15)

One could wrap up the story of Jacob's journey with God with this account. The entire narrative can accurately be viewed as "From Bethel to Bethel," that is, "From the House of God to the House of God." Although we did round off the story with Jacob's arrival at the border of Canaan fully reconciled to his brother Esau, this is not to minimize Jacob's return to Bethel. It deserves attention.

Jacob first met God in a personal sense at Bethel (28:10-22) where he vowed to return to his homeland: I will "come again to my father's house in peace" (28:21). Now that he has returned to Canaan, the God he met at Bethel appears to him and confirms the divine promises. With the return to Bethel the narrator moves to conclude the story of Jacob's life (25:19--35:29) before moving into the Joseph story (chs. 37-50). Jacob at Bethel again (vv. 9-15) puts a capstone on Jacob's life.

Jacob first came to Bethel as he ran from Esau's wrath. But just as Jacob has rid himself of Laban in order to return home, Esau appears with what is apparently a mercenary army. This time "the angels of God met him" and Jacob identified the place as "God's camp" (32:1-2). Soon he encounters the mysterious man who "wrestled with him until daybreak" (32:24). Now, with the family's status at risk with their Canaanite neighbors following several murders by his sons and the plundering of the city of Shechem, God again speaks to Jacob: "Arise, go up to Bethel and settle there." Arriving at Bethel, Jacob is told to "make an altar there to the God who appeared to you when you fled from [the face of] your brother Esau."

With the divine command to build an altar Jacob's relationship with God as the third patriarch is renewed. Patriarchal altar building in previous cases was either a spontaneous act or the reflection of responsive action. [235] Here God says, "do it!" God has enabled Jacob to "go back home again"! Jacob heeds the divine call to go to Bethel (vv.

---

[235] Genesis 12:7, 8; 13:18; 22:9; 26:5; 33:20.

1-8); the promise is reaffirmed (vv. 9-12); and Jacob worships at Bethel (vv.13-15).

At God's command to return to Bethel, Jacob's first response to is to prepare for the journey to Bethel as a religious pilgrimage. Jacob instructs his household to "put away the foreign gods that are among you and purify yourselves, and change your clothes." Included may be the household gods Rachel stole from her father as well as cultic figures fashioned as gods and goddesses brought by other members of the traveling clan. To experience God is to experience the holy. To bring foreign gods with him into Canaan is to undercut the centrality of the God who is to be honored at Bethel with the building of an altar . Jacob acknowledges that "the God who answered me in the day of my distress and has been with me wherever I have gone." He senses that these gods are irreconcilable with his post-Peniel life; religious maturation becomes evident as they depart for Bethel.

As they journey on toward Bethel, the aura of the holy with Jacob is such that "a terror from God fell upon the cities all around them, so that no one pursued them." Instead of Jacob being fearful of

Laban (31:31), of Esau (32:8), or of his Canaanite neighbors (35:30), it is Jacob and his party that is feared due to the mysterious "terror from God." Jacob's party reaches Bethel, "and there he built an altar and called the place El-bethel, because it was there that God had revealed himself to him when he fled from his brother." Jacob intensifies the name Bethel into 'El of the house of El, or "God of the house of God." In a new sense, Jacob perceives Bethel as a place of encounter with God. This time his vow has no conditions: "If God will be with me, and will keep me in this way that I go. . . . then the Lord shall be my God" (28:21-22).

A new name without conditions now fits Jacob. As God appears to Jacob this second time at Bethel and blesses him, his new identity, his new name, Israel, is reaffirmed: "Your name is Jacob; no longer shall you be called Jacob, but Israel shall be your name." From here on Genesis, Jacob will often be "called Israel"[236] What God shares with Jacob is in terms of blessing: "God appeared to Jacob . . . and he blessed him." Jacob will look back on this revelation at the end of his life (48:3-

---

[236] 43:6, 8, 11; 45:21: 46:1, 5, 28, 29; 48:8, 13, 14, 20, 21.

4), for it sums up all of the long-range promises God made to him. The promises now are pronounced, not on the old Jacob but upon *Israel*:

> So he was called Israel. "I am God Almighty: be fruitful and multiply; a nation and a company of nations shall come from you, and kings shall spring from you. The land that I gave to Abraham and Isaac I will give to you, and I will give the land to your offspring after you."

Jacob's new name signifies his future. Reflecting on the original creation, he is now told to "be fruitful and multiply"—the nation that will come from him is a "new creation"! Indeed, "kings shall spring from you," a promise made earlier also to Abraham (17:6).

In response to the promise, Jacob, for the second time with even more reason, sets up "a pillar in the place where he had spoken with him, a pillar of stone; and he poured out a drink offering on it, and poured oil on it." In memory of the earlier momentous event, he "called the place where God had spoken with him Bethel." Jacob, now Israel, has a future!

Leaving Jacob's return to Bethel, the narrator of Genesis includes some diverse materials from the corporate memory that touch the theme of land. We come first to a brief account concerning

Rachel and Benjamin
(Genesis 35:16-20)

Jacob's life descends from a high to a new low as he journeys on from Bethel toward Eprath, that is, Bethlehem. Sadly, and to Jacob's sorrow, Rachel dies in the process of giving birth. Her earlier wish for another son (30:24) entails her death. As "her soul was departing," Rachel named her second son "Ben-oni" meaning "son of my misfortunate." But Jacob renamed him "Benjamin," which may well be "son of good fortunate." As the child of Jacob's most loved wife, Benjamin differs from his brothers in two respects: he is the only child of Jacob's born in Canaan and he is the only child named by his father instead of his mother.

Jacob sets up "a pillar at her grave; it is the pillar of Rachel's tomb," a memorial in honor of his wife (28:18; 35:14; 35:20). Jacob now moves on with a heart, no doubt, deeply saddened with grief.

Before Jacob's brief appearances in the Joseph story that begin in 37:1, we take a quick look at the

Intervening Narrative
(Genesis 35:21—36:43)

Israel, as Jacob is here named, journeys on. Jacob continues to bear both names; Israel is still Jacob. Grace does not cancel out nature. It is not only the Jacob after Peniel that represents Israel, but as Kevin Walton expresses it, "it is precisely in that paradox of grace working with (and against) flawed human nature and striving that Jacob represents Israel."[237]

On his journey, Israel stops and pitches "his tent beyond the tower of Eder," a community near Jerusalem. While in that land, Jacob's eldest son, Reuben, enters the tent of Rachel's maid, Bilhah, and proceeds to "lay" with her. Bilhah is Jacob's concubine and the mother of two of Reuben's younger brothers, Dan and Naphtali. "Israel heard of it" and apparently says nothing.. The narrator does not record any criticism of Reuben's action until Jacob's later words of blessing over Reuben: "you shall no longer excel, because you went up unto your father's bed; then you defiled it" (49:4). Reuben's action appears primarily to be a political act in which he desires to assume the role of family leader now that Rachel has passed away and his father is

---

[237] K. Walton, *Thou Traveller Unknown*, 215.

immersed in grief. The narrator's use of Jacob's new name, Israel, is obviously ironic; Israel's silence does him no credit.

A listing of the twelve sons of Jacob follows the brief note on the behavior of Reuben and Bilhah:

> The sons of Leah: Reuben (Jacob's firstborn), Simeon, Levi, Judah, Issachar, and Zebulun. The sons of Rachel: Joseph and Benjamin. The sons of Bilhah, Rachel's maid: Dan and Naphtali. [26]The sons of Zilpah, Leah's maid: Gad and Asher.

The narrator identifies the sons according to their mothers as he reports the transition in leadership from Jacob to his sons taking place in the progression of the narrative.

The Jacob story as such concludes with a note about Isaac's death. Isaac. Isaac is said to be 180 years old when he died, meaning that he lived eighty years after he thought he would soon die (27:2, 4). His two sons, Jacob and Esau, lay him to his final rest (35:27-29).

A long list of "the descendants of Esau" (36:1-43) follows in the narrative. This list is introduced by the familiar Hebrew $tôl^e dôt$ formula that characterizes the structure of Genesis leading into what follows in the text, whether narrative, genealogy, or a combination of both. Here it is genealogy as the story turns briefly to Esau. Jacob, who now resides

333

in Canaan, appears only as Esau is described as living "some distance from his brother Jacob" (36:6), now in Edom. Esau had prospered materially a much as Jacob and was as well a "blessed" man.

Following the listing of Esau's family with chapter 37 the Hebrew *tôlᵉdôt* formula appears the tenth and last time in Genesis as the Jacob story continues with

The Family of Jacob: Joseph
(Genesis 37:1—47:31)

As "Jacob settled in the land where his father had lived as an alien, the land of Canaan," we read: "This is the story of the family of Jacob" (37:1-2). Since Jacob does not die until the end of the Joseph story (49:33), Joseph's story unfolds within the larger story of Jacob's family. Joseph is set apart from his older brothers as the son of Rachel, Jacob's first love.

We are told that "Israel loved Joseph more than any other of his children" and made Joseph a handsome "long robe with sleeves" (37:3). When his brothers saw it "they hated

him and could not speak peaceably to him" (37:4). Causing division in the family appears to be a habit with this father who is still Jacob. When

334

Joseph tells his brothers and father of his dreams that imply that they will all bow down to him, his brothers "hated him even more" (37:5, 8). But Jacob rebukes Joseph, but while "his brothers were jealous of him," his father "kept the matter in mind" (37:11). The old patriarch ponders this variation of the younger/older brother theme with spiritual sensitivity. Jacob's character as *tam* (25:27) prevails, a man of sensitive values that are not always apparent.

The continuing story has Joseph sold to the Midianites and then to the Egyptian official, Potipher. Joseph had been sent by "Israel" to check on the welfare of his brothers who were pasturing their father's flock near Shechem (37:12-36). The brothers then take Joseph's robe, dip it in goat's blood, and give it to their father. Seeing it, Jacob assumes that Joseph had been torn to pieces and "tore his garments, and put sackcloth on his loins, and mourned his son for many days" (37:34). His grief is such that he refuses to be comforted, saying "I shall go down to Sheol to my son, mourning" (37:35). Jacob knows how to love deeply, but cannot refrain from expressing it unwisely. Dysfunction continues in this family with Jacob as its primary instigator.

Jacob's son Reuben attempts meanwhile to rescue Joseph from his brothers' evil designs. To return Joseph to Jacob could bring him back into Jacob's good graces after questioning his father's leadership's by his affair with Bilhah, his father's concubine (35:22 More likely, however, Reuben is exercising his responsibility as the oldest son as he risks the disfavor of his brothers in his scheme.

As the Joseph story progresses, there is no mention of Jacob until after Joseph rose to power in Egypt and the Egyptian famine severely affects Jacob and his family. Jacob, still functioning as the head of the clan, hears that there is grain in Egypt and sends Joseph's brothers to buy grain in Egypt. He keeps Benjamin home with him "for he feared that harm might come to him" (42:4). Once they are in Egypt, Joseph is aware that the men before him are his brothers. When they are about to return home, Joseph demands that his brothers bring Benjamin to Egypt and keeps Simeon in prison as a guarantee.

On returning home, Joseph's brothers report Joseph's demand that Benjamin be brought to Joseph. Jacob, of course, objects strenuously: "I am the one bereaved of children: Joseph is no more, and now you will take Benjamin. All this has happened to me!" (43:36). But as the famine increased in severity and their grain ran out, Jacob finally consented that they take Benjamin and again buy grain. As they do, he calls Benjamin "your brother" (43:13) stressing his sons' responsibility for their half-brother with the wail, "As for me, if I am bereaved of my children, I am bereaved" (43:14). Jacob appears to be overly preoccupied with grief since his loss of Joseph.

When the brothers return to Egypt with Benjamin, they are taken to Joseph's house and to their amazement, they are seated at his table according to their ages. They are fed from Joseph's table with Benjamin being given five times as much as any of the others. They are then sent home with Joseph's silver cup in Benjamin's sack, but are arrested on the way and brought back. The one, Joseph says, who is found with the cup, will be his slave.

When the cup is found in Benjamin's sack, Judah, confesses the brothers' guilt concerning the brother before them. He appeals to Joseph pleading the effect on their father: "when he sees the boy is not with us, he will die; and your servants will bring down the gray hairs of your servant our father to his grave" (44:31). Judah offers to be Joseph's slave instead of Benjamin. At that point, Joseph is no longer in control of his emotions. Sending his servants away, he weeps loudly, and reveals his identity to his brothers, allaying their fears with a word on divine providence, "God sent me before you to preserve life" (45:5).

Joseph's brothers then return to Canaan with his instructions to bring their father to Egypt. Joseph sends them with Pharaoh's blessing and with good things from Egypt made possible by Pharaoh. On hearing that Joseph is alive and a "ruler over all the land of Egypt" (45:26), Jacob is stunned with unbelief. As Israel, he exclaims, "Enough! My son Joseph is still alive. I must go and see him before I die" (45:28).

So "Israel set out on his journey with all that he had" (46:1). When he came to Beer-sheba where God had appeared to Isaac (26:23-25), he "offered sacrifices to the God of his father Isaac" (46:1). There, in visions out of the darkness, God speaks to him calling out, "Jacob, Jacob." Jacob responds with "Here I am (hinēnî)" (46:2), and God repeats the promise,

> I am God, the God of your father; do not be afraid to go down to
> Egypt, for I will make of you a great nation there. I myself will

338

go down with you to Egypt, and I will also bring you up again; and Joseph's own hand shall close your eyes" (46:3-4).

God speaks to Jacob at night as at Peniel (32:22, 24) in a period of darkness like he did to Abraham (15:5ff.), repeating Jacob's name as he did Abraham's name at Moriah (22:11). The linguistic tie to the patriarchal era reinforces the continuity of the family's tradition in relation to God and his purposes. The passage of time has not dimmed the divine voice (35:9). Jacob acknowledges God in these "visions of the night" (46:2) and God assuages Jacob's fear of Egypt. God assures him of his continuing presence with him, and confirms his destiny as the father of the people of God with the promise of a return to Canaan as Joseph.

Jacob "and the sons of Israel" now set out for Egypt with the entire family and "all the livestock and goods they had acquired in the land of Canaan" (46:5-7). The narrative lists "the names of the Israelites, Jacob and his offspring who came to Egypt," sixty-six persons in all (46:8-27). They settle by Pharaoh's permission in Goshen where Joseph comes by chariot to meet his father. They fall on each other's necks and weep "a good while." "Israel" then exclaims to his long-lost son, "I can die now, having seen for myself that you are alive" (46:9-10).

Joseph brings his father to Pharaoh who asks Jacob how old he is. Jacob's answer speaks volumes as to who he believes himself to be: "The years of my earthly journey are one hundred thirty; few and hard have been the years of my life. They do not compare with the years of the life of my ancestors during their long sojourn" (47:9). Then Jacob blesses Pharaoh and settles with his sons in Goshen and lives seventeen more years (47:27-28).

As Jacob's death draws near, he calls for Joseph and asks for his promise that they not bury him in Egypt, but that when he lies down with his ancestors Joseph will "carry me out of Egypt and bury me in their burial place" (47:29-31). Again, both in Canaan and Egypt, Jacob *is* Israel. He knows that he is a child of the call and promise of God to Abraham and Isaac, confirmed dramatically to him as a "Jacob." Jacob is determined to be true to it and maintain his identity, even in death and burial. Jacob, a son of providence and the father of a nation to be born, will continue to carry out his destiny. His final duties as a patriarch begin as

Jacob Blesses Joseph's Sons
(Genesis 48:1-22)

Typically, when a patriarch approaches death he summons his male relatives and blesses them. In Jacob's dying words to his sons (48:1—49:32), the narrator sums up the theme of Genesis, points to the fulfillment of the promises to Abraham and Isaac, and repeats the promise that one day the land of Canaan will be theirs too as promised.

The theme of blessing with which the family of Abraham began reoccurs (12:1-3). Jacob is ill, and Joseph brings his two sons, Manasseh and Ephraim to his father's bedside. The condition of Jacob appears serious. But he rallies on Joseph's arrival and proceeds to repeat the promises of God given to him earlier at Luz (35:10-12) about fertility, the multiplication of the family, and that his seed will be an assembly of nations, with the further promise of land (48:3-4). Jacob then shifts to the future:

Therefore your two sons, who were born to you in the land of
Egypt before I came to you in Egypt, are now mine; Ephraim and
Manasseh shall be mine, just as Reuben and Simeon are.

Jacob elevates Joseph's two children from grandsons to sons,
now equal to Jacob's two oldest sons, Reuben and Simeon. Ephraim and
Manasseh can now also call Jacob "father." These two only, not
subsequent children born to Joseph, are co-inheritors with their uncles!
They will possess two tribal allotments. Is Jacob's gesture gratitude for
what Joseph has done on behalf of the family, or another instance of
favoritism? As the formal process of blessing proceeds, Joseph presents
Ephraim and Manasseh to his father: "They are my sons, whom God has
given me here." Jacob, embraces them affectionately saying to Joseph,
"I did not expect to see your face; and here God has let me see your
children also." After taking his children from Jacob's knees, Joseph,
with great affection and respect for his father, "bowed himself with his
face to the earth."

In order for Jacob to bless his sons, Joseph places his sons so his
father can bless his oldest, Manasseh, with his right hand, and Ephraim
with his less important left hand. Jacob's eyes were dim with age. But

Jacob, crossing his hands, "stretched out his right hand and laid it on the head of Ephraim, who was the younger, and his left hand on the head of Manasseh, crossing his hands, for Manasseh was the firstborn," and proceeds to bless Joseph's sons. Jacob's blessing covers the three generations of the patriarchs (48:15-16) and concludes with the prayer that God will "bless the boys; and in them let my name be perpetuated, and the name of my ancestors Abraham and Isaac; and let them grow into a multitude on the earth."

Joseph assumes that his father's poor eyesight has made a mistake. A blessing once given is irrevocable; he attempts to remove his father's right hand from Ephraim's head to that of Manasseh. But Jacob "refused, and said, 'I know, my son, I know; he also shall become a people, and he also shall be great. Nevertheless his younger brother shall be greater than he, and his offspring shall become a multitude of nations.'" Jacob ignores the law of primogeniture. His s denial of Joseph's request reflects his calm assurance that he knows exactly what he is doing. Jacob remains the patriarch, Israel, whose intuitive decision shapes the future. Being denied the blessing, Manasseh joins the line of firstborn in Genesis who are passed over.

What occurs are the inexplicable ways of God with Jacob, the mystery of providence. The motif of the unseen behind the scene does not end here but persists to the very end of the book of Genesis. The patriarch's attention now turns to the rest of his offspring as

Jacob Blesses His Sons
(Genesis 49:1-28)

Jacob is to fulfill his role as Israel! He summons the rest of his sons for the expected patriarchal deathbed farewell blessing:

> "Gather around, that I may tell you what will happen to you in days to come.
> Assemble and hear, O sons of Jacob;
> listen to Israel your father."

In parallel structure like in Proverbs, Israel's blessing of his sons looks to the future of the tribes as he employs the prophetic "in days to come." (Isa 2:2) or "latter days," In the many lines of the blessing (49:3-27) we sense the poetic power and beauty of Jacob's final blessings. Each individual blessing retains the individuality of the sons as the blessings recall incidents in their lives.

An appropriate summary brings the individual poetic blessings to a close by the narrator naming for the first time in the Bible "the twelve tribes of Israel":

> All these are the twelve tribes of Israel, and this is what their father said to them when he blessed them, blessing each one of them with a suitable blessing.

Jacob's dying words to his sons have summed up the theme of Genesis pointing to the fulfillment of the promises made to Abraham and Isaac about descendants and protection, and repeating the hope that one day Canaan will be theirs, too, as the Lord has promised. Jacob/Israel's blessing names each of the twelve sons and makes prophetic observations about each of them.

The tribal blessings are arranged roughly in the order of each of the son's births beginning with Leah's sons, Reuben first and ending with Rachel's sons, Joseph and Benjamin. Some tribes rise while others decline. Of Reuben it is predicted that "you shall no longer excel, . . . you went up onto my couch" (49:4) and Joseph is described as "a fruitful bough by a spring his branches run over the wall" (49:22). The overall word for the future, however, is positive because God is at work among them, saving and blessing.

We note especially the blessing pronounced on Judah, Leah's fourth son, which reads in part:

> The scepter shall not depart from Judah,
>> nor the ruler's staff from between his feet,
> until tribute comes to him;
>> and the obedience of the peoples is his (49:10).

The long-expected Messiah is to come from the line of Judah that (Matt. 1:2; Luke 3:30). The "new Israel" will come from the loins of the "old Israel," Jacob! The dreams of the very human Jacob about the promise to "Abraham, Isaac, and Jacob," now as the divinely touched Israel of Bethel and Peniel, will be fulfilled far beyond Jacob's wildest imagination.

The seal is now put on the narrative of the patriarch's life with

Jacob's Death and Burial
(Genesis 49:29—50:14)

In a final wish Jacob instructs his sons to bury him with his ancestors significantly in "the land of Canaan." Israel must settle in no other country than the "land of Canaan," the land promised long before to Abraham, Isaac, and Jacob. The narrator does not say merely that Jacob died, but that he "breathed his last, and was gathered to his people." He is rejoining those who have gone on before. The precise place of burial is "the cave in the field at Machpelah, near Mamre," which Abraham had bought from Ephron the Hiitte where Abraham, Sarah, Isaac, Rebekah, and Leah are already buried (49:29-53).

Joseph's response to his father's death is swift, he "threw himself on his father's face and wept over him and kissed him." This expression of intense feeling in his dramatic farewell to his father Jacob sets the stage for a new era. Jacob had received an earlier word from God that "Joseph's own hand shall close your eyes" (46:4). As one closest to the departed, this honor may have been reserved for Joseph who is clearly in charge of funeral arrangements (50:1). According to Egyptian practice, Joseph has his father embalmed by his physicians, a process that took forty days: "So the physicians embalmed Israel."

The text reports only Joseph's response to Jacob's death, not that the other brothers did not experience grief on Jacob's passing. The Egyptians mourn for Jacob in a grand way, for seventy days (vv. 3, 10-

11). Joseph gets permission from Pharaoh to bury his father in the land of Canaan in the tomb he had "hewn out" for himself. For Joseph, Jacob's insistence on being buried in Canaan is an affirmation of where Israel really belongs (50:2-7).

Joseph takes with him to the land of Canaan his household, his brothers, and his father's household. They leave their children and herds in the land of Goshen. With Joseph also were the elders of Pharaoh's household and "all the elders of the land of Egypt, . . . a very great company." On their way, at the threshing floor of Atad, they observe seven days of sorrowful lamentation: "This is a grievous mourning on the part of the Egyptians" said the Canaanite inhabitants of the land. The accompaniment by Egyptian dignitaries and a military escort are a reflection of the importance of Joseph and the dignity accorded to Jacob.

After Joseph and his brothers buried their father "in the cave of the field at Machpelah, the field near Mamre," Joseph with his brothers and all who had gone up with them to bury Jacob returned to Egypt,. The family of Abraham has truly gained in stature. God had promised to make Abraham's name great and to bless him. Now all of Egypt stops and pays attention with great pomp and circumstance at the passing of his grandson, the patriarch Jacob, now properly Israel (50:8-14): The destiny, almost hidden in Jacob's first description as a *tam* man has been fully brought to the surface: "Jacob was a quiet (*tam*) man" (25:27).

We too, like Joseph and his brothers, lay this patriarch to rest with gratefulness to the Genesis narrator who has given us a fascinating human (Jacob) and profoundly spiritual (Israel) story.

Bethel . . . Peniel . . . Bethel

Bibliography

Primary Sources

Alter, Robert. *The Art of Biblical Narrative.* New York: Basic Books, Inc.,
     Publishers, 1981.

_____. *Genesis: Translation and Commentary.* New York: W. W. Norton and Company,
     1996.

Brueggemann, Walter. *Genesis,* Interpretation: A Bible Commentary for Teaching and
     Preaching. Atlanta: John Knox Press, 1982.

Calvin, John. *The First Book of Moses Called Genesis,* Second volume, trans. John
     King. Grand Rapids: Wm. B. Eerdmans Publishing Company, 1948 [1847].

Delitzsch, Franz. *A New Commentary on Genesis,* Volume II, trans. Sophia Taylor. Minneapolis:
     Klock & Klock Christian Publishers (T. & T. Clark), 1888.

Fishbane, Michael. *Text and Texture: Close Readings of Selected Biblical Texts.* New York:
     Schocken Books, 1979.

Fokkelman, J. P. *Narrative Art in Genesis: Specimens of Stylistic and Structural Analysis.*
     Eugene, Oregon: Wipf & Stock Publishers, 2nd ed., 1991.

Fretheim, Terrence E. "The Book of Genesis," *The New Interpreter's Bible,* Volume I.
     Nashville: Abingdon Press, 1994.

Hildebrandt, Franz, Oliver A. Beckerlegge, and James Dale, ed. *A Collection of Hymns for the*
     use of the People called Methodists, Volume 7, *The Works of John Wesley.* Nashville: Abingdon Press, 1983.

Mann, Thomas W. *The Book of the Torah: The Narrative Integrity of the Pentateuch.* Atlanta:

John Knox Press, 1988.

Poteet, Margaret Ellis., *Literary Unity in the Patriarchal Narratives,* A Dissertation Submitted to
> the Graduate Faculty of the University of Oklahoma in partial fulfillment of the requirements for the degree of Doctor of Philosophy, Norman, Oklahoma, 1990.

Speiser, E. A. *Genesis,* The Anchor Bible. Garden City, New York: Doubleday & Company,
> Inc., 1964.

Sternberg, Meir. *The Poetics of Biblical Narrative: Ideological Literature and the Drama of*
> *Reading.* Bloomington: Indiana University Press, 1985.

The Torah: A Modern Commentary. New York: Union of American Hebrew Congregations,
> 1974.

von Rad, Gerhard. *Genesis: A Commentary.* The Old Testament Library. TranJohn H. Mark,
> Philadelphia: The Westminster press, 1961.

Walton, John H. *Genesis*: The New Application Commentary. Grand Rapids: Zondervan, 2001.

Walton, Kevin. *Thou Traveller Unknown: The Presence and Absence of God in the Jacob*
> *Narrative.* Waynesboro, Georgia: Paternoster, 2003.

Wenham, Gordon J., *Genesis 16-50,* Volume 2, Word Biblical Commentary. Dallas, Texas:
> Word Books, Publisher, 1994.

Westermann, Claus. *Genesis 12-36: A Commentary.* Minneapolis: Augsburg Publishing House, 1985.

Other Sources Cited

Barth, Karl. *Dogmatics in Outline,* trans. G. T. Thompson. New York: Harper & Brothers,
> 1959.

Bernard of Clairvaux, *"Sermon LXXXIV on the Song of Songs, 2;" Late Medieval Mysticism,* The
> Library of Christian Classics, Volume XIII, ed. Ray C. Petry. Philadelphia: The Westminster Press), 74-75.

Bonhoeffer, Dietrich. *Letters and Papers from Prison,* Dietrich Bonhoeffer Works, Volume 8,
> ed. John W. de Gruchy, trans, Isabel Best, Lisa Dahill, Reinhard Kraus, and Nancy Luiens. Minneapolis: Fortress Press, 2010).

Curtis, Edward. "Structure, Style and Context as a Key to Interpreting Jacob's Encounter at
> Peniel." Unpublished paper read at the 1983 meeting of the Evangelical Theological Society.

Erickson, Millard. *Christian Theology.* Volume 3, Grand Rapids: Baker Book House, 1983.

A. Hunt, Irmgard A. *On Hitler's Mountain: Overcoming the Legacy of a Nazi Childhood.* New
> York: HarperCollins Publishers, 2005.

Merton, Thomas. *The Sign of Jonas.* New York: Harcourt Brace Jovanovich, 1953.

Otto, Rudolf. *The Idea of the Holy,* trans. John W. Harvey. New York: Oxford University Press,
> 1923.

Robinson, Bud (Reuben). *Chickens Come Home to Roost.* Beacon Hill Press, 1958.

Stewart, James S. *Walking With God,* ed. Gordon Grant. Edinburgh: Saint Andrew Press, 1956.
> *Union-Tribune San Diego.* August 26-29, 2012.

Von Rad, Gerard. *Biblical Interpretations in Preaching,* trans. John E. Steely. Nashville:
> Abingdon, 1977 (German 1973, *Predigt-Meditationen*).

Young, Frances M. *Brokenness and Blessing: Towards a Biblical Spirituality.* Grand Rapids:
    Baker Academic, 2007.
Westermann, Claus. *Blessing in the Bible and the Life of the Church,* trans. Keith
    Grimm. Philadelphia: Fortress Press, 1978 (German 1968).
Wright, N. T. Wright. *Simply Jesus: A New Vision of Who He Was, What He Did, and Why He*
    Matters. New York: HarperCollins, 2011.

Expanded Outline: From Bethel to Peniel
(For Reference)

Preface

Prologue: Why Jacob?

Part One: To Bethel
(25:19—28:22)

I.
Isaac and Rebekah
(25:19—26:30)

Chapter One: What's In a Name?

> Issac's Family
> The Pregnancy
> The Birth

Chapter Two: Whose Birthright?

> The Twins
> The Sale

Chapter Three: The Promise Goes On

> Abraham's Promise
> Isaac's Sister?
> Isaac's Prosperity
> Isaac's Blessing

II.
The Brothers and the Blessing

(17:1—28:22)

Chapter Four: The Blessing: Jacob

Esau's Hittite Marriages
Isaac and Esau
Rebekah and Jacob
Jacob and Isaac

Chapter Five: The Blessing: Esau

Esau and Isaac
Rebekah and Jacob
Rebekah and Isaac
Isaac and Jacob

Chapter Six: Jacob at Bethel

Jacob's Flight
Jacob's Dream
Jacob's Response
Jacob's Stone
Jacob's Vow

Part Two: To Peniel
(29:1—33:17)

I.
Jacob and Laban
(29:1-31:55)

Chapter Seven: Rachel and Leah

Jacob Arrives at a Well'
Jacob Meets Rachel

Jacob Loves Rachel
Jacob is Deceived

Chapter Eight: The Children

Leah's First Sons
Rachel/Bilhah's Sons
Leah/Zilpah's Sons
Rachel's Bargain
Leah's Children
Rachel's Son

Chapter Nine: Jacob Prospers

Jacob's Request
Jacob and Laban Bargain
Jacob's Cunning Strategy

Chapter Ten: Jacob Leaves for Home: Part One

Jacob and His Wives
The Flight from Laban

Chapter Eleven: Jacob Leaves for Home: Part Two

Laban Overtakes Jacob
Jacob's Rebuttal
The Watch

II.
Jacob and Esau
(32:1—33:17)

Chapter: Twelve: Esau is Coming

www.ingramcontent.com/pod-product-compliance
Lightning Source LLC
Chambersburg PA
CBHW070339090426
42733CB00009B/1231